THE ROAD
BY THE RIVER

A Healing Journey for Women

DJOHARIAH TOOR

1817

Harper & Row, Publishers, San Francisco

Cambridge, Hagerstown, New York, Philadelphia, Washington
London, Mexico City, São Paulo, Singapore, Sydney

To my husband, Arthur
my children, Abraham, Herbert, Mariam, Sarah

To my spiritual grandparents, Fred and Katie John,
tribal elders of the AHTNA

And to all those whose stories are told here—
May all your roads meet.

FIRST EDITION

Library of Congress Cataloging-in-Publication Data

Toor, Djohariah.
  The road by the river.

  Bibliography: p.
  1. Women—Psychology.   2. Self-actualization
(Psychology)   3. Women—United States—Psychology.
4. Femininity (Philosophy)   I. Title.
HQ1206.T67   1987   155.6'33   87-45255
ISBN 0-06-250861-X

---

87 88 89 90 91 RRD 10 9 8 7 6 5 4 3 2 1

Contents

Acknowledgments

I am very indebted to the many women who generously allowed me to use their dreams, their stories, and growth experiences to illustrate the material for this book. Had they not shared their own journey with me, this book could not have been written.

I am also greatly indebted to my husband, Arthur, and to my children, Mariam, Sarah, and Herb, who have generously supplied me with time and loving patience while I have written this book; and to my editor, Roy M. Carlisle, and to Rebecca Laird, Christine Anderson, and Harriet Crosby at Harper & Row who all gave me invaluable help in preparing this manuscript. I also wish to thank my many friends who have generously given of their time and editing skills in creating this book, especially Nora Martos-Perry and Margaret McClelland, whose many hours of work on the text have been a great help. I am also indebted to Marion Woodman, whose work with women has been a real source of inspiration to me, and whose encouragement to stay with the labor of the book was a real gift. And most of all I am grateful for the Grandmother I discovered on the trail of my own journey, and who patiently guided me along its edges.

Introduction:
As Long as the River Shall Run

O our Mother the Earth, O our Father the Sky,
Your children are we, and with tired backs
We bring you the gifts that you love.
Then weave for us a garment of brightness,
May the warp be the white light of morning,
May the weft be the red light of evening
May the fringes be the falling rain,
May the border be the standing rainbow.
Thus weave for us a garment of brightness
That we may walk fittingly where birds sing,
That we may walk fittingly where grass is green
O our Mother Earth, O our Father Sky!

SONG OF THE SKY LOOM (TEWA)

When I was in the Southwest earlier this year, I was struck by
the stark beauty of the desert. Although I have been there many
times, this time the trails I walked seemed especially ancient
and powerful; my roots seemed to be reaching up through the
ground and calling me to listen. Hiking along the cliff base at
Bandalier in northern New Mexico, home of the ancient Anasazi
tribe, I was aware of another presence: a Grandmother spirit
who walked with me.

I sat for a while under one of the higher cliff dwellings and
meditated in the hot sun, praying for my clients, my kids, for
peace. Then, opening the deeper windows to the soul inside, I
sat in silence and took in the sounds of life around me. After a
while the swallows darting overhead into their nests above the
cliffs caught my attention, and I stood up to go exploring for
petroglyphs.

After I had walked for quite a distance in the hot sun, I
paused at the foot of a tall red rock and sat down in the warm
dirt to rest. An unusual object on the ground caught my eye.
Turning it over, I discovered a beautiful pot shard, painted in

the traditional black and white stripes of the Anasazi. As I held this fragment of the ancient ones in my hand I experienced a profound moment; something inside of me warmly and silently acknowledged the rough beauty of the hands that had formed this pot over eight hundred years ago. I was awed by the feel of those old hands, which seemed to touch mine in spite of the centuries.

Later, I hiked up to a ledge under a small opening in the rock; it was a shallow rectangular cave. When my eyes grew accustomed to the dark I saw that the inside was piled high with stones, all the same size, as though something was buried there. Rather than enter the cave I sat in the dark entryway, feeling the cold air from the inside of the mountain on my face. As I sat there, imagining these Old Ones and their simple way of life, a stream of tears began to run down my cheeks. Spontaneously, I began to sing into the cave. I asked our ancestors, whose life I could still feel in the ground under my feet, to pray for us in the world who have forgotten to live in peace, who have forgotten what sisterhood and brotherhood is, and who have not remembered how to weave for ourselves a garment of brightness.

One of the reasons I am drawn to the Native Americans is because many of their nations were in possession of a spiritual holism, which I feel an innate need to hang on to. Years ago I began to paint the desert of the Southwest; whether I was working from a photograph taped to the wall of my studio or from some inner image, scenes of the desert simply kept appearing on my canvas. Sometimes when I worked I hummed to myself, singing old songs and simple rhythmic chants. All during the time I was painting these scenes (or they were painting me), I felt a strange sense of affinity to the ancient high plateaus and to the people who walked them.

When I traveled to the Southwest years later, I felt immediately at home and at peace. Everything was familiar to me: the arid land, the red rock cliffs, the caves and trails; the women sitting on the square in Santa Fe selling their bright turquoise jewelry, their handmade pottery and breads baked in the earthen

ovens called *hornos*. Wrapped in colorful wool blankets and holding themselves in a proud reserve, they were always for me a
profound reminder of women who knew something holy. These
women knew the earth and lived in communion with it. Their
inner strength and peace anchored me, pulled me out of my
fast lane and brought me closer to the still more ancient soil of
my own soul. For me the desert was the place where life was
happening. And these women, whose dark faces reflected all of
nature in secret alignment with itself, spoke to me of wholeness.

In my personal inner growth work over the last few years I
have come to understand why I felt so grounded by these women.
The Navajo and Hopi women of New Mexico and Arizona em-
body the balance of masculine and feminine energies. They
have a quality of naturalness, a quiet strength in their ways. But
more than that, the spirituality of these women is rooted in the
earth. My inner conflicts suddenly felt quiet in the presence of
these women and their simple lifestyle. I always arrived fragmented and weary, and there they were, sitting like earthen
vessels of praise on the streets of the square. They walk barefoot
on the soil, while we walk on plush carpets and on the edge of
neurosis.

The Hopi word *koyaanisqatsi* means "life out of balance." At a
world level there is no question that poverty, hunger, injustice,
and violence are on the increase, and the soul of humanity
struggles under oppression. We are moving too fast, and we are
moving without true consciousness. Over this last century we
have somehow polarized ourselves from nature, and our humanity suffers because we have relegated the essence of heart
and soul to the far corners of the psyche. Many of us have lost
the ability to touch our roots or to be in communion with
ourselves and life around us.

Rather than heed the personal human power of the heart
and the incalculable power of the spirit within us as our steady
guides to life, we have made material worldliness the dominant
power we serve. And when this happens we are not in charge
of the technology we have created; instead, technology is in
control of us. This is *koyaanisqatsi*.

This summer I saw a movie called *Broken Rainbow*. It told the story of Big Mountain, a sacred land in the Southwest, which has been shared by the Navajo and Hopi for a long time. Now political and mining concerns have colluded to relocate the Navajo so that these companies can mine coal and uranium from a soil the Native Americans consider sacred. The old people who have suffered relocation from their reservation and from the land of their ancestors say that we have taken away their dignity. We have made them live like the white people, which to them is not living at all. For Native Americans our food, our cement, our fast life, and our need for money is a sacrilege. They say we have taken their dreams away.

I have always had a love for these peoples; I have drawn their faces, studied their myths, collected the artworks of their craftspeople, and resonated with their ways. I am drawn to them spiritually because many of the elders don't just talk their religion, they live it. When I saw the old grandmothers cry on film, when I saw their beautiful dignity crushed, I wept. My friends who saw the film with me wept. The old ones were stunned by the reality that the whites are digging up sacred soil to make weapons with (from uranium comes the plutonium needed for bombs). They asked why we thought Mother Earth would ever want us to make bombs from her soil, weapons for the destruction of her children.

To the Native Americans we are a paradoxical people who have not sat enough under the night blanket of Father Sky. We are too busy with our "progress" to listen to the Great Spirit. We have not contemplated the mysteries of the seasons nor taken our children into holy places; and we have not remembered our ancestors. We have not only broken our treaty with the Navajo once again, we have broken faith with our own integrity as a human race. Just as we cut the Native Americans off and "relocate" them for the sake of progress, at a deeper level we cut off a spiritual heritage that we cannot afford to forget: the heritage of a people who still know that they are one with the earth.

Humanity seems lost in the technology we have created because the very nature of this technology separates us from our essential inner spirit. Somehow we have fallen out of communion with the sacred intent of life. The elder ones among the

Navajo refuse to leave their land because they say it's where their roots are. They say they were born on the land, that their relatives have walked there for centuries and the ground for them is familiar and holy. But there are fewer and fewer pot shards we can pick up to remind us of the simplicity and integrity of a lifestyle lived by our ancestors long ago. In this age, when the mind has somehow become estranged from the heart, there is no balance between these forces in the psyche; and a preoccupation with power and the acquisition of a material lifestyle is the result. When anyone, man or woman, adopts these traits in an unbalanced way, we become *koyaanisqatsi*.

Until we recognize the imbalance of these conditions within ourselves and face our own inauthenticities, however, we have little business pointing the finger either at the overtly technical lifestyle around us or the people who program it. The task that is essential to women on a healing quest is that we find and heal our own personal *koyaanisqatsi*. Our task is to know our own identity as individuals and as women. Our work is to reestablish contact with our essential self, and with the force of the spirit of life within us. Our work is not to prove ourselves in the world of men, but to come to that world as women unafraid to speak of the sacred intent of life itself, and to speak it as women.

Many of us have no roots as women: We lack an awareness of what feminine identity means. We have made long strides in the male corporate world, but these personal and social accomplishments have somehow only masked our confusion, and we still can't say who we are. Defined by roles and governed by agendas, we lose contact with the vital elements of our own nature. We lose touch with our feminine roots; with the earth in our nature; with heart, instinct, intuition, and feeling; and with the ground under our feet.

Many places within a woman's soul need healing. In these times especially, human consciousness needs to be open all the way down to the soul level. The feminine spirit itself, an autonomous movement of life-giving forces within the human psyche, needs recognition and restoration.

The inspiration to write this book emerged from my own personal growth and crisis experiences, and through those of the women who have shared their lives with me. The struggle to break past our wounds and to unearth the human spirit within each of us has been a profound learning experience for me; I am often awed by the ability to survive and to grow that some women have shown. But more than that I marvel at the great strengths I have seen being born out of struggle; at the incredible power that suffering gestates in the soul.

There is no doubt that trial strengthens and purifies, and that crisis sharpens our awareness. But it is equally true that wounds, if they are not healed, can darken the heart and cause life to be withheld. I have always been fascinated by the work and the dynamics involved in the healing process. I am endlessly amazed by the fact that some people can and do move toward healing and wholeness. I am likewise intrigued by what factors stand as obstacles to the work of healing, those things within the unconscious that keep us victimized by life rather than in charge of our destiny.

This book deals with a healing process; it is a story of how we get wounded and how we grow; a tale of what brings life to the human heart and what takes life away. It is a poke at the mythologies and assumptions about ourselves that tend to pull us off the track. It is a story about the detours and summits of the journey to the feminine self. It is a song to the soul and to the One who made the whole experiment possible.

I have changed all names and identifying details. In some cases the material from the stories I have used does not belong to one individual, but is a composite of several individuals. I chose this kind of illustration in order to present a point while preserving anonymity.

1. The Road by the River

O Great Spirit, whose voice I hear in the winds, and whose breath gives life to all the world, hear me! I am small and weak; I need your strength and wisdom. Let me walk in beauty, and make my eyes ever behold the red and purple sunset. Make my hands respect the things you have made and my ears sharp to hear your voice. Make me wise so that I may understand the things you have hidden in every leaf and rock. I seek strength, not to be greater than my friend, but to fight my greatest enemy—myself. Make me always ready to come to you with clean hands and straight eyes. So when life fades, as the fading sunset, may my spirit come to you without shame.

NATIVE AMERICAN PRAYER

The older I get the more I find deep healing power in simple things: in nature, in the caves of my ancestors, in songs, in religious celebrations of all kinds, in dreams, in my children, through my clients, in rocks and rivers, in sea and sand, in the eyes of life's lovers. Yet the two main helpers in my own healing process have been the inner reserves of heart and spirit and the natural gifts of the earth. In both these gifts I have found myself alternately impoverished or blessed. Poverty happens to us when we lose the reality of who we are; when we abandon our essential nature for the counterfeit feminine images that the world values. Blessing happens because we discover in ourselves both the clay of the earth and the essential nature of woman and spirit.

The Native American prayer that begins this chapter clearly expresses the feminine spirit, and as such it is a good companion for the journey. In my own vision seeking I often experience this need to draw myself aside, to sit apart from the people in my life, from my work, my agendas, and from the fast lane, which has no time for red and purple sunsets. In these times there are few rites of passage where one can draw away to face oneself and ask for a vision; few quiet refuges where one can sit still and ask for inner wisdom and strength. Yet without this sort of movement inward to reflect, to ponder, to empty out our excesses, to face what needs work, and to reclaim the roots of our own being, there is no vision. If we are to be healed and remember who we are, then we need a vision for our lives. We need to remember to stay close to the inner woman who periodically leads us into silence; the one who laughs good naturedly at watches and agendas and who bids us come and sit on the earth. She is the guide we follow to the deeper self.

I have been a potter, a painter, a teacher, a therapist, and a mother. But my favorite role is that of a student; a disciple of sorts, a kind of follower of the river. I have strayed from the road during my journey, but the mistakes I have made in my life have been some of my most faithful teachers. Some of the wounds I have carried and wrestled with have originated from the world of my parents and society; some are of my own making. Yet the process of healing for us is never totally outside ourselves. The work of healing is an inner work, and that work is a journey.

To journey means to undertake an inner walk that eventually leads to the vision of who we really are. It is a search for the self the world has obscured; a reaching inward to the place that we knew long ago, but have since forgotten and covered over. It is a gathering up from within of what is denied and repressed, what is unacknowledged and unseen; a collecting of all the different sides of ourselves we don't like, can't embrace, or don't want to see. It is an acknowledgment of all the "enemies" within, which we have disinherited or projected onto others; it is a calling together of all the orphans of our humanity, a bringing forth of the remnants within the self that are incomplete .

When we embark upon the journey we begin a walk into ourselves; into both flesh and spirit, into the leaves and rocks of our being. We make a foray into that within us which is not only denied and unseen, but undiscovered: into the self we do not yet know. When we journey through the personality to the deeper self, we touch not only what is wounded and incomplete, but we tap into that which is also potentially a treasure. The journey is a vision quest in which we might learn to walk in beauty, to reverence the sunset, to walk in peace with ourselves and with the others around us. To heal the feminine is a woman's journey toward wholeness.

THE ROAD BY THE RIVER

Healing is an ongoing process. Women on such a journey are open to life and to its unfolding, no matter where the river seems to run.

Every year my husband and I go fishing on the Klamath River in northern California. This trip has become a renewing ritual for us, whether or not we catch any Steelhead (a large Rainbow trout that has been to sea and returns to spawn in its native waters after two or three years). Part of the beauty of the trip is the river.

The Klamath is magical. I fell in love with it the moment I first saw it. On that cold fall morning when we first hiked down along the canyon toward the river, fishing rods in hand, I was aware of how ancient the land around the water felt. How familiar it seemed. It was like coming back to a place that I had known long ago. The excitement of this discovery made me run like a child along the trail by the water, half expecting to find some old friend there waiting to greet me.

I have fished the river's shores and walked its paths in many stages of my own growth. The river has seen many of my growing pains, many moods and transitions. Whenever I am there I dream profusely and my journal is never far away. If the fishing is slow I sit on the banks and play with the stones, making rough altars of polished river rock, singing to myself, and whispering secrets to the wind that sings back to me up the canyon.

The river always has something to teach me. In some places the pathways of the water changes; enormous quantities of it tighten and swirl through narrow canyons and gorges. Rolling and tumbling over rocks and boulders and clamoring over log jams in the winter months when the rains have swollen its banks, the river makes a wild sound. There are times in my life like that: times when all my energies seem suddenly swirling through tight and confining places; times of crisis and change where I find myself suddenly flooded and close to being out of control, clamoring to break through my own internal log jams.

In other places the river runs wide and smooth, quietly winding its way down to the sea, almost silent in its passing. Here the land spreads generously away from the water, allowing it to make a wide flow across a shallow channel, where one could almost wade across. My own life is sometimes like the river, still and safe, where the rushing waters have calmed and the land of my life gives a spacious container to my soul. These are times in my own journey for silent pondering, reflection, and expansiveness.

Last year, when we tried to find the old familiar trail down the mountain to one of our favorite fishing holes, we found that a storm had wiped out the path and nothing was the same. All the recognizable landmarks had changed and the old worn places in the trail had simply vanished. The only thing that remained the same was the pitch of the descent and the sound of the river below. Nonetheless, we made our way to our old spot.

Later on in the day, with my pole in the water, my thoughts wandered back to the trail and to the huge patches of erosion made by the storm. When a sudden storm causes us to lose our way, when we can't see the old landmarks anymore, then we simply have to feel instinctively for the next step.

It somehow reminded me of a friend who had recently lost her husband after a long struggle with cancer. She said she thought that this was the hardest part of her journey because it was so uncertain. The death of her previous life with her husband had simply eroded her own path, and for a while she was unable to see the next bend in the road.

One day, as she was meditating, she saw the image of a great tree. The roots of the tree ran deep and were firmly planted in the ground, and when the wind and the storms came the tree swayed but did not fall. The power of the tree, with its deep roots and its protective branches that could shelter the forest creatures around it, was a healing symbol that came when she most needed it. In spite of the fact that her own paths had eroded and washed down the mountain, her own inner tree was secure. In time she would carve a new path, born out of the depth of her own journey through crisis, and made secure by her own inner work and her walk to soul.

The road by the river is the road we walk in life. Whenever I sit by the Klamath, thinking nothing and filling my tired body with the gifts of Mother Earth, I remember something vital: Ultimately, *I am not in control of my life.* I do not really make it happen specifically the way I want. I am subject to life more than life is subject to me.

The task of the first half of my life has been to repair my personal and relational incompletions and to find the ground of my own autonomy, and I congratulate myself as I accomplish those things. But as I sit by the river I suddenly recall that I am not supposed to get lost in my ego, in striving and agendas, in proving myself, or in having my autonomy. Along this road I am only a child, a guest, a follower of the river. The only important thing is the journey itself and the way I learn to walk it, to surrender to it, to pray—like the old Navajo who sing chants and praises while they work, like the Old Ones who have gone centuries before me.

As it flows to earth from the mountain and the clouds above the mountain, the river is like life itself. Its origin is from the sky and from the Grandfather who lives there dreaming up creation. Sitting by the river I remember that I am a small but meaningful part of that creation, that my life flows down through Mother Earth to the sea, carving itself through rock and sand and clay until it reaches its destination and becomes one with creation again.

Our journey is like the river's path to the sea. When the waters of the river spill into the ocean, they lose their identity as a river and become one with the wider body of the ocean. The river yields itself to the sea and its journey is done. In the beginning of our journey our ego needs to develop a strong identity; it needs a solid container for a while, like the river needs the canyons and the land that shapes its passage. In the first part of our lives we need to find ourselves, to develop our strengths, to make our own individual statement. Clearly, we cannot give ourselves away to life until we know ourselves authentically. But at some point in any spiritual quest, the authentic personal and relational self must reach the sea. At some point we must let go and give ourselves back to life, like the river gives itself back to the sea.

2. Beginning the Journey: A Time for Change

TURNING POINTS

The journey back to our self, no matter how uniquely each woman embarks on it, always begins with some degree of pain and the awareness of a need for change. A young woman who had just completed her studies for a Ph.D. told me the story of her own crisis: *"When I was back home last summer I experienced a profound emptiness, like a deep hole inside myself. For the first few days it was all right—my parents were happy to see me, to know that my studies were finished and that I'd soon be working and on my own. It was good seeing old friends and being the center of attention for a while, and it was nice to relax for a change.*

"But then something strange started happening. I suddenly began to experience a feeling of anxiousness that just seemed to drop out of nowhere. Then everything began to seem increasingly shallow and inside I felt bleak and empty, like there was no one home. In spite of all that I had attained over the last few years at grad school, something was missing.

"I stopped sleeping well and began to awaken in the middle of the night with a feeling of restlessness, almost a kind of panic. I felt like I was standing right on the edge of some incredible precipice about to go over. 'Great,' I said to myself, 'now that you've got your Ph.D. you're going nuts.'

"One evening, not too long after this began, I was taking a walk and suddenly I began running. I must have run full speed for blocks and then I collapsed under a bush in some neighborhood park. When I caught my breath I started to laugh hysterically and then I burst into tears and cried for a long time. By this time it was night and the sky was dark except for some patches of fog. I lay there watching the clouds roll over the skyline and around the hills over the town. A cop startled

me by asking me if everything was OK. I told him I was fine and I walked myself home.

"*Not long afterward I went to see a therapist in my home town. He gave me some pills to take. But I hate pills. Why medicate this thing when I don't even know what it is I'm feeling? He told me I was experiencing some stress. But he never pursued it with me. I told him he could take the pills himself.*

"*Everything seemed to fall apart for a while. But somehow it needed to happen. I suppose everything crashed because I was too top heavy, too driven in my life. For the last three years I have worked and studied nonstop—during that whole time I never even paused long enough to walk on the beach or watch the sunset. This anxiety also felt like a kind of paralysis around leaving home, being fully on my own and facing the real world outside of my parents and academia. A ridiculous dilemma for a twenty-eight-year-old woman, but that's what was up.*"

Another woman I know, who had recently left a difficult long-term relationship, told me: "*I was sitting in a restaurant looking out the window when I realized I was about to start screaming. When it came—this sense of utter disintegration—I felt trapped and panicky. My personality seemed to have dissolved like Kool Aid in a glass of water. I was left with only my body, which I didn't know how to work. In that moment I suddenly felt like a mistake, a ghost in the machine, a void; unable to gather enough crystals of my humanity together to face another person, to hold a life together.*

"*I told a therapist that an image for this had come to me so clearly: I felt that I had no house for my soul to live in. But she failed to sense the power of this image. She tried to show me that my self-concept was mistaken, that I was approvable and just as 'cool' as the next person. I appreciated her loving efforts, but they failed finally to ground me, to address the deep disconnectedness I felt from my own humanity and womanhood. I felt like the woman in the parable who loses one coin of ten. I have nine left, but they are not enough.*"

When this woman and I met, and she began to scream somewhere in the middle of our session, I knew her anguish was real. I also knew she wasn't going overboard for good. She was in a crisis and she needed to know it was all right to fall apart.

The false ways by which most of us learn personal identity are often entirely misleading. One way or the other, these coverings have to be lifted. Most of us have been told by our parents, our peers, by the world around us, "This is who you are." But few of us have broken free of the myths of our personality and stood through the process of disintegration thoroughly and honestly enough to say instead, "This is who I am." And that's what this woman was doing; she was creatively dissolving and coming in courage to her essential self. The relational impasse from which she was emerging, however, was not the end of her crisis. At the deepest level her work was to face the inner void she felt in relationship to herself.

The confusion of identity most women experience for at least the first half of life is a result of a variety of factors both personal and cultural; but the overall effect of that confusion is to block our growth. Many of us are wounded because we don't yet know the woman beneath the roles we play. Most of us have not yet asked the question of what our real identity is, or how we can be who we are without a need for apologies or rewards.

Crises in the couple relationship often impels us to seek a more authentic identity. A midlife crisis can be an especially compelling stressor for a relationship. Some women only seriously begin to take stock of where they are when this sort of dilemma erupts. This was certainly the way in which I began a major part of my own journey.

"What are you doing to us?" my husband shouted at me. "I'm not doing anything!" I shouted back. "Well, whatever you're doing is making me crazy!" he rejoined. My head was starting to spin and I could feel myself fading. "You're not the only one who's confused," I said. "I don't know what's going on either. I can't help it that I've fallen in love with this man, and I don't know any more about it than you do!"

I walked away from him and went outside into the back yard, to the hot tub. Peeling off my clothes I stepped into the dark water under a full sky of stars, still angry and confused. This will never do, I thought. For years I have been happily married, I've got four kids, I'm a therapist, a competent mother, a spiritual devotee. Life is good. I should know better. Why do I have to be bothered by this sudden craziness in my life? My thoughts tumbled together and mingled with the rising steam from the water. Suddenly, the back door opened and my husband walked out onto the porch. Fully clothed, he strode right into the hot tub and sat down beside me with an enormous splash. "Oh," I said in disbelief, "now what?" To the sound of bubbles rising vigorously from his cowboy boots, he said, "What do I have to do to get your attention? You're ruining our marriage and I can't stand it. Either it's him or me. Period."

I don't care what anybody says about romance, falling in love out of a clear blue sky is chaos. Aside from the outer distress it causes a family, the inner distress it causes the individuals concerned sometimes seems insurmountable. The unconscious, when it floods the conscious mind with its strong draught of Eros energy, is a tough thing to assimilate, even in my business. But having run from these encounters many times before, I knew that this one was serious and that there was no getting out of it through denial. I was going to have to see this crisis through.

The crises women must sometimes face range along a continuum that can penetrate even to the soul level. A woman I met this summer at a workshop told the group the following story about a profound awakening experience she recently had. *"At the beginning of the summer I was walking along a trail in the mountains, as I often do. I enjoy getting out alone hiking, it gives me a sense of peace. To this day I am not sure how it happened, but during a down climb off a slope I lost my footing and fell off a cliff.*

"Suddenly, I found myself on the ground below with a broken leg. Somehow I managed to pull myself over to a river near by and I sat with my leg in the water to keep the swelling down. For the next few hours I sat there praying for help. I put my hands over my foot and soaked it with prayer, sending in as much healing energy as I could for a person trying not to go into shock. Not long afterwards two men came along in a kayak and waited with me until a raft came down river.

"Recuperating in the hospital for the next week or so, I couldn't believe that this whole thing had even happened; but the casts I wore soon brought it home. You know, my whole life I thought that if I believed in God and took my vitamins, nothing like this could ever happen to me. Normally, I am a very busy person and always complaining about it. Now I had plenty of time to spend in reflection! One of the things that came to me after a while is that somehow my life was out of balance; that I was running too fast in almost everything that I was doing. As much as I was tempted to say, Listen God, why did you

have to do this to me? I felt that my whole life was off center and that my falling was somehow a reminder to slow down. The quieter I got in my meditations, the more I felt this to be true."

Since the original blueprint for us is a holistic one, in which body, mind, and spirit begin life together, a major part of our work is to remember how to integrate these forces within us. Somehow, when things get crazy and we forget where we came from and what we're doing here, the transpersonal force within us will rally for our attention. We will come to all kinds of cliffs in life. Some will be real ones, some will be emotional, some relational, and some spiritual; but all of them are like edges from one state of awareness (or the lack of it) to another. It is only when we have closed our eyes to these edges and deny them from view, however, that they become dangerous.

No matter what kind of crisis we experience, its impact can often lead us to a deeper experience of ourselves. Somehow, the ecology of crisis brings us face to face with our deepest self. When women complain of the sudden eruption of repressed feelings, depression, confusion, anxiety, a relational dilemma, a sense that everything is falling apart, undoubtedly it is a frightening and unsettling experience. Sometimes when women are experiencing this interior kind of crisis they feel they are going crazy or over the hill. But the truth is, it is often necessary to feel momentarily crazy or out of sorts in order to open and to lance the wounds in our past. In some cases it is a divine summons to higher personal and global consciousness. To pay attention to this process is to acknowledge that something holy within us would like our attention back.

HEALING TASKS

We can identify three levels where women are most wounded and most in need of awakening: (1) The personal level (the psychological self); (2) the sociocultural level (the social and relational self); and (3) the spiritual level (the inner soul).

Personal wounds and limitations are formed early in life and go back to our family of origin. This is where the basic building blocks of the personality are formed. Women who have had relatively healthy beginnings at the personal level may be wounded at later developmental stages by the social structure in which we grew up. We may be most hurt or misled by the ways we learned to adapt to the world around us, or by the masks and roles we assumed in order to fit in. These wounds at the personal and sociocultural level inevitably affect the spiritual level. When wounded, we often get defensive, and our defensiveness cuts us off from growth at any level. Whatever the nature of the wounds which have left us numbed or unconscious to the truth of who we are as women, our task is to awaken ourselves at all levels.

PERSONAL HEALING

To awaken consciousness we must not only deal with those attitudes, habits, thoughts, and feelings that are conscious, we must also journey into our deeper psyche. Every event from our past is recorded somewhere in the unconscious mind and, at some level, in the body itself. Although I can clearly recall certain events from my own childhood—like Saturday movies for a quarter, neighborhood baseball games, the smell in the air before a summer storm, the time I fell in a mud ditch just before church—there are many more things I don't consciously remember. Any number of unrecalled events, impressions, and feelings can lie buried in the folds of the mind.

Healing at the personal level almost always involves some work with the unconscious memories of childhood. Sometimes children block out whole segments of childhood, especially when times of crisis and deep trauma become too painful to acknowledge. We cannot dismiss these memories altogether, however; we simply drive them into the unconscious where they will not be so hurtful. Yet if we do not bring these unconscious impressions to awareness and work them through, either we will eventually act them out or they will act through us symptomatically.

For instance, in a household where there is marital conflict, invariably one of the children will amplify that conflict. In some families a child forms an unconscious allegiance with one or both parents and covertly agrees to "carry" the family dysfunction. For example, a young girl who is anorexic may be acting our her mother's own unlived life. Perhaps the mother may be depressed or dysfunctional, yet avoids working consciously with her problem or its cause. She may go on from day to day simply hanging on. She may speak out her pain or not speak it out, but one way or the other the child picks up the emotional turmoil. The daughter, thinking her mother's psychic conflict is somehow her own, punishes herself by not eating. The mother's starved psyche eventually becomes mirrored in the fragile body of her daughter.

I had a young girl at my house last summer who was anorexic; she was the daughter of a friend of mine who lived in another state. She had been struggling with anorexia for about three years, and by the time she came to our house everybody was used to the idea that Angie just didn't eat. When she first came to stay with us she had begun to gain a little weight and she was looking like she was going to stabilize, so nobody felt nervous. But after the first week she got chicken pox, and by the end of the second week she had lost a lot more weight and I began to feel panic.

I alternated between loving her (because she was incredibly lovable) and wanting to wring her neck. I threatened to take her to the hospital; we fought, she cried, I relented. I woke in the middle of the night wondering if she was still breathing. I was caught between trying to be both therapist and mother to her. Then, miraculously, I began to gain confidence in the fact that the Almighty was somehow looking over us. I relaxed at the table, she relaxed at the table. When it came time for her to return to home I took her to the airport, and after a long loving embrace I let her go home. After she had been home for some months, she finally decided that she wanted to stay on the planet. I got a beautiful photo of her later on with a big smile on her face and some long-prayed-for weight on her body.

Another example of the child who carries an obvious parental process is the adult child of the alcoholic. One of my clients said to me, *"In order to get along in my family I had to be numb. I had to completely ignore that there was anything wrong with my mother. She drank, she broke promises, she was never there for me, and I wasn't supposed to notice. She was the secret we all protected. To this day I still carry that numbness."*

One young woman whose childhood had been marked by mistrust of her father's alcoholic process said, *"Growing up I was always very careful not to allow anybody access to my inner person. I was very shy around men in general and tended to stay away from boys my own age. Because my father is an alcoholic, I grew up in an environment that was very unsettled. I never knew when he would be drunk or sober. He couldn't even remember events from day to day. I knew he meant no harm, but that didn't help the pain I felt. If this man who was the most powerful male figure in my life couldn't be trusted or relied on, then surely that applied to all other men too."*

The woman who has survived a childhood of chaos has a similar unconscious program of defenses that must be broken through. One friend of mine told me, *"I suppose my biggest issue throughout childhood was survival. My mother was violent and abusive and sometimes psychotic. But she never got any help for herself. She used to beat me unconscious sometimes. Once she broke my nose.*

"I survived by pulling in in every possible way; by shutting down and not talking to her. Not feeling. I could sense when she was going to go into one of her psychotic rages and so when I knew it was coming, I just shut down.

"I think the hardest part of healing myself was coming out into the open. There were lots of times I didn't want to allow any part of myself to be seen. Times I was afraid to engage openly with anyone. I shrank back a lot from my fullness because I was so afraid of being hurt for being alive. I still struggle with that, but it's getting better. It's hard, but it can be done. I've had some good therapy over the years and a strong spiritual refuge in my life that's been very centering for me."

Clearly survivors, and convinced that they would not be in a victim role forever, these women eventually reached out and got help for themselves. But some women allow the crises they have endured in childhood to become a chronic way of life. When hurtful childhood memories are buried, they result in an unconscious program of defenses designed to block pain. Yet in truth these defenses not only inhibit us from feeling pain, but also effectively cut us off from feeling life.

When our basic self-esteem is wounded early enough, we tend to recreate that early impression for years to come. A child's self-image, once bruised, will be difficult to mend. One of my clients said to me, *"I felt rejected by both my parents. My father abandoned us when I was five and my mother and my sister and I had to go live in a home of some kind. My mother was depressed a lot and she neglected us much of the time. I remember feeling invalidated as a kid, as though nothing I did was ever good enough. In a way I wondered if I was responsible for my mother's unhappiness.*" As a grown woman my client carried this same sense of unworthiness into her relationship with her husband, her children, and all subsequent relationships. Walking into every new situation with that same fear invariably meant that something would always go wrong. Dreaming up the idea that people felt critical and un-accepting of her, and rejecting others before they had a chance to reject her, her social life was a source of great pain and confusion to her. In effect, she was unconsciously living out her mother's dream at high cost to herself.

Anxiety, the complaint of many women, is the result of an-other kind of unconscious process. In some cases a consciously held attitude will force our less conscious feelings underground, and the resulting avoidance creates anxiety. When anxiety is felt unconsciously, and when the reason for the anxious feelings is not faced, the problem can begin to manifest psychosomatically. The body itself begins to register the internal distress.

In my early twenties I entertained some vague anxieties that I could not seem to shake. Sometimes I fantasized the weirdest things happening, a host of catastrophes over which I seemed to have no control. I worried about accidents, about my kids, about the dark spaces in the hallway, about making a fool of myself. I hated these fears and nefarious tricks of the imagina-tion, and bravely tried to reason them away, but they persisted in sometimes obsessive ways.

As a student in college just a few years before, I'd had an impressive knowledge of classic literature and philosophy. I could reason anyone out of their religious beliefs, played a great game of chess, and loved a challenging debate. Intellectually, I was accomplished; but emotionally, I was a powder keg. Although there was no severe emotional manifestation of these vague anxieties I felt from time to time, my body tried over and over to signal me that something was wrong. Sometimes I hyperven-tilated, I regularly entertained colds and flu, and frequently I experienced strange heart palpitations. My whole system seemed to sound a chronic alarm.

The neurotic split I experienced was happening because I was living solely out of my intellect. Feelings were not my allies, because they were likely to make me vulnerable. I had learned to cut them off early in adolescence because they seemed somehow untrustworthy. I was intellectually polished, but emotionally fairly primitive. The disparity between these two sides of my personality was part of an unconscious process of which I was not aware; my body registered the emotional tension I was feeling somatically, but "I" remained in the dark.

Sometimes the results can be more serious. For instance, the woman who eats to fill an inner void is caught in an addictive process. Any addictive behavior—whether it involves food, alcohol, drugs, buying sprees, or an addiction to ideals and perfectionism—is generally reflecting an unconscious process. The message deeply ingrained in the unconscious is that life is unlivable without some kind of overcompensation. The addictive process is a signal that the hunger a woman feels goes far deeper than what she uses to fill the void; it is a crisis of meaning which can never be met by the food she eats or the perfectionism in her routines; her consumerism or her alcohol will never satisfy the still-deeper craving in her soul for personal meaning.

Addictive behavior—because of the complex of variables that underlies the addiction—can be a result of causes that originate at either the personal or the sociocultural level. One example of a food process at the personal level is the woman who is still enmeshed with the mother and is unable to break free of her. Because the eating pattern of the daughter often reflects a tangle with the mother's unconscious process, the issue here is one of a struggle for autonomy.

In the bulimic process, for instance, the mother-daughter territory becomes confused in a number of ways. Sometimes the mother has not been present to the child, and a healthy separation has never taken place. In this case it is the child who unconsciously clings to the mother and wishes to prolong the maternal attachment. In other cases the daughter may try to establish her own identity as a child but the mother intervenes, comes too close, remains fixed on the child in some way and unable to detach herself. Then it is the mother who clings to and lives through the child. In some cases the daughter covertly gets the message that the mother cannot live without her; that she cannot be separate from her; that she has no right to her own independence. The eating (and vomiting) cycle that accompanies bulimia is a symptom that says to the internalized mother, "I am eating because I am starved and cannot get enough. My terror is that because you have lived through me, I have nothing of myself inside. I am empty. You infuriate me because you won't let me be myself. You have fed me too much of yourself and I would like to throw you up. I need you and I feel overwhelmed by you. I cannot stand you, I cannot stand to be without you."

Women who are living life unconsciously because of some childhood trauma or incompletion are often women who have been betrayed by life. Yet, to become conscious of what has made us victims and what holds us in some sort of self-destructive or self-defeating pattern is the first step in our healing process. Clearly the influence of our parents, whether conscious or unconscious, is something that must be dealt with if women are to move beyond the personal myths that bind them. The key to this initial work at the personal level is to own what behaviors and defenses we may have needed as children in order to survive; to sort through the ways these self-limiting patterns no longer work in the present.

SOCIOCULTURAL HEALING: BEYOND THE MASK

Aside from some of the unconscious parental programming a woman must sort through in her quest for personal identity, there are often a number of myths to challenge at a more collective level. The late mystic Thomas Merton speaks of the inauthentic side of a person as the "false self." Any part of us which doesn't reflect the truth of who we are, whether that part is a stereotypic behavior, a social mask, or an unhealthy attitude, always has to face the fire of crisis before it loses its hold over us. To a great extent we are the product of the society which has shaped us, and as such our identity has been something of public property. Subtly programmed to live according to a fairly collective identity, it takes most of us years to catch on to the fact that the status quo has us by the tail.

As a painter, an intuitive, and a woman who moves through life experientially, I have often felt I was on the wrong planet.

As a child I remember often feeling disconsolate and disconnected in school, somehow distinctly not a part of the adult world into which I was being lured. I am certain I remained in my own inner world longer than most. By living in mud and trees and as close to Mother Nature as I could get, and playing endless games of make-believe, I hid out from an adult world I felt little impetus to seriously explore.

As an adult I am aware that schools, religious systems, and the people that staff these institutions are merely upholding a status quo of one kind or another. Most have little investment in anything that isn't rigorously ordinary. A child can temporarily survive the system by hiding out in play, in mud and forts, and in the concoctions of an adventurous imagination, but not forever. Sooner or later the world of convention catches up with us, and when it does we have to conform or to risk the embarrassment of being an ugly duckling.

To begin to fit into the whole academy of linear thinking—a predominantly left-brain approach to learning—means that most of us must sacrifice this inner world of creativity. More and more of a child's natural spontaneity begins to subside with the application of a more technical and pragmatic approach to learning. Along with a loss of the inner world of our childhood, the expression of feelings, intuition, and spirit is also often quelled. In short, the whole feminine approach to learning— which is experiential, intuitive, and right-brain—is discouraged. More and more we become engaged in a world that honors intellectual pursuits and technical efficiency over matters of the heart. Because our educational systems are all based on a patriarchal model of competition and performance, the feminine has had few places to turn.

Without a conscious awareness of her own inner woman, a woman who adopts a strong social script can begin to feel alienated from her self. One of my clients who is in the midst of breaking through her own mask relates, *"If I let myself slow down for any length of time something unnerving invariably happens. I begin to notice I feel slightly on edge, a little restless or sad. It seems like I'm in the middle of some new territory that I just plain don't like. It makes me want to leap right back into my busy life and ignore this gnawing thing inside, but I know I can't. The truth is that I've worked hard to prove myself professionally; but inside I'm in a kind of fix. Inside [she thumps her solar plexus] I sense that there's something I'm not proving at all. As though there's this other woman inside who feels like a kind of orphan. If I look at her long enough she's going to make some demands on me that I'm afraid I'm not going to like."*

I can understand this woman perfectly. I don't like orphans either. For years I clung tenaciously to the little house of my ego, which I fortified with a full agenda. For years I measured myself by the kinds of things I could accomplish well. My whole identity used to be built around them. I prioritized the performing, masculine side of my nature because I was alienated from the feminine. To me the male world was challenging and vastly more compelling. That's where all the rewards lay—and, ultimately, some of the trouble.

A woman who is identified with her mask experiences a crisis when she wakes up from her role to find she doesn't know who she is without it. If our self-esteem comes from what we do rather than who we are, then some form of crisis is not far away. When we take another look at some of our so-called strengths, we find that some of them are not strengths at all. They are learned behaviors, roles, socially adapted patterns of response to the world. But they are not us.

Some of these behavioral patterns are not strengths as much as they are defensive structures; they may be attitudinal or actual—but they are little more than social masks that give us the appearance of being self-sufficient. If a woman has over-compensated for some childhood pain by becoming accomplished, or if she has become stoic by enduring some chronic problem, this mask may seem like her own identity. But as we work further down into the ego and all it has so carefully built up, we see that many of these women—competent in their careers, brilliant as strategists in their own fields of interest—do not feel very secure or self-confident at all. When a woman overidentifies with her mask, with a show of strength and achievement, or if the social role she plays is too heavily invested in a masculine status quo, then this role clouds the inner woman.

Neither does a woman gain much authenticity by following behavioral styles that are traditionally feminine. A woman caught in this stereotype values those things which are culturally esteemed, what women are "supposed" to be all about: self-sacrificing, living for others, devoted to causes outside themselves, submissive to men, always smiling, the girl next door—sort of a religious ideal. That's not the authentic feminine either; it's simply another stereotypic model that identifies women as pleasers, as servers of another status quo.

One such woman puts it this way: *"I'm one of those women who has simply lived for others. I've given myself away to endless good works; I've volunteered for just about every work-day in the children's school. When Bill or the kids or the church or the local women's auxiliary needed something, I was always there. I always seem to know about the needs of others, sometimes in very intuitive ways. My problem is that I seem to use my women's intuition on everybody but myself. I don't know whether I'm a saint or the village doormat."*

Other crisis situations that commonly act to bring one to attention can also involve separation, divorce, or the stress of a chronic dysfunction between individuals. Many women tend to enter partnering in unconscious ways. Asleep to herself because of problems and incompletions at the personal level, a woman's relational skills are not fully awakened; communication with another is difficult for the woman who is unaware of her own identity or who has not gone after some degree of self-awareness.

One woman describes a relational impasse in her marriage: *"Everything between us seems dry. We're at one of those awful places where we're not going anyplace and both of us know it. I think we've both been avoiding working on this mess because neither one of us wants to admit we've failed. I can't fool myself anymore into thinking everything is all right—I know that because I've been depressed lately.*

"Life just barely happens when the two of us are together, and that scares me. It never used to be that way at all. There's just no joy in our partnership, no delight. He watches TV and I clean house or read; I hide in the pages of my books where there's a little excitement and some fantasy. But I'm not making anything happen in my own life. I hate the thought of what's ahead, but I've got to face this thing between us because I feel like I'm dying inside."

HEALING AT THE SPIRITUAL LEVEL:
WHEN EVERYTHING FALLS APART

A spiritual crisis may perhaps best be described as an intense interior shift that involves the total person. Generally, it is the result of some major imbalance that occurs when our personal and relational problems have gone unchecked for too long.

At this level we are dealing with the core of the problems that block our growth potentials. Let's say, for instance, that a woman has had an ongoing problem at the personal level. The good news is that perhaps she has so far been able to function and to get along in spite of it. The bad news is that she has used up a major portion of her energy keeping her issue concealed or under control. Since it takes a lot of work to sit on a tiger, many of her most valuable resources have gone toward maintaining her balance—she has spent herself putting on a good show.

A woman who has been effectively cut off from her deeper self finds most of her energy being sucked up in a vacuum of pretense. In time, a voice within her at the soul level begins to cry out for attention and restoration. I once knew a woman who was chronically frightened about her self-image. Her fear of being rejected made her afraid of being herself, appearing vulnerable, or being wrong. She said once: *"I feel like I control so much of myself that most of my energy goes into self-preservation. I have a problem being myself and I know it, but it's really hard to uproot. I'm scared I'll say the wrong thing, make a mistake, appear like I don't know anything. When I talk to people in a crowd my whole body gets tense and this strained smile stays on my face until it hurts. Whatever I say comes out all wrong, or somehow it's not good enough."* Whether the root cause of her insecurity was parental rejection, abandonment, or some other early stressor, she was locked up emotionally and unable to do anything about it. When we let these conditions go until our fear and denial become almost bigger than we are, our control starts working against us. In fighting to keep control over herself, this woman became a prisoner of her own fear. Her spiritual crisis inevitably involved a headlong crash right into the very heart of what terrified her the most: her self.

Whatever its root causes, we must be forced to confront our

own daemon of insecurity until we are free of it. This sort of crisis can be anything from a mild shakedown to a full-blown psychosis. Of course, we do not always intentionally "choose" at a conscious level to wrestle these things through. But for the sake of our inner ecology, something within us arranges such an appointment. If we are to become more conscious and awake through these disruptions, then we can work our way out of the impasse. Having passed through such a crisis, we are free to create life rather than to guard against it.

At the heart of any spiritual crisis is always an attempt by the human system to regain its balance, its totality. In my late teens and early twenties I was fascinated with philosophy and I filled up my mind with all kinds of erudite stuff—I even took Lucretius on picnics. All of that would have been fine had I also honored my feelings. But I suppressed feeling and withheld my emotions, and my heart grew constricted while my mind gained by leaps and bounds. I was an avowed agnostic, furious at the inhumanity I saw in the world, and fairly well defended. My life began to lose meaning. Although I was outwardly accomplished and seemingly content, inwardly something was missing. After a while I grew melancholy and restless. Right around that time I experienced a series of anxiety attacks. I also experienced some major heart pains over an extended period of time. I was only twenty-three and I was beginning to think I was falling apart at the seams. Lucretius and I were just about at the end of our picnic.

For some years we may go about life performing roles, perfunctorily fulfilling the obligations and demands of life; then all of a sudden we suffer a crisis, a loss of personal meaning. Why? Because the "false self" has taken up far too much space. We have choked off the vital and authentic self at the soul level, and the only way it can get through to us is by getting our attention with some kind of crisis. In the best sense this creative disintegration is a complete falling apart of the old order. This is where our very foundations begin to be shaken and torn down so that a new awareness and a new vision can emerge.

I dealt with the crisis I experienced in my early twenties by immersing myself in a spiritual discipline and following it seriously for several years. Initially, the discipline quelled my anxiety and gave me a sense of well being and balance. My strange tensions eventually gave way to a long period of inner peace.

This period marked the beginning of a paradoxical process that has raised some interesting questions about the spiritual life. In the first place, the problems that I experienced at the personal level were undoubtedly remnants from my early childhood. Modeling myself after my father's more intellectual approach to life and disdaining my feminine side—feelings and intuition—made me a likely candidate for this early psychic log jam. By throwing myself into a new and profound stream of consciousness, I spared myself an emotional crisis of greater severity.

On the other hand, I simply threw water on the fire by submitting myself to this spiritual practice; and for years I practiced sublimating my feelings, my emotions, my hurts, and my passions. Rigorously adopting this inner discipline gave me a profoundly new meaning for my life. I *experienced* God rather than just approaching him/her intellectually. Yet, at some very subtle level, I also sublimated my authentic self. Unfortunately, not only the negative side of my personality came into abeyance. Unknowingly, through the rigors of this spiritual practice, I also withheld my own deeper nature as an individual.

Some years later I experienced a crisis at the relational level that was also a profound spiritual crisis. It went that deep because the triangle I had unconsciously created between my husband, my new friend, and me reflected a deep dichotomy inside. Because for so many years I had both tended and hidden the split between thinking and feeling, and consequently between flesh and spirit, I had become polarized. Half of me was a spiritual devotee and in control of my life, and the other half was a woman who had simply pacified a wounded child. Half of me was a respectable pillar in my church and a weekend mystic, and the other half was a wild woman who had repressed spontaneity, passion, and honest self-expression. I find it remarkable, however, that whenever this sort of denial goes on for too long the universe and the angels invariably arrange for a crisis. It is intentionally, I am sure, a benevolent act; one designed both to purify our woundedness and to restore us to balance. But initially crisis is a shaking that no one in her right mind entirely welcomes.

As I continued to try to balance this midlife crisis, some interesting things happened to my own inner orphans. I was forced to see a number of things about myself that I had simply never taken the time to deal with. The impact awakened my slumbering senses, beckoned me to look at how I was repressed, challenged me to confront the weak places within myself, and invited me to deeper self-knowing. What's more, it broke my personal and social myths of being in control, being perfect, being the woman others expected me to be. It wrecked my pillar, threw doubt into the mind of most of my friends, and alienated my church community. My children had nightmares, my husband threatened to leave or throw me out. And, because his shoes were not waterproof, the soles eventually fell off his cowboy boots.

As time went on and the dust settled I became much more aware of who I was, who my husband was, and where our own relationship needed work. I also became aware of the hidden sides of my personality that wanted attention and caring. I began to meet the orphans within myself that I had always denied or kept under wraps. I allowed myself license to face my father complex, to look at the ways I felt both abandoned and mistrustful of (yet dependent on) men in my life; to see the ways I had projected the missing hero-father onto this new man.

Finally, I learned to allow myself to trust being completely open—to follow the river. From one day to the next nothing was predictable, and the safe and known world of the past gave way to the emergence of the more cloistered elements of my nature. I gave myself permission to feel, to be vulnerable, to break past my defenses, to rage and cry, to laugh in the midst of chaos, and to learn to live with paradox.

It became a spiritual crisis because I had denied my feelings and postponed my inner work for too long. I had previously thrived in the spiritual world: I loved my meditations, I had unusual experiences in prayer, my life seemed in order. But intuitively I knew something was missing. I knew that I was nice, but not authentic, that I was safe, but not real. Consciously, I prayed to be a saint, but in my dreams I saw the seductress. I ran from the darkness and shunned all shadowy things, but eventually I ran headlong into my own inner daemons. I lived in the masculine, patriarchal world of good sense and reason and played by all the rules. But I had forgotten how to be myself; and the wounded woman inside me demanded to be heard.

In retrospect, this time of crisis was an invaluable ruin of the false world in which I had proudly lived for years. The Great Choreography had my holism in mind when I entered and painstakingly worked through this impasse. I am indebted to this experience in my life because it has been a faithful teacher; the wisdom it taught me humbles me in profound ways.

If we do not catch these imbalances between soul and psyche in time, the results can be even more serious than a midlife crisis. One woman came to me for therapy some years ago because she was experiencing a marked increase in anxiety and was beginning to feel she was having a nervous breakdown. She noticed herself entertaining awful fears. Rationally, she knew these fears were ridiculous, but emotionally she couldn't seem to reassure herself. During the night she awakened, plagued by frightening thoughts, and couldn't go back to sleep. During the day she became increasingly afraid to be alone because she imagined something might happen to her. She arranged to have her husband or her mother rotate their schedules in order to stay with her, but this soon proved useless and she grew more agitated as the days passed. Her doctor told her she was experiencing some stress and he prescribed a sedative for her so she could relax. At that point she entered therapy.

She was pleasant, docile, agreeable, intelligent, and previously had been happy in her marriage. But now she was a wreck. One day, after we had talked for a while, she began to stiffen up in a curious manner. She said she had just had another terrifying thought. Suddenly, without any warning, she fell to the floor with a shriek and began screaming that she thought she would die; that she couldn't stand these thoughts anymore and that she wouldn't make it. Not knowing what else to do, I got down on the floor beside her and held her, talking to her and rocking her in my lap.

Later on in treatment she told me that as a child she had experienced incest, that her uncle had fondled her and embraced her sexually on several occasions. She came from an extremely devout religious family and she grew up thinking the whole thing was not only hellfire material, but that it had some-how been her fault. When she started to share the terrifying thoughts she'd been having, they turned out to be sexual thoughts; thoughts of rape, of invasion, fantasies of men fon-dling her, long-forgotten memories of her uncle's face. Like many adult children of incest she never told anyone, but buried her experience. As she remained religious and somewhat devout in her faith, one side of her psyche contained her religious imagery and the other contained this dark secret. Because she had not dealt with the secret, and because it had festered in her unconscious, the incident had begun to contaminate her sense of decency and self-esteem. These two sides of her psyche had become enemies; she could no longer bear the conflict unconsciously and so it erupted into her conscious mind. She was experiencing this crisis now because she and her husband, married for about a year and a half, had begun to experience sexual problems. He wanted to start a family, and she grew increasingly afraid of sex and wanted nothing to do with it; for her making love was tantamount to recreating the incest, and her unconscious constellation of memories threatened her sense of normalcy.

In the struggle to take responsibility for our lives and to bring a painful past into the healing process, there are other struggles to be faced that can create an inner crisis. One of my clients told me that her oldest daughter and she had recent-ly had a very painful conversation. She had confessed to her daughter that the girl's natural father was not the one she had always known; that her biological father lived in another state. The mother promised her that when the time seemed right she would inform the girl's natural father about her and that she would ask for a paternity test. The results of the test, taken the following year, were negative; this man was not her father.

Describing this to me, she said, *"I felt betrayed and devastated, totally stripped inside. The pain I felt was overwhelming. And a journey began. In my struggle to deal with this I talked to a lot of people, trying to make sense out of what I had just put myself and my daughter through; trying to make sense of where my life was going. Nothing seemed to ease the pain; I felt as if my soul were scorched, like I had* this great abdominal wound that was deep and abscessed. To look into this whole thing, to work with my past and with the confusion I felt in the present, felt to me like volunteering for death. It seemed like insanity to open up more pain; but the alternative, to shut myself away from it again, with food, drugs, sex, alcohol, or some other superficiality, was to me known death. How to choose between deaths? I chose the way unknown to me—to immerse myself in the pain.

"I decided to go on a five-day retreat, a silent retreat where I could allow this thing more space. Where I had some solitude. One afternoon in my room I began to feel like something inside me wanted to be born; maybe it was a birthing out of this pain I felt. I began to visualize the birth of a very dark girl child with enormous teeth. She was hideous and frightening to me and I could hardly bear looking at her. From my room I carried her into the chapel where I sat Indian-style on the floor before a large crucifix. Words seemed to well up inside me, and looking up at the cross I said, 'I have birthed this child and I cannot love her, can you?' A look of intense compassion came into this Christ's face, and I fell over weeping. In my inability to love the dark, misshapen and ugly part of myself, I found the knowledge that there was a power in the universe that could and would love her, no matter what I felt. My healing had begun."

One woman came into my office one day and announced she had just taken a paid sick leave from her executive responsibilities at work, so she "could get her head together." Feeling fragmented and in a constant state of inner anxiety, she had wisely decided to circle the wagons in her psyche. "I am experiencing the strangest sensations. Sometimes I feel like the room is moving around me, like it's spinning just momentarily. Whatever else is going on around me at work seems far away, like it all recedes into a tunnel. I can't seem to focus when I get this sensation. Have you ever felt like someone was pulling the rug out from underneath you? Well, it's like that. These things don't last long when they happen, but when they're going on I feel completely disarmed. Like my world is collapsing around my ears. My immediate thought is that I'm losing it.

"My one concern when I was an adolescent was getting somewhere in life. I'm an incurable perfectionist and I want to be so good at my job that I make impossible goals for myself, I create unreachable heights. I catch myself being utterly grandiose about what I can do; sometimes I promise my boss things that I cannot possibly do on time. I'm endlessly

*saying 'yes' to the company and I make demands on myself I would
never impose on anyone else. So, here I am, right on the edge."*

As we talked more she told me that one of the things she had
learned in a stress reduction course her company had offered
was how to meditate. *"I've been doing this meditation practice for
about a year and it has been one of the few things I have in my life
that's grounding. It steadies me. I actually feel myself getting quiet
inside when I do it. The only problem is that it doesn't seem to last very
long. I try to practice it whenever I remember to, but it's not enough.
Or maybe I'm not doing it right."*

Undoubtedly, some forms of meditation are grounding. But
after working with this woman for some weeks we both began
to discover that for her meditation was a foray into the unconscious world, with which she was completely unfamiliar. Indeed,
the trek inward seemed at first to open up a previously hidden
anxiety, a fear of failure. She felt she was losing control and
that things in her life were beginning to "spin." The meditation
was lifting the lid on her defense system and she was staring
straight into her fear. Like some forms of therapy, some kinds
of meditation simply open inner doors that can be unsettling.
Defenses are clearly there to cover our childhood wounds, but
they cannot be pulled off like an old bandage. Lifting them and
working through them deserves care and wise pacing.

Second, what made this a spiritual crisis for her was that she
had known very little about the practice she was attempting to
do. The moment she walked past her rational, fairly contained
way of being in the world, she felt like she was going in over
her head. The spiritual world cannot be approached like a
business venture. When we rush into it in order to "accomplish"
something (like reducing stress or gaining psychic insights), we
create another imbalance. One simply cannot go plunging into
these depths without some sense of pacing and reverence. Coming to soul is a holy venture that our Western penchant for
productivity and increase has trouble computing.

If our childhood has been painful and we have hidden that
pain by what we have managed to accomplish, crisis signals us
that it's time for a change. Whether we've been fighting against
depression, anger, anxiety, or fear, the moment we peer inside
this repressed voice will certainly speak to us.

At one time I had a wise old man in my life. His name was Bapak, and he was like a spiritual father to me. He called this crisis process "purification." Once we begin to clean house, everything we've not dealt with in the past is likely to show up in the present.

Bapak was from Indonesia, and what was often so enlightening being near him was watching the way he walked, the way he moved and laughed and seemed so at home in the world. He accepted everything that happened to him with the same peaceful countenance; whether it was fortune or misfortune, he smiled at it. In the West most of us—myself included—expect that when we get into the soup we must find an immediate way out, an instant answer to our fix. We often seek remedies that tend either to eliminate what we are feeling altogether, or we throw ourselves toward the possibility of a cure; and yet seldom are willing to see it through to completion. The idea of allowing ourselves to balance naturally is foreign to us. But alas, there are often few shortcuts to this work. And sometimes the best way to clean and sanctify the house is to take it room by room. At some point one must simply get synchronized with a more cosmic timepiece.

Most women are either forced into the journey through a personal or relational crisis, or are slowly coerced into wakefulness because of some more chronic problem. Because crisis implies some sort of shifting, unsettling, or change, it can be creative. The way that we greet it, survive it, work through it, and then take the next step can make a profound difference. The women I know who have most often turned to embrace the crisis and then somehow managed to integrate it are the women who have the most to show for their trouble. They are the ones who have refused to give in to the thing and who have become authentic and powerful individuals.

3. The Deeper Waters of the Self: Awakening Consciousness

When our oldest son, Abe, was sixteen, my husband and I took him and his friend Bill backpacking into the Mother Lode country of the Sierra. The two boys, anxious to see what lay beyond the ridge we were crossing, forged ahead and soon left us in the dust. When they reached a wide river swollen over its banks with an icy spring runoff, they decided to wait for us. We walked up and down the banks. Looking for a crossing but finding none, we decided to brave the icy water and wade across. My husband went first, then Bill. Packs, pants, and boots slung over their shoulders, they each carefully inched their way across the wild current.

When it was my turn I gritted my already chattering teeth and began to cross. About two-thirds of the way across I discovered just how swift the water actually was. One false step on the slippery rocks underfoot and no telling how far down the river I might end up. I began to picture what might happen if I slipped, planning what I would let go of first, trying to calculate whether or not the weight of my pack would give me a permanent seat at the bottom of the river. Glancing down at the frozen water swirling around my hips, and realizing what a dangerous predicament I was in, I promptly froze on the spot.

With no second thoughts about my pride, I called out for Bill—who was just putting on his pants—to come in and give me a hand. He waded back in and reached for me, and I was amazed that the mere touch of his hand gave me just the confidence I needed to finish the crossing. Once across, I wondered how I could have frozen up like that.

A few years later, during a time of mourning for this young

man's untimely death in a motorcycle accident, I often recalled the image of his hand stretching out across the waters to me. And I wondered what the crossing might have been without the grounding of his presence.

Although many women make an honest effort to follow themselves inward through working at some sort of therapy, most of us make only a partial descent. For many of us the authentic inner woman is still repressed and the deeper waters of the self remain uncharted. Undoubtedly, there will be times in our journey when the obstacles in our crossing become difficult or dangerous, times we feel stuck and unable to move. But these very obstacles are the barriers in our growth, and it is these we need to pay the most attention to.

I have heard it said, both in contemporary theological circles and growth awareness groups, that the meaning of the word "sin" (aside from suggesting a life out of harmony with God) is a life that is incompletely lived. It is my intention in this chapter to review the ways we fail to live out our fuller potentials; to point out some of the more vulnerable places in the journey where we can become stuck, ensnared by some sabotaging element in our own nature. It is my own experience that sin happens when we neglect our potential, when we fail to bring to life our highest self. We neglect to make life happen within us and consequently around us because we have become somehow separated from ourselves and have lost our way. When this happens, for whatever reason, the soul becomes like an unmarked path, overgrown with years of untamed growth and pocked with places the soil has eroded and washed away.

In a moment we will look at some of the reasons why many women fail to enter or to fully cross these waters of the unconscious, but first let's examine something of the nature of the unconscious itself.

THE UNCONSCIOUS: A KEY TO HEALING

In my own inner work I have found the unconscious mind to be my best teacher. In that realm I have encountered alternately the best and worst sides of my nature. There I have met both my most formidable enemy and my best friend, and have struggled with the paradox of the coexistence of the strangest of bedfellows. Over time I have been amazed and mortified to discover a diversity of characters who both please and terrify me. Attitudes, thoughts, feelings, and behaviors belonging to not one, but seemingly several different and even opposing inner figures, sometimes vie for my attention—or worse, somebody else's. At best, I must confess to the complexity of my own inner house; in its rooms I continue to discover that within me which is a potential treasure, and that which is most wounded and liable to error.

The unconscious is an energy field of the greatest magnitude. Far below the surface of our ordinary awareness, there resides an inner life, a deeper field of knowing that waits to be found out. The more we plumb the depths of this inner life and seek to tap its resources, the more genuinely conscious we become. According to C. G. Jung, the mind is only the tip of the iceberg.[1] This metaphor implies that there is much more psychic energy available to us than what the conscious mind has so far shown us. Yet discovering this inner domain takes both work and cooperation with oneself. It is a sometimes intense, sometimes frightening and querulous journey, yet the truth it explores is the only real liberation.

The unconscious can house both our potential strengths and our greatest weaknesses, and in this there is an unsettling paradox. If we picture the unconscious as a coin with one side exposed to the light and the other side hiding in the dark, then the idea of the dual nature of the unconscious becomes clearer. On the light side of the coin lies all the best of our human and divine potentials. Herein are many of the qualities and character strengths we need for psycho-spiritual growth, but perhaps have not fully developed. On the dark side lies everything we have not seen or acknowledged about ourselves—past hurts and rejections, early life failures, present resentments and repressed feelings are but a few of the many potential ingredients for trouble that have slowly piled up in the dark.

ON THE LIGHT SIDE

Once we have begun the psychological work involved in confronting and healing the false images of the self, we can begin to discover the authentic self. Housed within this more positive side of the unconscious are all of our hidden talents, potentials, and treasures. Here is strength, honor, beauty, and integrity. Here are the reserves of the best of human nature and its unfolding—the resources of our own highest and most unique human possibilities. And, ultimately, it is here we will meet the true feminine soul, the mystery of ourselves as woman and spirit.

One woman I worked with last year experienced a particularly painful divorce. She had begun to feel overwhelmed by a tide of grief and rage that seemed unsurmountable to her. Yet after some time of working through these hurts, she began to find an inner strength. The deeper she dove into her own unconscious waters, the more she was able to access some reserves she didn't know she had. From time to time when she entered her active imagination (a technique for getting in touch with unconscious images), she noted that a certain presence seemed to visit her. Over a period of weeks this presence spoke to her, offering her words of direction and challenge, giving her hope and reminding her to believe in herself. This inner woman seemed to be her deepest feminine strength, an internal figure whose work it was to bring a powerful light into the dark side of her life.

Another woman I know who has been working to reconstruct some of the forgotten treasures within her own unconscious recently said, *"I had a secret place as a child where the whole world had to take off its shoes and just be quiet. It was a hedgegrove up the coast by the sea and I used to sit in the branches of one of the old junipers there and listen to the wind. I had great adventures sitting in that tree, hidden away from everything, imagining I was making up my life from day to day. I think it was the one place for me that was always sacred. Like a sort of healing place.*

"In the quieter moments of my childhood I discovered that there were hidden spaces within myself that had answers and guidance, spaces that brought me closer to some sense of well being inside. I spent hours playing alone, creating a lot of my own intrigues and games, allowing the dark gifts of nature to restore what the world had sometimes bruised or overlooked."

Often children innately know how to use the unconscious as a hiding place, a place to rest and refuel through play, imagination, and daydreams. As adults we can call on this same creative resource in our own healing work.

The moment I began to pay closer attention to my own unconscious a few years back—to dreams, fantasies, spontaneous images, moods, occasional unconscious murmurings and little Freudian slips—I began to discover that I had a number of seemingly autonomous characters inside. One of these fellows was an inner figure of sorts, a sort of Koshare,* whose job it appeared was to look after me in this life. This figure was always willing to tell me the truth, whether I liked it or not. Time and again he appeared in dreams, in impulsive moods, in moments of abandon. He seemed to appear as a devilish thought, a hint of capriciousness, a mad whim, as if to remind me that in my ordinary life I wasn't giving that side of my personality any breathing room at all. His devilishness, far from being some darker aspect of myself, seemed unequivocally directed at poking some light into my dismal status quo.

Another figure frequently showed at about the same time, an impish adolescent who appeared off and on in my dreams. She did the most outlandish things, things only a child would do. In these nightly dream visits I was frequently chasing after her to punish her (because my adult side couldn't take her antics). But she usually ran away in fits of laughter, leaving me to fume at her impudence. Ironically, she came at a time when I seemed to have lost the joyful spontaneity of my childhood, a time when I needed to remember the bright wildness of my own youth. I think I had known many such inner friends as a child, but in the spaces of my growing up, I had unknowingly covered them all, one by one.

ON THE DARK SIDE

On the other side of the unconscious is a storehouse of a different kind. Often the split-off psychic contents contained here are all of our unacknowledged or unacceptable attitudes—negative thoughts, feelings of anger, rage, fear, and hatred. Here too are the more irrational sides of our personality, things of bizarre fantasy, and other nefarious phenomena of the mind

---

*The Koshare is a Hopi spirit figure who is generally associated with the village trickster. He is also associated with restoring balance in situations of disharmony. Where there is folly he becomes wise; but where there is ego inflation and hubris he becomes the devil's advocate and a reminder to come back to our senses.

which we cannot ordinarily explain to ourselves, much less others. These unconscious contents—when unleashed to conscious awareness—threaten our sense of normalcy or "niceness." Most of us clamor to keep such untoward sides of the personality under tight control, and some of us deny we have a dark side at all. But the truth is that all of us have such thoughts and feelings and must sooner or later consciously deal with them, or they will certainly deal with us. Undoubtedly, if we have something cooking below consciousness that we try to ignore or repress, eventually it will try to surface either behaviorally, emotionally, or through a physical symptom.

This side of the unconscious can also manifest as our *shadow* side, about which I will speak more later. Briefly, the shadow side of the personality refers to one of the more prominent characters housed in the unconscious, the one from whom we have split off most surgically. It is that side of the self that carries the unlived energy within each of us. My own shadow side is the woman I most dislike seeing in myself. She is the very antithesis of what I want to be consciously, the opposite of my ideal self. I am aware, for instance, that consciously I like approval. But if I continually prioritize an agenda that seeks approval, and if I miss seeing that my behavior be an attempt to cover a fear of failure, in time I will be off balance. My conscious mind may think I have everything under control and that I'm just helping humanity with these behaviors, but my unconscious mind smells a rat. Surely, then, something in me will begin to dream up just the opposite of approval. The shadow is the woman in my dreams who everyone disdains; she is the one who loses face, who makes a fool of herself; the one in the parade who wears the emperor's new clothes and winds up a laughingstock. She wrecks my false sense of achievement and inevitably reminds me that, underneath my show of competent behaviors, I have some insecurity I need to work through.

In this inner work we soon find that not only are we likely to divorce from the shadow and other repressed sides of the personality—we are probably also cut off from our center, from the vital place of the soul.

DESCENT TO THE SOUL

Because psychological and spiritual healing go hand in hand, this work of self-awareness with which we begin the journey is also a descent to soul. Aminah Raheem, author of *Soul Return: A Guide to Transpersonal Integration*, says that once we sort out and clear away the imbalances in our personality then the voice of the soul will begin to reveal itself. Accordingly, when we work through the more static sides of the personality, then we are freer to come to what Raheem calls "soul awareness."[2]

Yet the way to the self and soul within is not an ascent, but a descent. As the mask of the personality breaks and new potentials and realities emerge, we often find that we need to face much more of our weaknesses and frailties than we may have imagined. This process of breaking through the false self can be unfamiliar and frightening, but there is no getting to soul without taking this plunge.

In the account of the Dialogue of the Savior from the *Nag Hammadi Library*, Jesus says, "If one does not stand in the darkness, he will not be able to see the light."[3] In the story Jesus is showing Mariam, Matthew, and Judas a picture of the heavenly sphere. Below the sphere is a picture of a fiery pit, which the three were terrified to see. Jesus then goes on to tell them that from heaven a seed fell into the pit, reassuring them that heaven would send that seed a word to redeem it; a word that would come forth from heaven to the depths and bring redemption. The inference here is that before we are able to come to the heavenly place (light), we must descend to the pit (the darkness in our own nature).

In any sort of work on the self a woman must identify which of her seeds has been "cast into the pit." The temptation for many of us is to want insight and wholeness before we ever have to deal with the darkness in our nature. Our whole socio-religious structure shuns this sort of inner work. For some reason we have been taught to get rid of the darkness, to deny it, repress it, to turn toward the light. But real awareness can only come from walking right into the dark pit and facing the trouble in the personality. This lost or condemned part must then be nurtured, called into life again, and redeemed.

Women especially need to acknowledge this place of soul. We must try to give it a new meaning that is not based on religious rhetoric, but on experience. For the purpose of the journey, soul must manifest in us not because of some understanding of theology or religious ritual, but because of a longing to meet the truth of life within us. Many women misunderstand the concept of soul and often equate it with religion. But awareness of soul does not mean simply following a particular religious practice; it does not come from ritual or from a specific set of beliefs common to a particular body of the faithful. Soul is the little vessel that houses the spirit; it is an interior essence all of us have, but with which most of us are not in contact. Many of us have followed religion; some of us stay and some of us leave; but few of us have come to soul.

Inner work and soul seeking is difficult, and no doubt that's why so few venture it. Once we turn inward for the identity which we have so far sought outwardly, the way becomes narrow indeed. But once we begin to touch our weakness, to plumb the depth of the wounds in the unconscious, we also begin to experience the real meaning of a holy presence.

In a prayer dialogue with the Savior, St. Augustine once said, "In my deepest wound I saw your glory and it dazzled me." This insight infers that it isn't until we touch our weakness and our interior poverty that the full glory of the soul is free to emerge. This interior life that we begin to uncover is at first a small inner voice; a subtle whisper of some divine process that waits to be found out, a gradual awakening of the voice of God within. It speaks no condemnation, only words of empowerment and mercy.

A FEAR OF THE UNKNOWN

Many of us seem stuck in the waters of our healing process because we have become complacent and comfortable, too dependent upon things running smoothly. When we look more closely at complacency, however, we often see a subtle emotional paralysis. When we allow ourselves to become caught up in our work or in causes, and claim to be too busy to get into the waters of the self, at the bottom of everything is often a fear of change. To move inwardly at all means work; it means facing interior conflict that we may not even be aware of initially. It means entering paradox and letting go of the tight controls we have prescribed over our destiny; facing the denial many of us have built into our system about who we are.

The unconscious is the unknown part of our psyche, after all, and some people will have a hard time getting their feet wet. The known for many of us, as disagreeable or painful as it may be, is often preferable to the unknown. And, too, change can be agitating because it beckons the traveler into new territory. The following dream illustrates such an impasse:

"I am at a border crossing of some kind, in a foreign country. Maybe it is Russia. I am trying to get across into another country and the border patrol has stopped me. They are checking my belongings, everything I have with me. I have something I know they want and I am hiding it in my purse. It is a document of some sort which I am taking across the line, and I know if they find it they will detain me and not allow me to cross at all. I am terrified they will find it in their searching, but they don't. I pretend everything is all in order and that I am just vacationing. But in my heart I am planning not to return at all to this place. At one point I can't find my passport and have to look through all my belongings to find it. People are waiting in a long line behind me and I am holding everyone up."

The dreamer is a woman of about forty who wants to make a career and a relationship change, but is apprehensive about what this might mean for her. She came to me to discuss her options. She had been working to unearth a more assertive and goal-directed side of her personality. At one level she had decided that she wanted more adventure; she had goals toward more personal power and change. These were her conscious intentions, anyway. But as she spoke, her body language said something different. Every time she mentioned wanting to leave her present relationship, for example, she crossed her arms and legs. Verbally, she seemed to come forward, and there was even an assertiveness in the tone of her voice; but as she spoke her whole body tilted backward and seemed to press in the opposite direction from her words. When she spoke she held her breath slightly and did not exhale fully.

The more we talked, the more the border-patrol guards in

the dream seemed to take control of her body. Perhaps they represent those aspects of her ambivalence that want to hold her back, to detain her. Maybe they personify the voices of her own doubtful, self-critical thoughts, jeering at her from the sidelines of her mind, ultimately keeping her afraid or intimidated.

Such body-mind incongruities are often a signal that a person is caught at a crossing she lacks the courage to make. Whether or not she finds her passport, however, will depend on whether she is able to confront her inner judges. The ambivalent voices that sometimes interfere with her growth movements might sound like this, once found out: "Well, I know you'd like to get on with your life, but really, this is a pretty tricky business. Suppose you make a big mistake and lose everything? Nope, I just don't think you're ready. Might as well stick around here with us and kick back for another decade."

These are the inner voices we all must confront; they are the edges of our own ambivalence that immobilize many of us on the journey. These are the unconscious voices that keep us suspended in a fear of avoiding conflict.

In the journey to the self there are endless dreams like this: We are on a crossing, a journey, a descent; then suddenly there are obstacles and we are held up for one reason or another. Seeking consciousness is hard work, there is no doubt about it. It takes a constant wakefulness to ferret out the obstacles to the inner life. It takes a stout heart to be willing to wade all the way into the unconscious and to follow through with it, once begun.

At this point in the journey a woman must make an agreement with herself that she is willing to come all the way into the waters of the self. She must agree that she will try to embrace the paradox that she meets, to go with some things unanswered or unresolved for a while. This is the dark night of the soul; it is the place of silent wondering known by mystics both East and West. A woman must make a pact with herself that she will not be frightened or helpless in the face of her own weaknesses, her own shadow side, or the external obstacles she may meet. She must give herself a helping hand, or reach out for another who can help guide her across.

MEETING THE DARK INTRUDERS

Some time ago I had the following dream: *My husband and I and our two daughters are in a sea coast home on vacation. Everything seems very pleasant until I see a young woman outside who seems to be crazy. As I watch her through the window she walks up and begins knocking on the front door. She wants to come into my home and to be with my family, but something is definitely wrong with her. She slurs her speech, looks somewhat dazed and slightly weird. First I am frightened by her because she seems so out of control. I think maybe she is on drugs or that she might be capable of harming my children. Part of me feels sorry for her and the other part feels afraid to let her in. I wake up still trying to decide whether to trust her or not.*

This dream came at a time in my life when I had too much control over myself, and had been pouring myself into my work nonstop. I was also keeping a fairly rigorous watch over what I considered to be the unacceptable sides of my personality. Afraid of confrontation, and cautious about saying my real feelings, I kept my temper and my thoughts to myself. The young girl, an intruder who is by all appearances "out of it," is the opposite of this conscious vigilance. I had been so rigorous toward myself, so alert to doing the right thing that it took this young shadow figure to wake me up. Her out-of-control state delivered the clear message that I needed to relax the controls I was demanding of myself.

The reason the shadow figure turns up at all is because we have been wounded as children. Over the years we have padded ourselves sufficiently not to feel these wounds, and eventually we have collected an impressive defense system that ignores and denies that our inner child is hurt at all. Yet if we do not face the shadow side of our nature, eventually we will separate completely from any awareness of our own weaknesses or faults. When this happens the shadow acts out on its own.

Some women are shocked to have to share the same dreamscape with characters who seem to be misbehaving or acting out in some way. In most cases these dark intruders are ourselves: the unexpressed and ignored sides of the personality we refuse to acknowledge. For example, the woman who identifies with the role of being a good wife may find herself dreaming of strange intrigues with other men, or of amorous inclinations toward an old friend or lover. This woman may be devoted to her husband at the expense of her own independence; the dream will come to show her that there is a problem in the woodpile of her motives toward relationships.

Perhaps another shadow for a woman who lends herself unquestioningly to a mate (or to others) is the lost woman in dreams, the one who wanders aimlessly and never finds the keys to her car, misses her transportation, loses her purse (her identity), or is being driven someplace against her will. In her need to be needed she may be giving too much of her self away and become lost, without direction, always falling short of her destination. In short, the ideal of the good wife may seriously be crowding her autonomy.

I once knew a woman who sacrificed everything for her children. She was the kind of mother who simply spent herself on doing all the right things for her girls. But as the girls grew older and began to assert their independence, the mother grew increasingly fearful that they were rejecting her. The more loving and nurturing she tried to be, the more these two girls squirmed and pushed away. The woman began to have a series of nightmares which seemed to repeat a certain perplexing and frightening theme. *"In the basement of my house there is a noise, and I go down to see what it is. A sort of moaning is coming from a closet, and as I walk near a voice begs me to let it out. I grow frightened and stand there frozen, not knowing what to do. The voice grows louder and begins to wail. Each time this thing cries out the closet door swells as though it will burst. Suddenly, it dawns on me that this presence is evil and that if I let it out it will devour me and my children upstairs. I awaken feeling absolutely terrified. In other dreams there is sometimes a hideous witch trying to get in through the window and she is bent on going after my children. I try to find something to fight her with, but I never seem to have anything at hand."*

A mother who overprotects her offspring and cares for them too much may be using them for her own ego need. Underneath her apparent loving manner she may be rather demanding and manipulative. The mother who cannot allow her child to separate from her is in danger of penetrating and taking over her child's territory. Such a mother force is out of balance with her positive nurturing ability, and the shadow will turn up as an overpowering, engulfing presence—a monster locked in a closet or an evil witch trying to get in. The demonic sense this woman picked up from the closet in her basement was her own repressed self below consciousness. Her emotional need had entirely too much power and was threatening to engulf everybody.

Likewise, the woman who pursues religious ideals may find her shadow side in dreams as a bum or a harlot who lures her down from her achieving heights. If our conscious attitudes are a bit too regal, if we live too much in our heads and are too devoted to spiritual perfection, we can be sure to find the pauper or the tart among our nightly visitors. The bag lady always waits patiently for the woman who lives her life hooked into performance, perfectionism, and control. Here too for the woman solely identified with religious principles, are intruders from her own unexpressed instinctual side—Marlon Brando on a Harley-Davidson, tearing off her clothes; or the cave man running close behind with a wooden club near the mouth of a great dark cave.

However these shadowy figures appear in our lives, whether through dreams or through the pace of our ordinary day, we always have an opportunity to wake up and listen to the wisdom of their intrusions. Often they are a divine summons to look carefully at where we are not living out our potential. This is the role of the shadow.

In some cases we do not just dream about the shadow, we become it. We dream it up and act it out.

A recovered alcoholic friend of mine told me what it was like when she was drinking. Married and a mother of three, she was a normal housewife during the day. She'd put the kids to bed after a long day, tuck them in with stories—and then get out her bottle. By the time she realized how badly off she was she had already come fully into the alcoholic process. It wasn't until a friend of hers took her to Alcoholics Anonymous, where she had a deep conversion experience, that she was able to face the truth of how much of her life she had wasted in her closet drinking.

This woman's shadow side was the drinker figure. The drinker for her was a powerful inhibitor of her feelings and a temporary answer to her need to fall unconscious and ignore her problems.

Unlike this woman, who became her shadow without realizing it, some people are at first aware of an internal struggle, aware that an inner conflict of some sort is going on. A person who is awake to this can fight it, struggle against it, and try to work out an alternative. Others, however, are too far into denial, too locked into unconscious behaviors to battle their own weakness. Some go about like a will-o-the-wisp and never bat an eye at the lies they tell or the number of lives they hurt in the process of denial they live out.

Each of us has a place within where we are weakest or most hurt. Into this wound other hurts can lodge and build up over the years, so that the wound festers and worsens. Instead of trying to lance our hurts, to work through them toward healing, we often cover and defend them until we have completely isolated ourselves from the truth. Once hidden and unacknowledged, these inner wounds tend not to diminish but to grow. Eventually, evil gains its own autonomy and becomes a closed system that is almost impenetrable by ordinary means. It finds a closet to hide in where it cannot be seen and where it becomes cloaked in the dark world of our nightmares.

If we are not conscious about why we behave or feel a certain way, or why we say or do certain things, then we are living unconsciously. If we continue in this unawakened state, then in time we begin to lie to ourselves about our behavior. Since denial itself is born out of hurt, out of having once been victimized or betrayed in some way, it becomes a defense against being hurt again. But unless it's caught in time, denial itself becomes our victimizer. Rather than risk truth and admit error, we continue the lie and make excuses. To protect ourselves from the truth we have to become increasingly yet subtly dishonest.

A few years back, for example, I discovered how subtly programmed I had become at avoiding conflict. I literally would do or say anything to get out of an unpleasant situation. I hated the possibility of hurting anyone's feelings, having to be direct, or not being thought of as a nice person. More than just conflict avoidance, I used a subtle system of denial to cover my fear of getting into any true grit with anyone. The threat of that kind

of heat felt too overwhelming to me. My own wound was insecurity—I didn't feel confident enough to blast anybody or to
just let it all out. When things got hot I found myself becoming
less and less who I was and more and more the person I thought
others wanted me to be. I hid my anger, my gut-level response
to life, my real opinions. What's more, the more I looked at this
flight pattern, the more I saw that not only wasn't I telling the
truth, in some cases I just plain stretched the truth to get out
of my discomfort. My mother used to call small fabrications
"white lies"; I don't know what she called the big ones. I suppose I grew up thinking the white ones were all right, and that
it was the other colors that must have been bad.

One definition of evil is "something that brings sorrow, misfortune, and distress." In the broadest sense evil is that part of
us which fails to be healthy, the part of our lives which has
fallen into unknowing, into darkness. Ultimately, it's where our
heart becomes hard and we forget our basic humanity.

Evil is that little bit of compulsive behavior that we do without
much conscience: We see it in the woman who gets angry at
someone but will not honestly face her anger, and winds up
gossiping about it to someone else. We see it in the religious
woman who speaks sweetly, but whose words are laced with hints
of judgment, self-righteousness, or jealousy. It's there in the
alcoholic, who gradually yet helplessly reaches phase three of
the following dictum: "First the man takes a drink, then the
drink takes a drink, then the drink takes the man." I once knew
a terrific spiritual adviser. He had wisdom that made people
feel inspired and humbled, but every year he cheated on his
income taxes. There are many ways to live the lie, whether we
consciously acknowledge that we have a problem or not. Unless
we are conscious about how we create evil in our lives, it gradually sneaks up on us and slowly takes us on from behind until
we're had.

Few of us intentionally set out to lie or act in false ways. Few
people premeditate how they are going to create false fronts.
As a human race, however, we do act in false and unconscious
ways; in ways that make us blind to our faults as well as to our
highest potentials. This is why it's essential to get to the root of
our unconscious behaviors, and to honestly plumb the depths

of our own blindness. Once we're underway in this process we have already begun to turn around the negative effects of these strategies of denial. The energy we invest in covering ourselves up and staying "safe"—and ultimately stuck—then becomes free to go where it needs to go.

TO SEE THE TRUTH FACE TO FACE: SHADOW AND PROJECTION

Sometimes we don't go into the waters of the unconscious because we are afraid of what we'll see and the changes we know we'll have to make. Women are notoriously good at changing things and other people, but very few of us are adept at changing ourselves. There is no end to the women who come into my office wanting me to change their husband, their children, their situation. Those who manage to stay around for the truth—that it is internal change, not external change that makes things better—have accepted a vital ingredient in their own healing work: themselves.

Mahatma Gandhi once said, "To see the universal and all-pervading spirit of truth face to face one must be able to love the meanest of creation as oneself."[4] But why do some of us have such trouble with this, and why are we afraid to admit that we ourselves are the problem? One of the hardest things in life is to accept ourselves as we really are. This does not mean accepting who we "think" we are or who we sometimes pretend to be; it means embracing the one within who hides behind the mask. But all of us, men and women, have a hard time loving the faults of others, much less our own. Most of us can't love others, because we don't love ourselves. We can't accept other people's weaknesses because we haven't yet faced our own. So we say the problem originates outside of us. We are afraid to see the dirt in our own lives, so we see it in the lives of others. Such is the way projection works, as this woman's words illustrate:

"My daughter and I never got along. She was a holy terror. She fought me in everything. She rebelled from the time she was two. I could never do anything right. Even when she was a baby she rejected me. I tried to nurse her, she pulled away at the breast. I tried to hold her, she shoved me away. I could never do the right thing. Now she's a teenager

and she's still difficult. Sometimes I feel like I can't do anything well enough to suit her. Now she's bringing this boyfriend of hers around the house, and I just can't stand him. I hope they're not sleeping together, but these days, who knows?"

This woman has clearly turned on her daughter. By making her teenager the villain she is actually projecting her own self-hatred and rejection onto the girl, all along saying it is the other way around. Mothers with low self-esteem often "feel" their children don't think well of them; but often it is the mother herself who, expecting to be unlovable, pushes the child away in her own feelings.

When my husband and I first began consciously working on our relationship, it was often difficult to find and withdraw projections. They were endless. I complained that he lacked intimacy, that I couldn't get close to him emotionally. The more I looked at which of us was really afraid of intimacy, however, the more I began to see that *I* was the one who quaked at the thought of being vulnerable. I had a habit of making myself appear intimate by talking intimacy; but the truth was that my self-disclosure was a kind of ruse. I might initiate some attempt at close sharing and openness, but I was also the one to sound the first retreat.

Another example of shadow is where we begin to notice that we are different people in different circumstances. In my church I may give the impression that I want to be seen as holy; maybe at work I want to be seen as Wonder Woman; but at home people see me as I am. Children and spouses are often likely to spot the other side of the heroine we are so anxious to show others. Welcome or not, these intruding personalities, whether they come in the form of dreams or projection, have one intention in mind: to humble us.

Projection is such a popular defense for most people because it automatically guarantees its user from having to own up to the problem herself. Projection works ultimately to put someone else on the hotseat, while we ourselves pretend that we're not in the least to blame. There is a certain comfort, after all, in feeling blameless or victimized. But it is in this self-righteous state that many women become paralyzed and unable to face themselves. One of my friends in a women's group recently said,

"The truth is, I hate seeing my own faults. I'd much rather sit here comfortably and see yours than sit here uncomfortably and see my own." An honest woman aware of her own shadow is not going to be stuck for long.

Unfortunately, however, many women use others as excuses to stay immobilized. For instance: "I feel like I can't get away from the house. I'm tied to the kids, I'm tied to my husband, and I feel trapped. I'd like to go back to school, but what would they do without me? I just can't do what I want." Later this same woman complained again that her husband expected a lot from her and that she was afraid of letting him down if she wasn't somehow always "there" for him. The red flag that begins to show up here is that, in fact, this woman is not really ready to go to school because she is afraid to venture out on her own. But rather than face herself and her own fear of taking on a new career, she tells herself that it is her family that's stopping her; that it's her husband that keeps her in the pumpkin. This woman's primary inhibitor is not her husband, but herself.

AVOIDING INNER WORK AND CREATING ILLNESS

Some of us don't venture inward because we are afraid that when we awaken to the whole self, our long-repressed feelings will want to come up and take over. So we avoid the journey. One woman I know suffers from painful arthritis. She has been avoiding inner work for years because she feels it would hurt too much to make the descent to some of her deepest wounds. She fears that she would simply fall apart when faced with the things she has so long cut herself off from. Yet the sad part of this is that these interior wounds that have lain so long have not simply kept quiet and healed over, they have festered and grown in magnitude. Chances are that they control a lot more of her response to life than she would like to admit. Feelings, once we split off from them, have to go somewhere; and just because they don't get expressed is no sign that they have ceased to exist. Perhaps this woman's arthritis is trying to tell her something.

There is a parable in the Old Testament about Moses and the Israelites in the desert (Numbers 21: 4–9). Because the people had been rebellious and were causing all sorts of trouble, God sent down upon them a chastisement in the form of poisonous serpents. When the people saw the snakes they grew frightened they would be bitten and die—which is, of course, what happened to some of them. Not long after the serpents had arrived on the scene, the people came running back to Moses and promised to reform and get better. When Moses promised God that the people were serious, God relented. The story goes that God told Moses to have his artisans fashion a rod on which a bronze serpent was mounted. If anyone was bitten they were to go immediately to the image and look upon it. This would nullify the toxin from the bite, and they would be healed.

I was struck by this story because it symbolizes our healing process so beautifully. When we are plagued by something, or when something has bitten us, we must immediately turn and stare it in the face. When we confront the thing directly and acknowledge it fully, then we have control over its toxic effects.

Look at depression, for instance. It's a very toxic energy which, once in our system, can cause emotional chaos, a sense of hopelessness, and a real slowing down of our vital life energies. Metaphorically, it acts like the bite of a serpent in its effect over our whole system. Yet these toxins of repressed anger or sadness, if ignored long enough, sooner or later let us know they're there. Eventually, they manifest in a breakdown of one kind or another. So, to face the depression and to fix our gaze on it intentionally is the only way to get at the truth of why the depression is happening. If it's something we have repressed internally, then we need to dig it up and become conscious of what it is. Depression simply comes from holding feelings in; and if we are not consciously aware of doing this, the body will certainly be soon willing to tell us.

I once had a client who complained that she was out of touch with her feelings and periodically experienced a painful constriction in her throat. The first time we spoke, even as she was trying to tell me her problem, her throat began to ache. Her voice grew shaky but she was unable to cry. It is amazing what the throat can do, especially when it has been closed for a long time. Over the course of our work together, this woman and I discovered that all sorts of sounds could come out of her throat. Laughter, tears, cries of rage, long-overdue messages to the people in her life—sounds of all kinds rumbled and rippled out. And what beautiful sounds she learned to make with that throat of hers. Of course her throat constriction ceased almost as soon as she began to be conscious of the ways she was withholding the sounds of the heart. Not long ago she said to me, "I'm noticing that I can sing differently nowadays; I can reach notes I was never able to reach before."

Almost every complaint I hear that involves the ears, nose, throat, and chest has to do with repressing feeling. The ancient Chinese, who discovered and refined a system of internal energies on which the practice of acupressure is based, knew that the neck is the mediator between the mind (thinking) and the heart (feeling). When there is trouble in the neck area it often can be traced to some kind of emotional pain and withholding. This woman's throat was the ground for a battle between her conscious and unconscious, which were deadlocked, and her pain was letting her know it.

I had another client who used to complain of a tightness around her chest. Whenever she got anxious her breathing rate would increase until she felt as though she couldn't catch her breath. Sometimes she felt dizzy and faint, and at other times she experienced a sense of panic. As she worked to uncover the cause of the constriction in her chest, she found it to be a pattern of emotional withholding. She was unable to express herself because she feared making her already volatile husband even angrier; so she held herself in until she was nearly choking. As she learned to be assertive and to release her passive way of dealing with him, she began to find her voice. The more she found her voice (and her own rightful expression of anger and feelings), the less tightness she felt around her chest. The breath that we withhold is connected to our feelings; when feelings and words are held in, the breath will signal us by shutting down. I have also seen this to be the case with many people who are asthmatic.

Many women are wounded at the heart level because our culture has generally diverted itself from feeling. We can be emotional, but this doesn't mean we can recognize and articulate feelings. The fact is, a lot of women are *afraid* to feel. Most of us are too defended to feel pain, anger, excitement, joy, outrageous impishness, or to take risks. Emotionally we are immobilized, bound to convention and a masculine penchant to keep a stiff upper lip. Most of us don't trust intimacy, avoid deep self-disclosure, and run from saying who we are in any relationship. Most women are stuck at the level of heart because few of us ever learn how to use it.

A FEAR OF OUR INSTINCTS

Some women shy away from entering the waters of the unconscious because our society has not only taught us to deny our feelings, it has also endorsed a betrayal of our instincts. Beneath the layers of cultural refinement and the collective masks that we wear slumber some profound internal chemistries. Take, for instance, our sexual energy.

Sexual energy is a natural part of the instinctual energy harnessed in the body, yet it is also energy which is not specifically genital in nature. Sexual energy can also be described as a pulsation which can and does manifest in the whole body. It encompasses a whole range of human responses, and for this reason should not be confined to one specific area of the body. Yet most women are afraid of this more primitive natural self. Many of us polarize these instinctual energies by either acting out of the instincts promiscuously (unconsciously), or becoming intellectualized and avoiding the body altogether.

The fear of sexuality is a double bind for women who are on a spiritual quest. In order to explore the work of holism, one must go into the body and into the split between flesh and spirit which has caused us such woundedness. Many of us seem at home in our work and commitments, or in relationship to the significant others in our lives; but few of us have acknowledged any connectedness to our own flesh. We live in the body as if it were simply some shell that must be tolerated to get us around, but many of us remain significantly unable to feel at home in it.

When I was growing up I treated my body as though it were something slightly alien to me; I walked around in it, but the two of us were simply not connected. I was sympathetic to the ascetic St. Francis's endearing term for his own body—"brother ass"; I similarly saw the fleshy part of my nature as somehow inferior or less than the loftier place of mind and spirit. In many ways I lived polarized from the body and its earthy side.

In contrast, Eastern spirituality has long said that spiritual and sexual energies are very closely interrelated. To be strong spiritually we must also acknowledge our sexuality and admit that we are not cut off at the waist. Yet the fact remains that many women are ashamed of their bodies, out of touch with them, and not in communion with their own more earthy nature. For instance, for most of us bodily pleasure is something we rarely think about, consider, or allow ourselves to freely participate in. I am not just speaking of genital sexuality here, I am also speaking of touch, affection, foot rubs, massage, closeness, hugs, bodies next to us at close proximity. Most of us hurry through our day, taking very little time for any such pleasures. Women who focus outward, toward some goal or destination, often deny themselves the natural pleasuring that the body needs. Most bodies I touch in my acupressure work, for instance, are rigid, stiff, sore, and feel somewhat fragmented. Many women are afraid to be touched, and I often get the impression that many of these bodies are so used to being in transit, or on their way someplace, that they are altogether unable to relax. Why are so many of us alienated from our bodies?

One woman I worked with recently on integrating body and spirit commented that although she experienced sexual feelings easily enough, it always brought up some guilt. This woman had been in a religious order for a number of years before leaving to marry. In gathering her history, I learned that as a child she had experienced an unfortunate encounter with incest. We had worked on the incest somewhat already, and she had begun to release the negative hold that these early experiences had over her. Now we were coming to the place where we could address the whirlwind of her her mixed feelings about sexuality. One evening, during some guided imagery and a foray into the unconscious, she said that she could see a dark figure at the bottom of a black hole, which she described as evil. We jointly decided to approach the image and start up some dialogue to see where it would lead. I asked her if she could imagine giving this figure a voice. She said she could, and soon the show was on:

"What's it saying?" I said. "He says he's hiding, that nobody can come in. You can't come in here. No one is allowed. It's dark and there's no light."

"What else is happening?"

"I'm raising this cloak over my head because I'm evil. I'm the devil and I don't want anyone to see me," she said.

"Go ahead and be the devil then; and what's it like to be the devil?" For a moment she went blank, then she laughed as if feeling embarrassed. "What's happening now?" I said.

"It's hot in here," she said, "I'm feeling hot."

"So where is this heat happening?" I asked her. We waited in silence, and I started feeling a lot of heat in my genitals. "In the genitals? Is it getting hot in here?" I asked. She said it was.

"Let's stand up and blow off some of this heat, let's dance the heat and see what happens." I told her we could close our eyes and that I wouldn't peek and we danced around. Then I asked her to imagine she was a volcano, like Vesuvius, about to blow up. We danced the blowing up and it was marvelous fireworks. We were waving our arms and making great hot lava and boiling earth sounds, and the energy in the room was terrific.

"Now, what's happening?" She said the feeling of heat in her genitals had spread to her whole body, that her chest felt expanded and open, that her arms were tingling. It went on like this for a while, and then we decided to dance a little more—to dance creation energy, to dance the holy fire, to move to the rhythms of the Mother of creation. So we danced again, and we sang, and she felt good about this fire in her body for the first time in years.

These are the instincts that we begin to meet when we enter the unconscious. They will want to be recognized and reclaimed as a part of our totality. Whatever experiences we have had at the personal level, whatever our "training" has been at the sociocultural level, it must be called from the dark cloak of repression and healed. If we freeze our sexual energy and treat it like an alien, we lock up a lot of our vital life energy. Whether we choose to be sexually active or celibate, it is important to know and honor our sexual nature, to call it into healing and to allow it to become an expression of our wholeness.

Some years ago, when I was in the middle of trying to work through some of my own issues of sexuality and a fear of my instinctual side, I had the following dream: *I am riding in a car with some friends of mine. We are in unfamiliar territory and the terrain is very rough. My friends want to be taken back to town, but I want to stay in the country; so my husband drops me off at an old farmhouse in the wilderness. It feels good to be alone and I explore the grounds in peace. The farm is perched on a hillside overlooking a broad expanse of valley below.*

Just as I get inside a lioness comes down the hallway of the house, running to catch up with me. I try to escape from her by closing the doors of the room, but none of them seem to fit. Finally, I trick her into coming into the kitchen, and I climb out the window over the sink. Thinking I am safe at last, I turn around to walk away. Immediately before me stands a huge male lion.

I think I will be eaten, but he does nothing but stand before me, looking me straight in the eyes. I do not move but stare back, transfixed. In a moment this lion and I are holding one another in a powerful embrace. I can feel that he has an erection, and yet it seems perfectly natural. I am wondering if this great beast and I are going to make love. Then suddenly he begins a low, deep-throated moaning from the pit of his stomach, as though he were crying for something lost. We stand on the edge of this valley and it is daybreak and the sun is beginning to rise. His cry begins to fill the whole valley; it echoes through my whole body. As the sun rises there is a long and peaceful silence.

As I pondered the dream it became clear to me that the lion is my own instinctual side, from which I have consistently run in the past. The doors in the dreamscape which I use to close out the instincts don't seem to fit, however, and sooner or later this element of my nature and I must meet. This lion I fear and then finally embrace is a long-neglected wild side that I have somehow silenced in my race to keep conventions, meet schedules, and keep my own animal nature in abeyance. The dream seems to say that I have been suppressing and confining my deeper, earthier side. As I tried to make more sense of the dream, I suddenly remembered that at one level I had been compromising myself to please others; seldom expressing my-self, carefully measuring what I said, and saying less than I thought. At another level I was aware that I still entertained some duplistic feelings around my own sexuality, and I still felt polarities within myself. Intellectually, I have resolved my fear of the instincts; but emotionally, at some deeper level, I don't love my sexual nature.

The lion represents strength, power, king-like majesty, and animal instinct. In myth the lion often symbolizes a fiery principle, the power of the sun, courage and vigilance.[5] Aslan, the lion in C. S. Lewis's Narnia tales, symbolizes spiritual power, the power of Christ, the kingly nature of God. Throughout Europe sculptured lions stand at the entrance to many churches; they symbolize the guardian of the door, spiritual watchfulness. But in the dream the lion is also sexual. As we embrace there is a great feeling of power and at the same time an incredible sadness, a mourning for something lost. The cry that came from him was almost like some inner lament; a deep crying out over the essential split between that which is spirit and that which is flesh in me. A question arose for me so clearly: Why did I think that making love was somehow not as good as meditation? Why did I see it as less than holy—as an act of consecration? The dream seemed to be a promise of healing in which I am reunited with a potentially frightening yet powerful side of my self, a sign that the polarization between the soul and the body wanted a more honest integration.

Before the soul can fully merge into union with the deepest recesses of the mind and body, and before we can integrate what dark and light energies we contain, we must first come all the way into the unconscious. We must have begun at least to meet and face our personal and relational wounds; we must have wrestled with the very obstacles in the heart that have cut life off in us. Many of us have difficult tasks to face in our inner work and there may be times we don't feel up to the work ahead. It helps, however, to begin to reexamine the ropes we have been holding on to in the descent to the self; to reevaluate what has worked so far and what has not.

4. Routes to the Inner Woman

I THINK, THEREFORE I AM: GOODBYE DESCARTES

When I was in college I was fascinated with the old man who was chairman of the philosophy department. Roeloffs was a distinguished fellow with a thick shock of white hair and a provocative way of thinking that soon caught my attention. After four long and fairly unsuccessful years in high school, here in the archives of the philosophy department I found a challenge that seemed to make some sense. This was the beginning of a long preoccupation with things of the mind. I used to spend hours in Roeloff's office, smoking Turkish cigarettes and discussing the mysteries of metaphysical thought. I liked this man immensely because he was witty, clever intellectually, and something of a dreamer. On many occasions we confided our darkest secrets to one another.

I am slow to disdain the many happy hours I spent sitting at this man's feet learning how to debate, how to think, and how to ask meaningful questions. But the truth is I began to grow a little lopsided. By the time I left the halls of academia I had completely swallowed the old Cartesian maxim, "I think, therefore I am." It's taken me all these years to figure out that for the development of feminine consciousness, it goes the other way around.

In order to understand something of our basic feminine nature, women need to be aware of the differences between those energies in the psyche that are potentially masculine, and those that are potentially feminine. Before we venture much further into the journey, let's differentiate between these forces.

Historically, women have been overidentified with the patriarchal culture; we have been its victim and, more recently, its antagonist. Yet for the purpose of deeper self-awareness, we need to open more consciously to the gifts of our own feminine nature, in spite of what our roles or wounds have been. If the image of the feminine self has been dishonored or misunderstood in some way, as is the case in most of Western society, then we must make the commitment to do whatever we can to redeem it.

YIN AND YANG: SEEKING BALANCE

The ancient Chinese philosophy of the Tao holds that masculine and feminine powers manifest differently in us, and as such can be used as representatives of a universal truth about male and female. The idea appeals to me because, taking the concept a step further, masculine and feminine can be illustrated in terms of inner patterns of energy that both sexes possess as potential resources, rather than what men and women do differently. These energy fields, when deeply fathomed, are like guides to our deeper, more essential self.

YANG: MASCULINE ENERGY

In the tradition of the Tao the symbol for the essential masculine energy is the sun. This *yang* energy is composed of light, heat, fire; it bursts forth, it radiates and is powerful. Someone who carries this masculine energy manifests active, creative, and generative kinds of power and movement. It is a doing, accomplishing and making-things-happen kind of energy.

We need this male energy to direct and anchor us. Women need a certain amount of aggressiveness, strength, know-how, and an ability to push ourselves in generative ways. Without some share of the natural masculine strength, will, and focus, we cannot get around on this planet. My husband and I went cross-country skiing last year, in the Sierra, and on skis we hiked up a long trail to the top of a steep ridge. It took every ounce of strength I had in me to make it to the top; once I got there I burst into tears—not so much because I was exhausted (that too), but because I felt vitally aware of how exhilarating it was to feel this sort of strength in my body. Somehow this trek had quite unintentionally turned into a sort of ordeal, spontaneously thrusting me into a drive that tested me right up to the limit of my endurance. As I stood gazing over the snow-covered valley below, I felt anointed by a profound blend of human and trans-personal power. It was a pure generative force and I felt awed by it.

Women who exercise the relational aspect of the masculine, are not going to be passive about what they want. Assertiveness, confidence, and an ability to take a stand—all characterize the masculine quality a woman needs in her dealings with others. When this force is in balance, a woman is clear, direct, and purposeful in her communications.

At other times this masculine force comes up for me as strength of purpose, an ability to remain focused and rational in some task. This *yang* or masculine essence brings the mind and the intellect into play. It is the ability to rely on reason, logic, order, and predictability; it guides one's forays into the "known" world and teaches us to question life carefully when we have to. It's one's ability to read the "fine print" in some ventures and to learn to choose our direction wisely. One woman told me: "In the past when I felt excited about something, I ordinarily just dove right into it. Whether it was a task, a new venture, or a relationship, I made a wild forray right into the center of the thing. It was only later I might suddenly take a look around and ask myself. . . . 'Now how did I get into *this?*' Gratefully, these days I'm learning to stall myself long enough to consult with my wise old man inside, whose old and discerning gaze can tell me whether I'm actually inspired or going off the deep end." In its purest sense, masculine energy is personified by the wise old man, the "light bearer," who can bring clear vision to our endeavors.

YIN: FEMININE ENERGY

The feminine principle, *yin*, is symbolized by the moon. The feminine way of knowing something is to learn to see it by the light of reflection, the way the moon reflects the light of the sun. It represents that part of the personality which is inner, hidden, earthy, nurturant, womb-like. Following the *yin* side of one's nature means that one learns to drop inside oneself into the less-familiar sides of one's nature. To move with feminine energy is to learn to be comfortable with paradox, and with a certain element of unpredictability.

While the masculine gets its information in concrete, logical ways, the feminine gets its information in more diffuse ways—as though there were some sixth sense at work, some innate intuitive "seeing." It is a reflective, inward way of seeking answers and direction, a communion with the night time of our thinking process. Like the revelations illuminated by the indirect light of the unconscious, feminine energies allow us to feel our way by reflection and experience rather than by the direct light of reason.

Intuition is not limited to women, of course. Once my husband and I took about twenty kids on a wilderness experience, backpacking into the Sierra, while two of the boys forged a bit too far ahead of the pack and got lost. When the rest of us arrived at the meeting spot, it was clear that we were shy these two and my husband started back after them. He came to a fork in the trail (one of many) and simply "sensed" that the boys had taken the wrong turn. Following that trail about two miles he found the two boys by a lake, frightened but safe. This sort of inward "sensing" intuitively is not logical; it simply means that one learns to follow the quieter, more reflective way of knowing.

In the masculine nature the mind is a powerful, dominant force, with its ability to reason; but in the feminine nature the heart takes the lead. Here emotions and feelings come into play and their expression is vital to the whole person. Relational ability is inherent to the feminine nature; it is an innate penchant for sensitivity to others. Men and women with a strong dose of relational gifts can initiate feeling bridges to the things and people around them. A person who does not have enough yin energy is overly rational, unfeeling. Too much yin is exemplified by the woman who "loves too much."

Yin is the quality that enables a person to go deep into the contemplative realm; to feel out and become familiar with the ponderings, insights, and revelations of the human spirit. It is that side of our nature, whether male or female, which emanates from the right hemisphere of the brain, from the experiential side of our consciousness. Frequently, from this more diffuse field of experience of feminine consciousness, our spiritual life emerges. Children are often more open to this side of experience; like mystics of any age, they are frequently closer to the soul.

The feminine also comprises our natural earth energies. The

earth, another symbol for the feminine, is that ground of our being that reflects our more primitive side, our sexuality, and the soil of our more fleshy down-to-earth nature. To be human is to be in kinship with the earth within us; it is to be able to live close to our feelings, our instincts, to a gut-level honesty about who we are and what we feel. To admit our nature is to admit that we are liable to error and vulnerable to pain and paradox, to the elements of nature within us.

When understood with reverence, we can hold these qualities of masculine and feminine in balance and in mutual regard, without bias about either one. They are simply different energies within that need to be developed equally in all of us. Yet both men and women seem to be in a crisis of identity. Men seem out of touch with the authentic masculine, and women seem lost to knowing their deepest feminine nature. Few of us get past the most superficial aspects of either nature, and often we remain locked in the stereotype rather than in the essence of male or female.

Although some women have learned about how to be authentic with their new-found masculine strengths, a great many of us seem to get lost acting out the masculine rather than authentically living it. Unlike Native American women, who stay close to their earth roots, many Western women have become lost in a corporate male world; a world of agendas, cement, busy schedules, demands, wearing several hats at once. We are often guilty of approaching some aspects of our lives as a business contract. Some of us forget compassion, feeling values, and the art of allowing interior silence; some of us get stuck rationalizing and thinking rather than feeling and pondering; we hide in our heads and don't risk the heart; we don't speak from our own truth. Likewise, some of us remain unyielding and firm when we may need to let go and relax into the moment. A woman can act out traditional scripts of either sex in a multiplicity of ways and yet still be out of touch with her inner woman, her most essential self.

I AM, THEREFORE I THINK: COMING TO OURSELVES

I recently had the following dream. It illustrated to me clearly and powerfully that a woman's process of healing the feminine is often symbolized by a return to the waters of the unconscious; it is basically a descent through the outer layers of the personality to the deeper, more essential truth of the "I Am" of woman.

I am on a city street near a store. The store is familiar to me and I come inside and begin to visit with the people who are there. It is relaxed and pleasant and I feel as though I am among friends; yet after a while I grow uncomfortable, as though there is something else I have to do. Eventually, I leave these people, who seem to want to distract me, and make my way to a small back room which is dimly lit.

On the far wall of the room is an opening to a cave, not unlike those of the cliff dwellings of the Southwest. From the inside of the cave a light flows from some interior source and illuminates its sandstone walls. On the bare earthen floor of the cave I see a rattle or gourd and some other ceremonial items, as though someone has been interrupted in a ritual. Beyond the cave I can hear the sound of the sea. I crawl through the opening of the cave and come out its back passageway, and find myself by an ancient sea. Along the shoreline earth-colored cliffs rise majestically above the edge of the water. Then I find myself swimming in the warm waters of the lagoon, completely in tune with this ancient place. I can smell the kelp and taste the salt spray in the air and every part of my body feels enlivened.

Later, I find myself back on the street near the store, waiting for a woman friend to join me. As I walk along waiting for her bus to arrive, a young "ivy league" priest walks up behind me and starts up a conversation. He is wearing a three-piece grey flannel suit; his black shirt and white collar stand out noticeably. He is quite proper and reserved, but not unfriendly. Yet as I am talking I am aware that his eyebrows are raised and his manner rather condescending. When he sees I am resistant to him, he becomes increasingly paternal, as though he is going to give me some better advice; to keep me from some capriciousness. He makes it clear that he does not want me to return to the sea, yet I keep silent, simply aware that the sea is close at hand.

In this dream I am in the waters of my deeper self. Beyond the busyness of a crowded street, the everyday commercialism of a store, there is a passageway through a cave to the sea. It is an old sea and one I'm familiar with and long for. The passageway through the cave is the descent to the womb; a symbol for the feminine. A ceremony has taken place there, but it has been interrupted. The Native American gourd that calls for the rains and the harvest of new life has been abandoned, and waits for the hands of the dancer to pick it up to let it sound again. I am the dancer. The sea itself is the waters of the unconscious, the place from which the natural feminine begins to emerge. Throughout the dream, as I am talking to this priest figure, I am remembering the cave and the sea; feeling again the ancient landscape. Impervious to his polite conservatism and dissuasiveness, I know that to be there is right for me. Whether he represents my intellectual approach to life, or my preoccupation with masculine ideals and performance, I am about to abandon him for a while.

I awaken with a sense that there is another woman in me that I am finally beginning to allow a voice. She is the feminine companion that I have abandoned in my preoccupation with the masculine world, the woman whose company I need to keep now more than any male figure. The ivy league priest in me, who would have been so powerful a hold over my actions some years back, has lost his authority. He can no longer dissuade me from the waters of the woman within me who longs to break free from needing the continuous approval of a male corporate world.

I know innately that I can trust this dream because it is a feminine dream; all the symbols point me back to the earth within myself. The programmatic, technical world into which I was lured as a young woman is suddenly at a dead end; from here on my journey requires that I be in touch with the rhythms of my nature as a woman. The walls of the cave, which seemed so mysteriously lighted, are in fact lighted by the cave itself. I understand the message: Real illumination can only come from within myself.

The earthen ground, the humus in the cave, is a reminder that I am nature's child; that I can relax my schedules and demands and allow life to be more organic; to follow the river within myself and see what wants attention. The womb is the classic feminine symbol for waiting, for quietly listening to the sounds my inner woman wants to make. It tells me that if I cannot find immediate answers for what I/want to know about my life, that I can give myself permission not to know until later; later when I have learned how to feel my way through pondering, through making mistakes if necessary, through letting go of control. I am content to sit and wait in the darkness while a new more authentic feminine self begins to form. I do not yet have the answers for my identity and I am aware that I am still emerging.

ROUTES TO THE INNER WOMAN

When we walk on the path of self-awareness we need to pay attention to ourselves. A lot of us read copious amounts of literature, attend a variety of self-improvement workshops, join women's groups, AlAnon, Overeaters Anonymous, and are active in a variety of self-help channels. But until we get down to the inside of who we are, little that we learn from other resources outside ourselves will make a lasting impression. Certainly our goals toward change, and the support systems that tend to be helpful for many of us, are not to be overlooked. But in the journey to the self it is not a going out but a coming in that makes the difference.

To break the masks of our identity and unearth the self we need solitude, honesty, and the pursuit of an inner life. Through the use of dreams, journal keeping, meditation, and perhaps therapy, many women can find new awarenesses.

To learn to relate to the deeper self we need to take time with ourselves. Many women take time for outside interests, to pursue careers outside the home. But the kind of time I am talking about is the time we take to be alone; to sit still, to reflect, to write in a journal, or to meditate. This sort of time is not necessarily "doing" time; it has nothing to do with accomplishing anything in the usual sense. It is simply a time to be in deeper relationship to ourself.

The masculine way of knowing is logical, methodical, fact oriented. The feminine way of knowing, however, involves plunging headlong into the senses and temporarily releasing the idea of goals and performance. To come into the waters of the self we need to pay close attention to the deeper voices in the unconscious and to initiate a dialogue with the uncharted sites of the personality. When we come up against an unknown, we need to feel it out from the inside, to sniff it out, and to intuit its meaning from the heart or the instincts rather than from the mind.

One of the best ways to uncover the deeper self is through

dreams. Dreams strip away the false front of the persona, expose hidden feelings, and reveal the unseen contents of our nature. Often they conjure up for us, by the use of a language of symbols, the folly of our pretend world. Dreams often show us the absurdity of our "ideal" self, the coverings and shields we have built up over the years. They are compensatory, provocative, and insightful messages from the unconscious that invite our attention to correct some imbalance. Of course, dreams also have an ulterior motive: When they reveal our hidden faults or wrong paths, they also open up the possibility of new vistas and creative solutions. I suspect many dreams come as a means of enlightenment. One of my friends told me recently of a dream she had that was clearly a call to bring a neglected side of herself to life:

"*I am on a plain and I look up at these foothills and they are white and covered with snow. Every now and then I notice these little dark figures on the snow, like skiers. They look furtive, somehow threatening and scary. I am afraid of the whole thing. And then to the east of the foothills I see a range of enormous mountains, filled with light. Something like an alpine glow. I can still see them vividly; sheer, translucent rock or ice, but certainly inaccessible. I am awed by the light—whether it is internal and radiating from the mountain, or whether it is reflected light, like an alpine glow, it is amazing. But they are very far away. Forever far away.*

"*The dream haunted me for years. I couldn't figure it out. Then years later, after quite a bit of personal therapy work around some of my early childhood fears, I began to understand something more of the dream. The more work I did the more I started to trust doing some of the things I'd always been afraid to do. When I was a girl my mother was crippled from polio and had lost the use of her legs. The one thing I wanted to do as a child was to dance. But this threatened her in some way—she was always afraid I'd fall and break a leg, or an accident would happen and I too might become crippled. Of course, I danced anyway, whenever I could. I sneaked around behind her back and I danced, because for me it was life. But in spite of my rebelliousness, I've been afraid to take risks. Catastrophe is always in the back of my mind. The more I got into my therapy work the more I felt I had to confront this childhood fear thing all over again. To get to it once and for all.*

"I wanted to take up skiing again. At my age it sounded ridiculous, but somehow it was that thing in the dream that I was both frightened about and drawn to. I had to do it. At first I was terrified and was afraid of falling. But I gradually learned, and little by little I could actually do it. Over this last year, skiing has been for me not only a way to confront my fear of taking risks, it's also been a process of learning to let go. For instance, I used to be a compulsive giver. I think I defended myself in this way. I mostly related to people by giving; in a way it made me feel safe. In a crowd I'd talk a lot, I suppose it made me feel safe and in control. Skiing was a metaphor of growth for me. What I learned facing the slope was how to face my fear of falling, my fear of losing control. Off the slopes it meant I had to begin to learn how to receive without giving all the time. Learning to trust that the universe cared for me and that people could actually love me was like falling gradually down another slope; there was nothing to do but to let myself go and allow people to love me.

"Not long ago I had another dream. In the dream I am on those same mountains that had seemed so inaccessible, so unreachable. I'm not afraid anymore; I am actually skiing on this incredible mountain filled with light. I am there. The other skiers are friendly and I say to myself, 'How in the world could I have ever been so scared?' I realize that I can go to that mountain . . . whatever that represents in my life."

When a woman consciously undertakes the inner journey she removes the dam from the waters in her psyche. She opens the feelings she has denied and suppressed. She begins to acknowledge the paradox in her nature, and to dialogue with the mountain that has always seemed so frightening and inaccessible, and with the sea whose ancient waters have the power to transform and to heal and nurture.

CHARTING THE JOURNEY

Learning to use a journal to record thoughts, feelings, old impasses, and new awarenesses can be a valid way to keep a record of our inner movements. One of the greatest benefits of the journal for me is that it clearly records where my journey is moving and where it seems to be stuck. It's like a sort of yardstick that measures where I am. I was once surprised (and annoyed) to find, as I thumbed back over a year's worth of entries, that I hadn't really changed at all. I began to sense in myself a certain pattern of ambivalence. One voice inside would complain in a fiery monologue about some injustice I had to suffer; a later entry might address the problem in a more resigned way. After a while I began to see that I was lost somewhere in between these two conflicting attitudes.

The journal also provided me with an absolutely attentive and completely captive audience. It never judged or criticized a word I said; we never had any disputes when I thrashed out my feelings on the pages; and I could always trust it no matter what I said or did. The journal is the one safe place that many of us can keep the strange, untoward creatures that arise from the different sides of the self.

For some women sketching the fragment of a dreamscape can powerfully amplify an inner symbol. Symbols are the vehicles of meaning in the unconscious. Once we take the time to learn how to give them life, we begin to understand their language. For instance, in the dream of the cave through which I passed to come to the sea, there was a gourd, a rattle of some kind. As I began to recall the gourd, I sketched it in my journal. As I worked on it, I began to imagine the sounds it made. Then I could envision a ceremonial dance in which I became the gourd, filled with seeds, shaking out the rhythm of the seasons. I became the seeds for corn, for squash and beans, I became the seeds of the cottonwood, the sage and piñon. As I took this further in my active imagination I then became the dancer who danced the seasons and the fertile earth that took in the seed. The more this inner movement from the symbol of the gourd and its seeds evolved, the more I began to connect with places in my life that needed to celebrate new life. I felt the symbol leading me within to gestate what might want to be planted in me in order for some new thing to happen. If I had not taken the time to "play" like this in my journal, I would have missed the power of the symbol in the dream.

Fascinating to many women is the discovery, once on the journey, of a variety of different sides of the personality. When we get in touch with the unconscious side of the personality that we have repressed or stayed away from, we begin to give that deeper, unexpressed thought or feeling a voice. When we can give this creature a way of talking to us, telling us how she really feels, then we have let something more of the inner woman come to consciousness.

THERE IS A DREAM DREAMING US

The Kalahari bushmen have said of their own creation myth that "always there is a dream dreaming us."[1] I am struck by the notion that somehow creation is always dreaming me up; because to me that means I am an ongoing process of an evolution, that I am not just stuck here with my limitations and as some mere effect of the conditionings that have formed and shaped me. I am more than this. As individuals none of us is ever fully stuck unless we choose to be. The more we understand our own nature in this dreamscape, the more we can cocreate along with the Great Dream—with the soul—and the more we can gestate with new life, and change.

In this age, more than any before it, we are freer to experiment with what it means to be woman and to explore the nature of feminine energy. Many of us who have opened ourselves to the work of self-awareness have begun to look for ways to create the dream of who we want to be; unlike the past, where long-established social roles were givens, many women can now be cocreators of their own destiny. Much of the history for women over this last century has been involved in the work of awakening; and the dream continues. The work of opening up what it means to be fully in touch with one's innate feminine self is essentially a journey inward; it is a reclaiming of the inner territory of feelings, instincts, nature, and the *yin* side of our nature. To walk this journey in the feminine way is to drop inward and to explore. Each woman's discovery and expression of her own feminine essence will be unique.

Discovering our nature and its essential gifts, however, is only possible when we can identify what must yield to the healing process. At some point our work recedes into the past, into the personal level of our childhood, and begins to confront the obstacles and impasses we have experienced along the road to our adulthood.

5. Images of the Mother

The image of the family tree is a powerful symbol. Without roots the strongest tree will fall over. Without branches, it cannot generate life. One of the most important steps in exploring the ground of our ancestral tree is to study the women who are our roots and branches, the women who model our female experience. Healing the hurts and misunderstandings between mothers and daughters promotes a firmer sense of a woman's acceptance of her feminine identity. If we carry an estrangement from our mothers all our lives, we will likewise be alienated from the mother within ourselves. And if as women we cannot embrace the mother, neither can we embrace the feminine.

HEALING OUR MATERNAL ROOTS

It would be easy for most of us to find fault with the models of feminine behavior we find hanging on the branches of our own generational tree. No doubt many of these models lack authenticity, strength, or assurance. In my own family the women were high on long-suffering and low on self-esteem. We were skilled at creative manipulation and rather poor on assertiveness and an honest expression of feelings. Yet all these things have to yield to the healing process, because each of us carries both the refuse and the fruit of our maternal lineage. I may prefer to say I am my own woman; but I am also my mother, my grandmothers, and the women who bore them down through the ages. That we all share the same small apartment of my mind is a source of endless amazement to me.

The following prose by Meinrad Craighead, who both wrote and illustrated the exquisite book *The Mother's Songs: Images of God the Mother,* illustrates this kind of ancestral connectedness in both image and metaphor. Accompanying a beautiful painting of two women embracing around a central figure of a red pomegranate with bright seeds are the words:

Each year in June my mother put me on a train in Chicago and sent me to her parents for the summer. She could not go with me but she told me that it was good for me to be there where I began. I had to touch home, and through me she did also. When I was old enough to understand, she said: "Your flesh is growing there. When you were born Memaw buried your cord and membranes in the soil in Little Rock. You are rooted there like me and Memaw."[1]

According to Jung, women clearly share a more expansive sense of their identity than men. As women we go back into our mothers and grandmothers, and we also potentially extend forward into our own daughters. Consequently, there is a continuity to the feminine identity that has more truth to it than most women realize. And because we are all connected at a deep level, because in a sense we all bear one another, and because we are all joined as branches to the same blood root, women need to embrace the ancestral tree without too much condemnation. Over and over again on my journey to reclaim and to heal my own roots I have had to remind myself that the images I have of my own origins and the hands that molded me are the same images I carry within myself.

Part of the task of beginning to mend some of the broken shards of my own self-image involved a long and consistent review of how my mother and I had connected and what her agenda had been for me as a child. Early in this process I picked up an old family album and began leafing through the pages. I was surprised to find the changing moods of my childhood so clearly recorded in black and white, and I could not help but notice some subtle changes in my expression over the years. From a smiling, plump-cheeked three year old who looked like the Unsinkable Molly Brown without curls, I gradually began to see a much more sober look. By the end of sixth grade, although there was still a discernable twinkle in the eyes, the look had metamorphosed into mild reserve. By eleven the child in the pictures looked as though she had definitely begun to experience some second thoughts; something vital and alive had either been lost or postponed in the course of her childhood.

Because our feminine heritage has often come down to us with memories and impressions that bind us from authenticity, many of us as women are not who we would like to be. One of the reasons I began to review my childhood in the first place

was to confront an unhealed side of myself. I've always entertained a paradox in my personality, a duplicity of sorts. In spite
of a fairly successful and contented side to my life I still often
entertained some degree of self-doubt. Try as I might, I could
not completely shake the vague notion that a bag lady mysteriously peered at me from behind. For some reason I had a
number of puzzling thoughts about my self-image. Invariably,
no matter what I could accomplish, there often lurked some
feeling that I could have done it better. I often felt very self-
conscious with strangers or authority figures; in formal circumstances I found myself wanting to impress people, to appear
credible.

The irony was that I *was* a credible person, it's just that I was
never convinced. For a person who seemed outwardly independent, I somehow loved approval; yet the promise of being thought
well of ran counterfeit to my need for independence. Sometimes
overtly sensitive to the needs of others, my own identity often
vanished into thin air. I began to take a long, hard look at the
incongruity between my outward sense of accomplishment and
the seemingly unconscious fears I entertained about risking to
be myself.

THE ENMESHED FAMILY

Nancy Friday, in her book *My Mother, My Self,* mentions
the need a child has to experience a healthy degree of self-
centeredness—some "primary narcissism"—for a while. As a
child is allowed this permission to feel good about herself, to
learn to see herself as basically OK in spite of her mistakes, her
spilled milk, or her messy room, then her autonomy has a
chance to form in positive ways. But autonomy for most women
is scarce, because most of us are coached toward acting out the
will and the expectations of others. Consequently, believing in
the self doesn't happen easily for many women. Instead, little
girls are taught to see themselves through other people's eyes;
their own self-worth is often measured by how others see them.[2]

Most mothers seem to look to their own daughters as an
extension of their own personal self-worth, so a woman's sense
of self-esteem often becomes very invested in what her children
do. Although many mothers mean well and want the best for

their daughters, many are unable to see their offspring as separate from themselves. This is a major stumbling block for women who seek a separate sense of identity. One of my clients said of her mother, *"I know my mom loved me as a child, that's clear. But I'm also sure she was too concerned with shaping me, and in some ways she was too close. She seemed to want to govern everything we did as kids. As long as we did what she said, things were good. But when one of us stepped out of line or exhibited some overtly different behavior, we were in deep water."*

The enmeshed family is a family who cannot separate clearly. Identity in such a family thrives on the close connection of one family member to another, and there is no room for difference. In my house there were few spaces that would permit autonomy, and messes of any kind were never welcome. My room could not be a mess and neither could I. Appearances were important to my parents, especially to my mother. She spent hours laboring over interior decorating, planning parties, coaching us in social graces, lining up little occasions for the social page of the newspaper. For any formal occasion my sister and I, although not twins, were always dressed alike. On some Saturdays we were dragged off the baseball field and marched over to Neiman-Marcus for modeling sessions; then my mother, my sister, and I dressed alike and spent the afternoon smiling at photographers. Fortunately, not long after that my front teeth fell out, and that was the end of my modeling career. One injunction in my family that I will never forget was an unwritten prohibition against flatulence. I remember my mother thought little of the unpredictable workings of nature and it certainly held no weight alongside the power of convention. If one of us in the family had gas, unquestioningly the rule was to pretend it didn't exist. In my family we had clean rooms, clean clothes, and lots of gas.

Many times as little girls we learn to see ourselves not as how we really are, but as mother wants to see us. When this happens our sense of self-esteem as adults becomes subject to public scrutiny, or to the collective mother. The woman who gives herself over to the collective mother has learned to value giving behavior that will endlessly stereotype her role as a woman. These behaviors, aimed at pleasing, nurturing, and serving, are often performed at the expense of autonomy. In this sort of program such a life becomes increasingly polarized between being who we really are, and being the person everyone else expects us to be. Ultimately, getting approval means some kind of self-effacement—and there is no autonomy in that.

Part of our task in healing our own childhood incompletions is to review the factors that have shaped the self-image of the women before us. The more I dug around the roots of my own family tree, the more I began to see that part of my mother's need for a meticulous adherence to convention stemmed from her own insecurity as a child. My mother's parents had been poor, and my grandmother Ann had stoically endured an often difficult relationship with my grandfather. Benjamin was a carpenter with a great sense of humor and a deep baritone voice that I can still hear echoing through the house on cold winter mornings. I am certain things would have been good for them had he not had such a fascination for betting on the horses. His carefree attitude about life and occasional losses at the track were just another thing he easily took in his stride, but the loss to my grandmother was always a personal defeat.

In the end, however, no matter what his faults were or how they fought over money issues, my grandmother stuck with him and made the best of it. She was not in favor of divorce and she had a will of iron when it came to enduring hardships. To my grandmother, men were an enigma that women had to tolerate. Abandoned by her own father when she was a young child, Grandmother and her mother survived by hiring on to cook for a logging camp on the coast of Oregon. Although life was not easy for her, my grandmother had a pioneering spirit that emerged throughout her life whenever times were hard. Benjamin's occasional forgetfulness of their wedding anniversary or his outward lack of a show of affection for her were all things she heroically took in her stride.

My mother was not inattentive as a child to her own parental conflicts. I am certain she picked up her mother's unhappiness, her sense of defeat, her concern over money, her sense that men were not reliable. Somewhere along the way, my mother gradually got the impression that there wasn't going to be enough. Growing up, some of her friends lived in fine homes; yet hers was humble and unimposing, and a source of embarrassment and frustration to her. I began to understand that her preoccupation with social graces, appearances, and with two little girls who dressed well, was like a talisman that would somehow guarantee that the poverty of her childhood would not repeat itself. That we were all loving women and caring mothers cemented even more solidly our sense of connectedness to one another. The loyalty between my mother's bag lady and mine had secretly formed.

LACK OF CONNECTION

Many women come out of childhood lacking any essential connection to their mother at all. A child's ego in this case is not simply an overidentification with a mother's process; it is symbiotically tied fast to the mother not for the sake of self-esteem, but for the sake of survival. For many of us the wounds of childhood are far more extensive and painful to face than the wounds of adulthood. The absent mother is a source of conflict still for many women struggling with their own identity.

One woman who had lost her mother as an infant, and who had spent most of her life in foster homes, never felt a sense of security. *"I feel like I'm in this strange double bind. On one hand I realize that I've been looking for love in a lot of different ways for a long time. On the other, when it comes my way, I can't let go enough to trust it. There have been plenty of men in my life, but somehow our relationships don't last. The moment anyone gets close to me, something deep inside freezes over. I don't care how intimate I am with someone emotionally or sexually, I'm a million miles away."*

One of my clients—whose mother not only had to look after several children, but a disabled husband as well—experienced another kind of mother loss. This woman had never really bonded with her mother at all, and neither could she bond with anyone else. She came to therapy because her relationships all went awry. In childhood her mother's love had been very infrequent, never available enough, and often erratic. *"I remember just wanting my mother's lap for a little while. Wanting to spend time with her. But there were times she pushed me away or got angry and frustrated. I know now she had a hard time of it with Dad and she didn't really have a lot of patience left over for me, but I never really understood it at the time. All I knew was a lot of rejection."* Over the early years, out of her mother's often impatient and unpredict-able response to her, the child became afraid to leave her moth-er's side. An emotional whirlwind soon followed most of their interactions. The cycle became a wild pattern in which the daughter clung harder, demanded louder, and felt more and more afraid of the rejection she knew was coming. Getting love and attention was tantamount to a trip to Hades; it became a struggle involving desperate need, fear of rejection, anger, hurt, and longing. This dramatic interplay of emotions became the way in which she approached all her future relationships: Every-body became the mother from whom she never got enough and who was sooner or later going to reject her—no wonder she was stuck.

Another woman, who had been working on herself for some months in therapy and was feeling good about her growth, suddenly came to a standstill. As she began to uncover the memories of her mother which she had long suppressed, she found herself in turbulent water. At first she refused to acknowl-edge how significant these memories were and shrank back from wanting to face them at all. *"I feel like my work is going backwards. In the beginning of our therapy I felt stronger, relieved that I had some support. I had a sense of going somewhere finally. But this is just agony."* Suddenly, she had begun to feel frightened, help-less, and small in the face of her memories of early childhood. All the places where she had been neglected, hurt, and abused in relationship to her mother were surfacing and, after years of denial, her childhood pain was finally emerging. One day she said to me, *"I don't think you understand how difficult this is. Some of the memories I am recalling are things I'd vowed never again to think of. There was a time my mother fondled me; there was a time she stood by and watched a man sexually abuse me. These are things no one should have to recall."*

It is here, in this very fragile place, that the real work of unearthing the wounds of the child emerges. I have known some women to quit the journey at this point, turning abruptly away from the pain of childhood simply because the thought of reliv-ing it seemed too great a task. It is never easy to admit that as adult women we somehow still have unfinished business with our mothers that we need to face and sort through. For those of us who have to face these early wounds, to enter the pain and hurt we have suppressed over the years is essentially to touch the core of our deepest wound. For some women this sort of inner work is too threatening. But the fact remains that authenticity has a price. As hard and exacting as this work is for some women, it is a crucial key to healing and transforming the heart of the child. On the inner journey, getting to the personal roots of childhood is an essential part of the healing process. When we have our mother image in clearer perspective, and when we begin to sense how we are still attached to the roots of our family tree, then we can begin to prune the wild shoots in the heart that block growth.

SHARING THE SAME PSYCHE

"I used to think that my mother and I were worlds apart. After all, we lived differently, believed in different things; she had her life and I had mine. She was Catholic, I became Buddhist; she liked opera, I liked modern ballet; she was prejudiced and I can't stand that sort of thing. I don't know when it was that I began to wake up to the fact that I was just as fearful about intimacy as she was. We have all these miles between us and we do a lot of things independent of one another, but underneath I realize I'm just as much of a perfectionist as she is."

One of the most important areas in understanding our mother-child relationship is the work of becoming conscious about the ways we have been shaped at unconscious levels. Sometimes we see things we don't like about our mothers, things we consciously choose not to emulate. Some of us succeed at some level, but in other ways we fail. The problem is that often the very characteristic we consciously say we can't stand and would never repeat is often the very one that we have unconsciously identified with. Consciously, we may not think we're carrying on this rejected pattern; but unconsciously, we often are. When we carry a parental process, that means we carry something of our parent's way of experiencing the world. This phenomenon is like a hidden thread that connects us to our parents. It is the same thread that communicates feeling and thinking states, whether they are actually expressed or not.

MIXED MESSAGES

When a mother says one thing and does another, or when her actions don't match her words, the child is left with two distinctly unmatched communications. No doubt some women do manage to come across clearly to their children. Words, looks, gestures, and direct signals often leave little room for guessing what a mother might mean. But sometimes a mother gives mixed messages. When a message is not clear, a covert level of communication begins to take root.

One of the most common examples of mixed messages I come across in my work with women relates to the confusion many of us experience about our own feminine self-esteem. For instance, some women are confident in their role as mother to their offspring, and their communications to the child are clear. Trouble comes, however, when the mother doubts her confidence in other areas of relationship, when she doubts her role as wife or mate, or does not esteem herself as a person. Or a mother may be adept at her career and totally unskilled at showing warmth or human caring toward others. In other words, the mother who has not found a congruent balance within herself about her own identity is going to model her own ambiguity to her offspring, and ultimately the unconscious of the child will carry some of that same incongruity toward the feminine.

My mother, although basically a loving woman toward my sister and me, and certainly there for us as children, modeled a mixed message of self-esteem to us. With her woman friends and with us, for instance, my mother was uproariously funny. Often she was spontaneous, assertive, self-confident, and at ease with herself. With my father or in the company of men, however, she became reserved, polite, coy, and somewhat placating. Like Scarlett O'Hara in *Gone with the Wind,* she became condescending, politely seductive, airy, clandestine, and conforming. Her womanly independence seemed to fade into the woodwork and she became like a child. The message I got was, "You can be yourself with women, but there's a role to be played with men."

My mother must have discovered the art of manipulation at an early age. When she used her feminine wiles in polite but intentional ways, she got whatever she wanted. And she wasn't unsuccessful. She was a good-looking woman with dark hair and great legs and a build that stopped a lot of men in her day. For her, good looks were insurance against having to live under the thumb of a benevolent patriarchy, although she would never have phrased it in that way. Once she said to me that although men brought home the money and were the so-called boss of the household, in the end a woman would have the last say. According to my mother, if a woman played her cards right she would control the men. She had the slightly raised eyebrow of the infamous Mata Hari look as she spoke and it wasn't hard to guess what she meant. But in my household the tactics were undercover; precisely because men were in control, they could not be squarely faced or confronted. In her experience, if a woman wanted something she had to go about it nicely, seductively, or secretly.

As I explored more of my own unconscious process I began to discover that my mother and I were not so distant as I thought. In many ways we shared the same psyche. I suddenly began to see that my own unconscious need to please authority figures and to placate the important men in my environment came directly from my mother's script. Because she had never invested much esteem in herself, but in the other seemingly more important people who comprised her life, her sense of herself had always remained undeveloped. I began to discover that the impressive people I searched for (and made myself small in front of) were all part of the same unconscious program she had followed.

I found too that my own sexuality was just as repressed as hers. My own communications with men, especially authority figures, were just as filled with unconscious games. Consciously, I hated the idea of being clandestine, airy, and capricious, sometimes playing out the innocent child. But the Scarlett in me was being unconsciously repressed and unacknowledged, driven underground—and I had no idea that I was acting her out. She was my own shadow side of whom I knew consciously very little.

The mind is rather like clay: If we push on a wad of clay from one angle, it has to give somewhere else. When we consciously split off from one behavior and deny its effect over us, it's quite likely to show up some place else. Yet the more we are in touch with these hidden sides of ourselves, and the more we seek out the unconscious sides of our own nature, the more we are willing to forgive the unawakened places in our own feminine ancestry. If we are tempted instead to condemn the women in our past, we go down with the ship as well—because these women are undeniably a part of our own psychic blueprint.

CARRYING THE PARENTAL PROCESS

A child becomes vulnerable toward carrying a parental process because the connective thread between the parents has broken. A parent who fails to receive needed support and affirmation from the mate will either consciously or unconsciously select one of the children to catch her or his projections. If the mother, for instance, fails to get a sense of gratification and/or self-esteem from the father, she will turn to one of the children to be her source of self-esteem. Children are often called upon in this way to be something for the parent which the spouse has failed to be. Sometimes one child may be the "favorite" of a parent and will tend to carry the positive projections of that parent; another child may be in some kind of disfavor with the parent and will therefore tend to carry the negative projections of that parent. In some families there are children who tend to carry the hopes and aspirations of one or both parents, while others tend to carry the rejected shadow side. Thus sometimes one child can be seen as the "good" side of the parent, while another may be seen as the "bad" side.

A woman in treatment recently began to see that her oldest daughter, with whom she could never get along, had been carrying the projections of the worst side of herself. Ironically, the faults she repeatedly accused her daughter of were the faults within herself she had the most trouble seeing and accepting. Yet as she began to see how she had labeled her oldest daughter to carry her own rejected (shadow) side, she could then begin the work of withdrawing some of these negative projections from her. In time each of them was freer to relate in more genuine ways to one another, and the daughter could be released from her mother's own personal psychic conflicts.

Although in this case the daughter was often very clear about the signals of anger and rejection her mother verbalized, many times a child will get no verbal cues about a parent's feelings—especially when the parent herself is unaware of them. For instance, I knew a woman who seemed to have an unreasonable dislike of her son and whose treatment of him was clearly negative. Unfortunately for the boy, he looked just like his father. But because the woman hated the father, the boy's likeness to him recreated that same hatred and mistrust in the mother towards her own son. He got less positive attention, fewer presents at Christmas, and more chores than the daughter (who resembled the mother).

Francis Wickes, in her book *The Inner World of Childhood,* speaks of the unconscious mind of the young child as extremely impressionable.[3] Like fertile soil, a child's mind is always open to the seeds of the unconscious content of the parents. Most children are like sponges. They pick up not only the verbal cues of the parents, but the unspoken thoughts and feelings as well. These unconscious processes, although they are not sent in clear, conscious ways by the mother, can be just as powerful and lasting as some verbal messages. In sand-play therapy* with children, I not only see children playing out their own inner feelings and conflicts, but they are often "playing out" those of the parents as well.

We've had sand-play toys around our home now for some years, and our children have often freely had the chance to express themselves through the symbols of play. During the time of my midlife crisis a strange thing happened with our two younger girls. Not surprisingly, my husband and I were experiencing some tension around our own relational impasses at the time, but we were doing our best to keep it under wraps. To our surprise the children seemed perfectly attuned to our situation. I began to see that their sand-play themes spoke to the exact nature of our own conflict. The unspoken tensions and undercurrents of our marital issues were being enacted through the miniature toys of a play battlefield. Typically grand-scale uprisings and dark underworld creatures repeatedly threatened to invade peaceful domestic scenes. As tempting as it is to

*Sand-play therapy is designed to amplify the child's inner process through play with toy figures in a tray of sand.

underestimate what children can pick up from the environment, they nonetheless are wide open to the unspoken and unexpressed psychic content in the air. Somehow, although they were both involved in this process, it was our just-budding teenager who seemed most sensitive to my personal state and it was the following tray which caught my attention most sharply:

In the center of her sandtray was a mound of earth. At the top of it a dark, transparent glass ball was partially buried in the sand. At the right end of the tray, Native American women were performing domestic chores on a narrow strip of land, fenced in by a wall. Between the women and the center mound was a strip of water running the length of the tray; a kind of river. Young boys were able to come and go from the women's quarters, but my daughter explained to me that the women themselves were not allowed to venture out. At the bottom of the tray a narrow path led from the women's section to the inner circle where the "treasure" was, but the way was flanked by four or five cavemen brandishing clubs and spears. In another section of the tray a lone wolf sat watching everything in the women's quarters. He was planning to steal a turkey the women were cooking over the fire. A small bird sat atop the magic glass ball in the mound and a coiled serpent sat in a water urn listening to the women.

I gazed intently at the powerful metaphors unfolding through my daughter's sand play, and felt a rising lump in my throat. I asked her, "What's with these guys guarding the women like that?"

"They're guarding the women because they are afraid they will cross the water and find the treasure."

"Oh," I said, "and what is this treasure?"

"Just the little bird knows what the treasure really is; the men and women knew a long time ago, but now they have forgotten. But the men are afraid to let anyone else see inside anyway." She went on, "The snake spies on the women just in case they want to get away, and so the women have to be careful."

As I pondered the symbols in her work, I saw clearly that my daughter was expressing almost exactly the nature of my own conflict. Whether her sensitivity to me was out of our own enmeshed relationship or out of her own approaching need for independence, I don't know. But the tray was undeniably a picture of my own unconscious process struggling to come to life. In sorting through this work it became clear to me that the adolescent girl within me had never successfully come safely into the waters of womanhood. Frightened to venture forth into the forbidden territories of independence, and seldom encouraged to search for the treasure of my own autonomy as a child, the inquisitive, lively, and adventurous inner teenager within me was still sealed up. The more I thought about it, the more I saw that this other relationship in my life, and the stretching experience it was calling me to, was a large part of my individuating work. Yet, still enmeshed with my mother in some ways (or at least with the collective mother), I was caught needing a sense of parental approval even as an adult. In truth, I had never experienced a break through the wall myself. Like the women held captive by the men in the tray, I half expected that I would be clubbed ("struck from above") if I dared to leave the safe and familiar world of the status quo. Needing approval and afraid of being judged or misunderstood, I had failed to separate out from the traditional role of the corporate mother. I was still locked up within my own internal women's quarters and unable (or unwilling) to venture into the mound at the center of the tray—into the rich earth of the self, the treasure.

Part of my inner work at the time was to challenge the ways I remained a prisoner to the myths of womanhood; ways I felt afraid to cross the edges of my own need for authenticity. As children we are naturally inquisitive, endlessly filled with a yen for adventure. Life is an exciting discovery until someone closes the door on our seeking process, until someone pulls in the reins too sharply or demands too much conformity. For many of us the photographic images of our childhood do change noticeably over the years. The rakish smile starts to fade as we become less our own spontaneous child and more and more the child of our parents.

As I began to pay closer attention to the inner work I had to sort through, and to bring into consciousness some of my own inner conflicts during this time, I noticed that the themes of my children's sand-tray work seemed to change. I noticed that the more I began to become aware of my own internal issues and to deal with them, the less my children seemed to need to act out for me what I wasn't seeing. The moment I began to take responsibility for my own inner process, their play again became their own.

Since the interior and often unrecognized conflicts or other unconscious workings of the parents get acted out by the children in the family, it is essential for the parents to face and deal with what is going on with each of them as individuals and also as a couple. We must ask how our own unworked-through inner conflicts as adults may still be affecting our own children in the present. Likewise, when we as adults are trying to piece together some of the early dynamics of the family constellation of which we were a part, it is often helpful to consider that each of us most likely carried some fragment of the unconscious of one or both our parents. Each of us may honestly have to acknowledge what part we played, and may continue to play, in the unexpressed side of our parental psyche.

Let's look at another example of an unconscious process that goes on between a mother and child. This particular level of unconscious communication is one that is perhaps less well known, but it comes up periodically in the deeper levels of work with the unconscious and is well worth mentioning.

Some current research postulates that during gestation, probably somewhere around the latter months of fetal development, the psyche of the unborn infant is sufficiently formed to be taking in the thought and feeling processes of the mother. I have worked with adults whose impressions of rejection, for instance, may have been formed way back in the womb.

One such woman entered therapy with the complaint that she often felt insecure about herself. In spite of the fact that her scholastic achievements were unusually high and that she held a professional position she felt proud of, she continued to feel a deep-seated sense of unworthiness and was periodically depressed. During one session in which we were working at the deeper unconscious level, she spontaneously experienced an age regression and began to feel herself back in the womb. As she continued to work with some of the impressions in the deep psyche and to process through the intense feelings that accompanied them, she began to get the distinct feeling that she was an unwanted child. *"I don't ever remember being unwanted. Certainly my mother never told me anything of the sort. She's always been a loving mother. But I just can't shake this idea of feeling unwanted. It makes me wonder if my mother ever considered an abortion when she was carrying me."*

During a later visit my client reported that she had, in fact, asked her mother about this. Not surprisingly, her mother admitted to her that she had considered an abortion several times during her pregnancy. She had apparently felt apprehensive about this particular birth because of her age and because the family already had several children. In time, as the woman reckoned with and healed these impressions, her previous feelings of low self-worth began to recede.

RECONCILING OUR ROOTS

Other kinds of ancestral connections exist between family members that do not fall into the previous categories. These connections are different because they seem to exist whether or not there has been any direct communication or modeling. On many occasions, I have noticed these connections clearly in effect between two individuals in a family who have rarely even spent time together.

First, there is the mother-daughter dynamic that occurs first to the mother, and later to the child at about the same age. Second, there is the evidence that a woman is not only connected to her mother at the deeper level, but also to her grandmother, great-grandmother, and so on down the ancestral line. The connections here can be psychic connections, for want of a better description, and can range along a broad spectrum—from emotional problems to character likeness. At the spiritual level we seem to be connected to one another in ways that seem to defy both reason and coincidence.

One of my clients experienced a depression and some degree of crisis which seemed directly related to some unfinished business of her mother's. The issues of depression that my client was trying to deal with at the time were caused by a pronounced fear of abandonment and rejection, but neither one of us could figure out where these feelings were coming from. She had already worked through some important issues in therapy, she had just remarried, and her life should have been relatively stable. When repeated talk of her mother came up at each session, we decided to explore that.

As we dug around in her mother's history, trying to see what *her* depression might have been about, we began to discover some significant likenesses. We found that her mother's depression had happened at just about the same age as hers, and that several of the complaints of the two women seemed identical. During the long bout of depression her mother had experienced years before, her mother had often felt similarly rejected, insecure, and abandoned. Periodically, she had sometimes questioned her right to be. My client's work then turned toward trying to sort through what part of this depression was actually hers to deal with, and what part was a remnant of some loyalty to her family tree. We concluded that whatever this was, it seemed clearly more related to her mother than herself.

In her work on this problem my client created a family sculpture of as many of the women in her bloodline as she felt belonged (or that she could remember). Working in clay, she began to sculpt her mother, her grandmother, and great-grandmother in a line working back into the past. We decided to illustrate something of her ancestral heritage by symbolically placing in one hand (of each of the ancestors) something negative, troublesome, and problematic. In the other hand she was to place a symbol for something positive, some characteristic she liked about that person, a useful trait. For instance, in one figure, the left hand held a hickory switch and the right hand held a basket with a treble clef in it. One symbolized the disdain and disapproval that might come from that side of her grandmother; the other stood for her grandmother's ability to be musical and creative. Where she was uncertain just what traits there might be in a particular ancestor, I suggested she simply try to tune in as best she could; to feel out with her imagination what might have been handed down. When we work with the unconscious, we often find that what we "make up" is usually fairly accurate. I asked my client to be choosing as she was working, just what ancestral qualities she wanted to bring forward in her own life, and which she wanted to leave behind.

As she neared completion, we began to talk about how she might bring closure to her ancestral work. To ritualize that she was releasing the past and entering into the present of her own life she decided upon the closure of prayer. I asked an Irish Franciscan friend of mine, who understands about these generational impasses, to join us in my office and to celebrate a special mass for her and for her ancestors. We placed her family sculpture on a homemade altar in the middle of the room and began our celebration. We prayed for the women in her family and for forgiveness for all those things that had been held in the left hand that had kept her from living to her fullest potential. We prayed for the power to choose those qualities in the ancestry which came down through the symbol of the right hand; all those things which had served as strengths and as sound guides for a more integrated self. We asked for a releasing of the family bonds of the past, a reconciliation in the present, and for the grace to begin to embrace the real woman within her.

Another kind of ancestral link can happen between members of a family: I have found it to be true that grandparents and grandchildren frequently share similar traits. Although many of these traits do not specifically seem to follow sex lines, for the purpose of this study it is the grandmother-granddaughter connection that I want to focus on. It doesn't seem to matter whether or not the two may live in different places, or that they may not have spent much time together. In some cases a granddaughter has spent no time with her grandmother and yet may still carry some of her traits and likenesses. Likewise, the two may be connected in terms of carrying similar problems or being similarly symptomatic of certain things. Although we are clearly linked because of both genetics and modeling, we also seem to be linked with our relations without any apparent space or time connectors. These connections must be something like psychic bonds—we can only guess at how they are actually transmitted.

Some years ago I had a client who suffered from some bouts of acute anxiety and hypertension, mixed with depression and fatigue. She could not seem to pull herself together and tried hospitalization and antidepressants. Nothing seemed to help. After her stay at the hospital she came to see me, and by that time she was beginning to think she heard voices. She feared leaving the house, being alone, going crazy; she fantasized her husband getting fed up with her and leaving. She worried that she would get an illness of some kind and die. She was not a happy woman.

In delving into her family history I soon learned that her

grandmother, a native of Bolivia, had also been an unhappy woman. Frequently superstitious, withdrawn, easily frightened, and given to bouts of hypochondria and fears about her health, the old woman had a suspicious number of similar complaints. Although there was no evidence of any chemical imbalance in the family, there were some unmistakable likenesses between these two women.

Perplexing to me was the fact that my client had little or no current stressors that might support this level of depression. And since her family had moved from Bolivia when she was three, leaving the old grandmother with relatives, I also doubted whether her grandmother's modeling of these same complaints might have had much effect on her as a child. Unfortunately, she did not stay in treatment long enough for me to get much work done with her; it seems her family wanted to put her back in the hospital and keep her sedated. Not surprisingly, talk of ancestral linking and any kind of healing prayer to clear the family tree clearly made them all uncomfortable. Digging around the roots of the family tree is clearly taboo for some people.

One woman I know discovered, while in the midst of her own inner work, that her fears of drowning were actually not her own. She had never known her maternal grandmother, who had died when this woman was only an infant. But when she reviewed her family roots and talked to her great aunt, she discovered that her grandmother had a phobia about water. She had nearly drowned herself as a child and had always carried an obsessive fear of water, although apparently only her husband and sister had known about it. She had insisted no one else know because she wanted her children to be good swimmers. *"None of us ever found out Grandma had been afraid of the water until after we were grown. I can't remember anybody in our family ever acting funny around it. But even as a small child it terrified me. Thoughts of drowning used to plague my dreams as a child. I don't understand why this fear should happen to land in my mind, but it's always been there."*

We are also bound to our ancestral tree through character likeness. For instance, many women are not as much like their mothers as they are their grandmothers. In my own tree, it is my grandmother whose character I seem to favor. I not only look like my grandmother, but many of her traits and interests are also things I easily identify with. I spent very little time with my grandmother as a child; she lived in California and we lived in Texas and Nevada, and so our time with her was primarily vacation time. This would not seem to be sufficient time for a child my age to have picked up much information from modeling. I remember her as long-suffering and sometimes rather austere, yet she could also be mischievous and playful. She loved nature; she had a huge garden in which she worked long hours, and around her modest house there were always bright red geraniums and succulents of all kinds. When money was scarce, grandmother's garden was always sufficient. She baked her own breads, canned fruits and vegetables, and made great meals out of next to nothing. She had a great tolerance for sick people and not infrequently took them under her wing, made them strange soups from her garden, and nursed them back to health. Mother says she read her Scriptures often, prayed and sang in the garden, and found little inspiration going to church.

My mother once commented to me that she noticed how much like her mother I was, particularly in the content of the letters I wrote and the character strengths and weaknesses I exhibited. Visiting me one day as I was canning tomatoes from my own garden, my mother said to me: "Your grandmother used to grow and can her own tomatoes. It's amazing that everything you seem to do are all things she loved to do."

THE BIRTH OF ANOTHER CHILD

Tracing the formation of our own blocks toward self-esteem is often a revealing and sometimes painful discovery, yet this level of work in our personal foundation is vital to holism. Many women in this sort of work, however, are unable to go directly to their own mother for reconciliation. Some of our mothers have already died, and still others could not yet receive this emotional healing themselves. Some are simply unavailable for a direct two-way confrontation and healing endeavor. What we do have to do is become aware of our ancestry and its effects over us, because we are responsible for breaking from the negative aspects of our own lineage. Above all, women need to make a conscious effort to choose how we want to manifest these women in our family tree; to choose what we want to own in the present and what is better left in the past.

Like other organic processes, it takes time to heal the feminine tree. Some of the roots are buried deep and sometimes the work is tedious and uncertain. Sometimes it's difficult to heal to the point of releasing those old growths that simply bear no fruit. If my mother lacked ability in direct communication before men, if she winked and wiled instead of stamped her foot or standing her ground, my task is to find out how that happened in her life, how it re-creates itself in mine, and then to let go of the thing. If I hold her at fault because her model of the feminine has wounded my own self-esteem in some way, then my own healing process will be impeded. If her preoccupation with social graces and nice clothes over more human values offends me, what good are the spaces of my unforgiveness?

The moment I hang onto my incompletions and tag my mother with the blame, then I get into bad habits. When I can project my failures onto my mother, then they get to be "her fault"— and when that happens then I don't have to take responsibility for change myself. Healing happens when I can say to my mother, *"OK Scarlett, I forgive your poverty. I forgive your pretensions, your lack of assertiveness, all your covert agendas for living through others. I forgive your wounds; your hurts; all the times you felt you never had enough; all the ways you were afraid to say who you were inside."*

Our healing journey stretches both backwards and forwards; we are both the root and the seed of the same tree. We have a continuity of identity not only with our ancestry, but with the concept of womanhood. I've thought many times that I am not only my mother's daughter and my grandmother's child, I also belong to a rich tapestry of women who stretch back to the beginning of time. When our model of the feminine is inadequate and undernourished, we can draw upon other resources. Perhaps our psychic connections to our ancestors are unhealed and need work, perhaps they are there as solid wells from which to draw; but either way, *they are there*. Consequently, our healing process needs to stretch to include all of these possibilities in our walk toward wholeness.

I recently attended a women's workshop about discovering and empowering the inner woman. In one of the exercises we were to begin to move spontaneously in dance form, to move from an inner figure of the earth mother and her roots. My experience was powerful: *I found myself first dancing to the music in the room—not paying much attention to what the other women were doing, just listening to my own internal promptings, my instincts, my body. Then I began to find myself on the ground, squatting as though I were participating in some ancient birthing ritual. I imagined myself giving birth long ago, maybe thousands of years ago. I imagined that I was a primitive. My feet were large and soiled and very solid and I pushed them against the dirt as I strained to bring this child down. I made noises like a woman in labor, groaning and crying and singing this child into the world. Then I began to weep for something lost, as though I were rediscovering the truth of the women in my own blood from past times. I imagined myself in this tribe of women; they were all coaching me and some of them were dancing and singing in my labor. Their faces were dark and beautiful and there was an air of mysticism in their dance. Then this child came and they gathered around with deep smiles and sighs and took him into their arms and laughed with me. Washing me and dressing me in a woven brown cover of some sort, they handed me back my child.*

After the depth of this experience I needed quiet, so I went off by myself for a while. I found a spot of grass and sat down on it and closed my eyes and these women gathered around me again. All of them reached out and touched me and spoke a blessing to me. I was remembering that when I was a child, the clothes I wore and the manners I used were the ones my mother chose; Scarlett's wiles were all mine to learn too; the polite seductions, the apologetic asking for things in indirect ways, the childlike innocence before men. Tears of rage began to fall, waters from the years christened the grass below me. And the women stayed with me, looking at me, holding me, blessing me in a tongue foreign yet somehow known to me; they were my ancient mothers. They were my grandmothers from the past centuries. Their old hands were touching me, healing the imprints of the present misunderstanding of our feminine heritage. They were the Old Ones rebirthing me and the labor and groaning of my own inner work was going to bear fruit. Theirs was the same voice of the old Grandmother spirit that walked with me on the trail up through the red rock country of Frijoles Canyon.

And theirs were the same hands that yielded the ancient painted shard of pottery. I was a part of all of them before me and my heritage was clear. This baby in my prayer dance was my feminine spirit.

The dance experience had suddenly become transcendent. The ordinary limitations and incompletions of my maternal past were touched by a reality that was far more powerful and expansive than I alone was. The old women in my prayer dance were the essence of what it means to be a woman. Gently they removed from me the false sides of woman, and lifted from me the early imprints of wounded feminine esteem. Speaking directly to my heart with their broad, dark-faced smiles and their ancient knowing of themselves as women who are sacred, they gave me back a heritage I had lost. "This is who you are," they said. In as much as I could open my eyes to the beauty of these mothers within me, and to the sacredness of what it means to be a woman and a mother, I could begin to receive and to understand more clearly the feminine side of God. The road by the waters of my past was beginning to heal.

6. Fathers as Heroes and Adversaries

There was always something familiar about my relationship to my mother. Somehow I knew that we had come from the same mold. She was often more predictable and generally more accessible than my father. She had by far the most comfortable and often the most available lap. It was from her touch that apple pies emerged, wounded knees were bandaged, and stories were read late at night. But of the two of them he was the enigma, definitely a horse of a different color. Mysteriously weaving in and out of the fabric of our early family, his appearances were magical events I often planned my whole day around.

Our fathers are significant sculptors of our self-image. Of course, a child's initiative, her ability to stretch out beyond the security of her mother and to test the waters of her environment, is formed by both parents. In order to be in balance, she needs to be able to draw from the inherent strengths of both worlds. Yet it is often the father's leading, encouragement, and support that will set the tone for a feeling of safety outside the maternal nest.

The father is that first significant other in a little girl's life, the mysterious presence of the first man in her environment. If he is a positive influence she can idealize him and make him into her hero, striving to draw him into her child's world and anxious to please him, to be near him and to compete for the reassurance of his lap. Even if he is an absent father, either physically or emotionally, she may still idealize him, longing for what she never had as a child. Imperfect as our fathers may have been, whether in the role of hero or adversary, the first man in our lives has a profound effect on us as daughters.

A woman I know, who happens to possess a great share of self-confidence, says of her father, *"Dad was an incredible man. I felt free in his presence. He made me feel I could do anything. I don't mean he was permissive by any means, he wasn't. I knew when he disapproved of something. It's just that he was fair. If he didn't like something I did or didn't do he never attacked me with it. If I made a mistake or fell flat on my face in some project or effort of some kind, he helped me see what went wrong, how it might have been better, or what I might have done differently. As a kid failure wasn't ever a big deal. To him it was just another opportunity to try something a different way, to experiment with new possibilities. In a lot of ways he was a real hero for me."*

Not long ago my oldest daughter, Mariam, and I were talking over a problem one of her friends was having with her own father. She was amazed that so many father-daughter relationships among her peers seemed broken and painful. After reflecting about her own father for a moment she said, *"I feel like Dad gives me enough space to be my own person. He doesn't smother me with goals that are out of my reach. And he gives me room to make my own decisions instead of trying to force his on me. You know, it's been easier for me to really believe in myself when he's believed in me."*

Another woman said, *"I always knew my father had a special concern for me, I knew I was important to him. Sometimes he confided in me when he had problems, and he always had a way of making me feel like his friend—like an equal. He used to read us a lot of stories at night, sometimes tales from* Songs of the South *or from his favorite cowboy sagas. No matter how busy he was, he always gave us whatever time he could. Sometimes he sat on the floor and let us comb his hair this way and that, and he actually would walk around the house with his hair whatever outrageous way we had styled it. And he loved it when we sang. Sometimes we'd take trips and I'd stand next to him and sing the whole way. His patience for my songs was infinite."*

Just as some mothers show us great regard as children, a daughter needs respect and validation from her father. She needs to see him as her support, as one who affirms, protects, and enables her to move gracefully as a whole person. The daughter of such a father grows up possessing a natural sense of self-confidence and regards herself as a healthy equal to men.

From the father a child needs both a good model for the masculine and a clear sense that the feminine is worthy of his love. When she can trust her father she can hold a trusting attitude about men in general. If she has experienced her father as a friend, she will believe in herself as a woman. She will not be likely to choose a man or a role in life that does not celebrate her feminine giftedness. What's more, the daughter of a man who esteems the feminine will not grow up with a sense that her experiments and errors in life will be relentlessly judged.

A girl whose father has been her friend will have an easier time walking the path to her own inner masculine self. Looked at from a psycho-spiritual perspective, the father energy within the psyche is power, authority, protection, strength, integrity; ultimately, it is a hero force within. If a woman is nurtured and upheld by the father, then her internal sense of a transpersonal father will be healthy. If this is the case, then God and father do not align themselves as internal enemies in the feminine psyche, but are synonymous heroes from which she can draw strength. When the father is the enemy or the stranger, however, the feminine child has very little sense of masculine strength at any level.

THE ADVERSARY FATHER

A woman who had been working painstakingly to reaccess her own internal masculine strengths said of her process, *"Since my dad was taken away while I was still very young, I had only Mother's opinions and teachings to guide me. Without saying a word, Mom taught me that she didn't like men; to her they were untrustworthy. While I was still very young, my mother allowed me to be exposed to some very unstable men. I don't believe she ever wanted me to be hurt by them intentionally, but I think she just thought, 'That's the way men are'—a thought that gradually formed in my own mind."*

As a child, this woman was a victim of repeated sexual abuse. Her mother knew of it, but took no action to stop it. In many cases her mother stood by and helplessly cried as she watched her daughter's abuse. Her mother's model not only reinforced fear and mistrust of men, it also encouraged severe passivity in regard to them. Such patterns do not disappear. They are indelibly imprinted in the psyche, whether or not we are conscious of them as adults.

This woman naturally took on a victim role towards men. She married a man who turned out to be her adversary; one she could neither trust nor love. Bringing all her mother's predictions about men along with her over the years, the past continues to repeat itself in a variety of ways that have reinforced her childhood nightmare. To her men are still untrustworthy, and yet they must be tolerated.

This feeling continues to be carried over to her spiritual life. *"Since I've been a child, I've believed in God. In some ways that's been my only oasis. I've always thought that things would eventually change; that they'd somehow get better."* Even though her faith had been an emotional reservoir, God subtly assumed the characteristics of the men in her life that she could never trust or appease. For her he was both reminiscent of the father that had abandoned her and the men she fell victim to. Ultimately, her relationship to God was bound by overtones of a fear of condemnation, a fear of doing something wrong or displeasing. Over the years she became frozen by these powerful inner attitudes, which canceled her power to change or to believe in herself. Her personal experience of the masculine was so wounded that eventually God also became the inner adversary. To the little girl who never knew any real heroes, the idea of God as a loving father somehow doesn't ring true because loving fathers don't wound their daughters.

Most of the women I know are wounded in the father-daughter relationship. Instead of being free to relate to men with a sense of trust and a willingness to explore loving relationship, most women still bear the scars of incompletion in relationship to the first man in their lives. And it is here in the present that many women are stuck carrying the ghosts of that early experiment.

One of my clients who experienced a harsh father when she was a child says, *"He was a good father to us and I know he tried hard to make ends meet. He had a lot of pressure financially and he was always working at least two jobs. But he yelled all the time. It's like his fuse was always short. Ever since I've been a little girl I have tried to make everything all right for everybody, to smooth things over, to fix everybody's feelings. I can't stand any kind of chaos or disorder, so I'm always careful to sidestep trouble. I am an ace at staying out of arguments and I laugh a lot. I even laugh when things aren't really funny. I guess that's been kind of a hiding place for me. But I'm noticing that I'm depressed most of the time now, and I don't think I can hide my anger anymore. I used to hide it because I was always afraid I'd sound like my dad, and I just hate that kind of chaos. But I know that if I don't get assertive, if I keep holding this anger, I'll just keep smiling and be depressed."*

Clearly, any man who has developed powerful lungs at the expense of his family has effectively frightened his daughter away from a rightful sense of self-esteem. Not only that, he has damaged her image of the masculine by exaggerating it in ways that do nothing to boast of true strength. When a man feels fearful inside he tends to try and overcompensate for his fear and emptiness by taking control over others, and by acting as if he had everything under control. But a man who protects his own low self-esteem by attacking others or acting in overtly dominant ways alienates others, and among them are the women in his life. The daughter of a harsh father has not only her own mistrust and fear to deal with, she ultimately must heal the broken image of the masculine which has been imprinted on her deepest memory.

In short, some men make such a bad show of masculine characteristics that a woman has no recourse but to deny her own positive masculine strengths and risk becoming passive, or to follow her father's negative suit and become abusive herself. Whether the abuse is physical or emotional, abusive fathers tend to produce daughters who are either prone to anger and rebellion or lack any assertiveness at all. Whether a woman plays the aggressor or the victim, the effect of the father's abuse on her self-esteem is always the same: One way or the other her spirit is crushed, and she often suffers from a poor self-image.

In order for a man to be sensitive enough to respect the feminine, he must have touched and shown reverence for his own authentic masculine strengths. A man who is secure in himself naturally feels secure with others. He is neither too strong and domineering nor too weak and passive. But since this is generally not the case, and since a man's own models for masculine and feminine are often incomplete and lacking in themselves, what is the effect on the daughter of a passive father? *"I don't think my Dad was ever a model of strength for me. He was a loving father, but sort of ineffectual as a man. There were a lot of times he seemed afraid to take initiative, to take risks. He was always quiet if there was the slightest possibility he might be wrong about something. I can see a lot of places in myself that are similar to him. For one thing I tend to draw back under any kind of pressure or competition, especially if the competition feels threatening. I just seem to lose myself."* When the significant male in a daughter's life fades into the woodwork, her own masculine empowerment may be much less accessible, and in some cases, barely intact at all.

A woman may hesitate to take power and to stand on her own because her father was passive himself, or because he took too much responsibility for her and overprotected her. Another woman comments, *"My father was a good man basically. But he seemed sort of lukewarm as a father. He had trouble saying no to me— or to anyone else in the family, for that matter. I think he wanted to please everybody and he wanted to be a good guy, but he came off as sort of passive. He indulged me a lot and almost never denied me anything. Not that that's bad, but I think it would have been better for me to know there were limits.*

"I had a hard time setting limits for myself after leaving home. It was hard for me to meet the real world in a way, probably because my father had protected me from the hard knocks. It took a long time for me to stop expecting others to take care of me. I was very dependent on other men for years. When I was a little girl I loved it when he took charge of everything, but expecting that as an adult woman somehow didn't work the way it used to."

Fairy tales are full of stories of the favorite daughter, the little princess who seems to have everything. But a father who does everything for his daughter effectively leaves her without much independence because he has taken the initiative for her too many times. Like an overprotective mother, he takes from her some of the vital steps in mastering autonomy.

When a father is passive and ineffectual toward his daughter, she misses out on a potentially valuable model for power and assertiveness. She has no model for action, for that father force of the sun, for the movement in her life of *yang* power, and for an expression of vital and dynamic energies. She is up the creek without a paddle until, if she is fortunate enough to have the chance, some later model or circumstance causes her to fashion one for herself.

VARIATIONS ON THE THEME OF INTIMACY

When we experience intimacy with our fathers in childhood, we innately know that we can trust life—and men. Yet Western culture rarely models intimacy in relationships for men. Instead, it reinforces goals that have little to do with loving. Culture rewards the man who is the achiever, who is a performer, a responsible provider, sometimes a stoic. But men who have been locked into goals and achievements are seldom good at intimacy.

There is no doubt in my mind that my father raised me in the best way he knew how. Without a doubt he gave me what he could of his own self-confidence and know-how. As I grew older and he traveled less, he taught me a lot of skills and shared many of his interests with me. He encouraged me, affirmed me, and believed in me. He loved the outdoors and taught me about mountains and streams and sagebrush and showed me how to build fires and bait my hook. He showed me how to shoot skeet and how to patch the tires on my bicycle. But risk feelings and honesty with me, he could not. He never told me much about himself as a person. My mother and father never knew one another either. Their quiet denial of feelings sheltered both of them from risking to be who they really were with one another. I grew up watching them play these defensive games with one another. It's taken me years to discover the fear I've had about intimacy, the ways I've hidden from being vulnerable.

Some of us had fathers who, like mine, were basically fair men who tried their best, given all that they knew of life and human nature and things of relationship, but who just could not get it. Others of us had fathers who themselves were deeply wounded men without an inkling of how to go about safely in the arena of relationships; men who were not only inadequate models of intimacy, but who were emotionally impoverished themselves and unable to function in the father role at all.

One woman whose father was a preacher said of their relationship, "*My dad was wonderful with his parishioners. He treated each of them with incredible sensitivity. People idolized him—they came to him with everything, our phone rang day and night. But he showed his family a different side of himself. Sometimes he seemed far from any sensitivity or kindness. He could be a terrible grouch, moody and arrogant. In his robes he was like a real man of God, but at home he was just a man with a lot of his humanity hanging out. I remember feeling jealous sometimes when he'd spend all day with someone else's problems and then had little patience with mine. I saw him as intimate with others, but I never experienced that side of him much at all. To this day I feel ambivalent about the whole idea of intimacy. The thought of it brings up a lot of anger in me. It's real hard to trust men when they get too close. It's like I want it but I'm afraid of it at the same time."*

The daughter of an alcoholic said, *"I never knew anything about closeness as a child. I was terrified of my father. And although I've worked through some of my fears of men, it's still an underlying theme for me in all relationships. I've done a lot of things to keep myself safe with men, to keep myself distant and not vulnerable. I've created a lot of blocks to intimacy, ivory towers, smoke screens, high standards, moodiness. Just when somebody thinks I'm getting predictable, I do something chaotic. Chaos was the only thing I knew as a child, I don't feel at home without it."*

Until she squarely faced the painful memories of chaos and broken trust in her own childhood, this woman had been caught for years in destructive relationships; ones that would always assure her that she wouldn't have to get too close. Brilliant in her field and endlessly creative with whatever endeavors she tackled, her relationships were inevitably chaotic. The men she chose were an ironic mixture of eccentric, artistic, intriguing, and schizoid—but they were exciting. *"I never got into a relationship that was ordinary. These men were incredibly talented and creative, but they were all slightly mad. I suppose I chose that because it was something like what I knew as a child. I had no concept of normal."*

The child who is the victim of incest from a male family member is similarly victimized by a sense of low self-esteem and a fear of intimacy. If a child is molested, raped, or fondled by someone she should be able to trust and look up to, the effect on her experience of men is disastrous. The little girl who must suffer being held and touched in ways that she is afraid to speak of and can only silently cry about is bound in deep guilt and rage.

All too often the little girl blames herself. Because she has been taken advantage of and sexual intimacy has been forced on her, gaining her footing both emotionally and relationally will be a task that may take years to sort through. Even more than the child who has lost her father and suffers from a sense of abandonment, the sexually abused child suffers a betrayal from the first man in her life that will be difficult to heal.

THE ABSENT FATHER

In my work I have been struck by the fact that for many women, the father was not present at all. Either he was absent altogether because of divorce, death, or separation, or he was home but ineffectual as a father. He may have been a successful and active businessman outside of his home and a passive and emotionally withholding man at home, or an alcoholic and out to lunch most of the time. He may have been socially at ease with other people, and yet as a husband or father he may have been in the background when it came to relationships, feelings, or intimate contact.

Elyse Walkerman, in her book *Father Loss,* covers in detail the essential effects of early father deprivation. She says that there are some important differences between the child who has some conscious recollection of father, and the child who has not.

> Just as her stage of development will largely contribute to the child's reaction to death, there is one circumstance which, because of its timing, separates its victim from other fatherless daughters. The girl whose father died when she was an infant must struggle with the . . . void of never having known him. Try as she might to plumb the hidden corners of her memory, there is no image for her to recapture, no man to claim as father.[1]

One of my own early childhood friends, whose father had been killed in action during World War II, experienced such a loss. Not only was she minus a father's presence and attention, she also lacked the presence and nurturance of her mother. Financially, the family just got by—but that meant her mother, too, was absent. Among all my friends I liked her best, because she was the wildest. A dare made her day. To this day I am missing a small chunk of my left ear because she wanted to see how close she could come to restaging the drama of William Tell using her bow and arrows and my ear. In the fifth grade my family moved out of state and we lost contact with one another. During a visit back to my home town later on in high school, however, I looked her up. I was surprised to find her even wilder and more out of control. But she was no longer playing with bows and arrows. Instead, she was going through boys and alcohol and was only about three steps ahead of juvenile hall. Our meeting filled me with a lot of sadness and concern that summer. The next news I had of her was that she had married a successful lawyer and was attempting to settle down. Some years later I was stunned to learn that at twenty-five, married to a man who somehow failed to fill her early losses, she had committed suicide.

Clearly, not all early father loss ends in such tragedy; but neither is it uncommon that such deprivation has a profoundly negative effect on the daughter. Feelings of abandonment, rejection, emptiness, self-doubt, and loss all characterize the child whose father has died at an early age. Young girls who have experienced father loss also tend to idealize their fathers, as perhaps their mothers have before them. When father is idealized in the imagination of the abandoned child, then chances are that in real life no one can measure up to the child's image of the lost father. Consequently, no man can take his place.

In approaching men relationally, the daughter of loss may often be engaged in a frustrating paradox. At one level she may approach a man, hoping he will fill her needs in some way. At the same time she may push him away, because she fears he will die to her—not be there for her—in some metaphorical or real sense.

One of my friends said of her own father, *"My biggest issue with him was abandonment. He was an alcoholic who just couldn't stay sober. He tried several treatment centers, but he and my mother never got along and he always wound up drinking again. Some of their fights were because of the way she treated my brother and me; because of the beatings she gave us. I know it upset him, but somehow he never got on top of it. When I was about fourteen he left for the last time and never came back. I was stunned that he would leave us, that he wouldn't want to protect us from my mother. It was incomprehensible to me that I was now left with such a dangerous woman."*

Another woman caught at a relational impasse said, *"I feel like the minute I let down, the minute I trust this guy into my life, he's going to leave. The adult side of me says that's ridiculous, but the child side thinks she's going to be abandoned again."* Because the adult child of loss fears more loss and abandonment, she seldom grows to trust the normal wear and tear of most relationships. To her, relationship is more apt to be a deadly game of winners and losers. In such a game she cannot afford to be vulnerable, to lose face, to relinquish control, and she cannot bear the necessary independent or autonomous spaces that healthy relationships require. To her, normal separation doesn't imply wholesome creative breathing space, it means emptiness and isolation—and aloneness, to her, is frightening.

Many fathers, although present, were emotionally unavailable to their daughters. They may be good at what they do professionally and may provide for the basic needs of the family, but may not come through at other levels. In some cases their secure provision for the family may camouflage any real sense of caring. The following story illustrates this kind of loss: *"My father was at the top of his field professionally. Everyone at work admired him and most of the people in our town had heard of him. My mother was proud of him and sometimes we read his name in the newspaper. But he never came to a single one of my soccer games, nor to any of the events other girls' fathers came to. Aside from confirmation and graduation, it was always my mother who supported me. He was either too busy or out of town. I missed ever really knowing him as a person. He was a great provider and we always had everything that we needed. But I never had a father who could reach out and let me see who he was, and he never asked me who I was either."*

A woman I know, still struggling to come to terms with losing her father to alcoholism, said, *"No matter what I do, I can't seem to shake this sense of abandonment. I'd like to think I've forgiven my dad, but he always seems to be in the background of all my relationships. A long time ago I told myself it didn't matter that he wasn't there for me. I said it was OK and I didn't care. I said I could get along without him. But the truth is that even though he isn't there, he really is there after all. He's behind every relationship I have. I always go for the man I can't get. I set up this pretend relationship. I mean I pick the most unavailable man in the book and then I pretend everything is all set, and then when we get right down to the line and I'm feeling like I've got it together, then he says he's unable to make a commitment, or that maybe he's given me the wrong impression, or that maybe it won't work after all. I thought I was through with my dad, but I keep doing this over and over. I endlessly choose the kind of man who's not ever going to be there for me.*

UNCONSCIOUS IMPRESSIONS

When a daughter idealizes her father as hero she will not only act like him, consciously by picking up his values and his way of doing things, but she will also pick up and act out the less conscious arenas of his nature. Paradoxically, even if a child experiences her father in negative ways, there will still be something within her that wants to connect with him, to make it right, to redeem the relationship. Even if he is an adversary father, she still bears some unconscious likeness to him.

Another woman whose father had been an alcoholic, and who wanted to deny his effect over her, told the following story: *"My father drank a lot periodically. Sometimes he'd try to stop and he'd even go to AA. He even had my mother go to AlAnon. But usually he fell back into drinking anyway. We all rallied around his drinking problem and tried to help him, but eventually he always went back to drinking and we all gave up. He and Mom divorced, and I suppose in a way I divorced him too. I felt sorry for him. It was something he just couldn't overcome. I put him out of my mind and went off to school. I studied hard and did well. I never drank. I tried hard to make it out there, and in some ways I succeeded. But something went wrong somewhere. In my senior year I had a nervous breakdown. The doctor said I was working too hard, worrying too much about my performance, my grades. I couldn't stand the idea of being second best. I was plagued by dreams of being a failure, not making it. I dreamed often of being drunk and unable to function. I always woke up in a cold sweat. Eventually, I began to see that I'd become addicted to success, that ironically I was not unlike the father I was trying to forget. Just as he had become paralyzed by his drinking, I had become paralyzed by my fear of failure.*" Although she denied her father's influence, this woman had covertly taken her father into the corners of her psyche where he and she collaborated, in spite of their different paths.

Speaking of the unconscious and covert spaces some fathers and daughters seem to share, a friend of mine working on a weight problem, recently said to me, *"My father told me once, 'I don't ever want you to have to depend on anybody.' And I never really have. It's taken me all these years to make the connection between those words and what I'm actually doing. I've always been self-sufficient, I like living alone, I'm responsible to no one, and I thought I always liked it that way. Now I'm beginning to wonder. But if I look at the truth of the thing, I'm scared of relationships and I can't stand not being in control, because I hate the thought of being dependent on anyone."*

We had been talking about the covert seductions we felt from our fathers when we were younger. The irony of her story is that she had been living faithfully but unconsciously in her father's play. He was the director and she was the actress, stuck in between the first and second acts. When she was an adolescent she fell in love with a young man and they started going together. But essentially she felt afraid of the relationship and feared that she would be taken advantage of or somehow made dependent. This was a vulnerability she felt she could not afford. She is a professional teacher who has excelled in every academic pursuit she ever laid her hands on. But there is a wall between her and life, and inside of it she has begun to feel rage and despair. Clearly, something in her unspoken contract with her father not "to depend on anybody" is about to be brought into light. After all, this is a loyalty she can afford to break.

Often even the positive father has got to be wrestled with, and not infrequently the hero father for some of us has the undeniable markings of a father complex. Women who look to men, or to a sort of patriarchal validation for everything they do, are often caught in such a trap. The girl who adores her father because he was always there for her is in one way lucky to have had a father presence at all, especially in this day and age. But this sort of affinity to the father can actually stand in the way of a woman's own initiation of her deeper feminine self.

Likewise, the young woman who grew up in some sort of silent but mutual pact of loyalty to her father's values must also be held accountable. A woman engaged in this kind of pact holds herself in a psychic bondage to the father, because as long as a woman esteems the father too much she will never break free of wanting his approval. Innumerable women literally become unavailable to themselves and untouchable partners to their mates because they are unconsciously still connected to the father. This is psychological incest.

One of my friends told me once that at the heart of her inability to be able to make love to her husband freely was an unconscious attachment to her father. As a child her father had been terrified of his own sexuality and was constantly projecting this fear onto his own daughter. From the time she was very young, he made sure she *always* kept her legs together and frequently became irate with her over anything in her play that was even remotely suggestive of sexuality. In effect he instilled the same kinds of anxieties in his daughter. He withdrew all physical affection from her from about the age of ten on, and the only affirmation she ever got from him was for performance—for good grades, for excelling in sports competitions, and all things related to achievement. The child gradually got the message that getting her father's approval meant she had to remain well above her body. Naturally, performance was acceptable, perfection was even better, but anything sexual was taboo—including being in relationship to anyone else. She said to me once, "Making love to my husband was like saying 'no' to my dad; I just couldn't do it." This woman had always regarded her father with a great deal of love and respect, yet her allegiance to this unconscious program needed to be challenged and called to truth.

Once in a women's group we were discussing things that had affected us as our father's daughters. Someone opened the issue of sexuality, saying that her father had been very Victorian outwardly, consciously abiding by a rather rigid morality. But he had acted in seductive and suggestive ways with her and her sister. She recalled that he would often tease her about her developing body, sometimes patting her on the fanny when she passed by and making suggestive comments. Other times he would turn around and berate her for wearing something he thought was too sexy, scolding her for what he saw as a lack of decency.

Others in the group shared similar incongruities that came up over the course of their adolescence, similar ways their own fathers had handled—or mishandled—their developing pubescence. One woman's father had been affectionate and playful with her until she developed breasts and began to mature into young womanhood. Then he abruptly turned away and withdrew his attentions from her altogether. Another woman experienced her father as caring and supportive to her in front of her mother or other members of the family, but when they were alone he often seemed angry or withdrawn, suddenly defensive about his former show of attention.

The unconscious behaviors of these fathers always has an effect on the daughter's impression of herself as a woman. She is directly or indirectly influenced by the content of her father's communications to her, whether the messages are verbal or nonverbal. If a father is consciously controlled about his own sexuality and yet unconsciously gives the daughter mixed messages by teasing her, being suggestive with her, or touching her in seductive ways when she passes, then her message about her sexuality and her self-image is also bound to be divided. Consciously, such a father is saying "no"; but unconsciously, he is modeling "yes." She is caught in his ambivalence and eventually may act it out in her own life. He may even have set her up to act it out by his suggestive behavior and messages. In effect he is saying to her, "Go ahead and do what I am afraid to do."

Likewise, the father who turns away from his daughter when she is entering her sexual development is clearly afraid of his own sexuality. Possibly he has never dealt with his own sexual issues, and his daughter's development makes him nervous and afraid of his own sexual response. He may fear he is being aroused and, rather than risk that, he cuts her out. It is the same with the man who treats his daughter well in company but who is afraid to be alone with her.

A girl can pick up cues about the unconscious of the father in a multiplicity of ways. The danger is that she lacks the know-how to say her father has a problem with sexuality. She doesn't always trust her own intuition that there is something wrong. She can't articulate it or sort it out yet, so she grows up often thinking there is something wrong with her or that she is to blame. She may flaunt her developing body or try to hide it, but always there is the underlying guilt that it's *her* fault if she turns somebody on. She may choose to play out the other side of her father's ambivalence about sexuality by acting out in promiscuous ways. Yet she still may be ashamed of her sexuality and may feel confused about her body when she grows up because of the mixed messages she got as a child about herself from her father. Or, going to the other side of her father's mixed feelings about sex, she may be afraid of it. For instance, she may feel afraid of being alone with boys or men for fear something will happen, unconsciously carrying the same fear about handling herself as her father carried.

It is clear that, given these incongruities, a young woman can and does get confused about her sexual identity. Take the previous example of the father who has a dualistic view of sex. Consciously, he warns his daughter to remain chaste, scolds her slightest decolletage, and censors her television programs. Unconsciously, he would like to be reading *Playboy* and having a better sex life with his wife. His beautiful daughter in fact turns him on. In a clandestine way she is exciting to him, a reminder of the days he and his wife used to be sexually freer and more spontaneous. But his mind won't let him admit it, and so he represses it. These conflicting thoughts come out as incongruities in his behavior, and he becomes unconsciously seductive (perhaps overprotective) with his daughter. He does not carry out the act itself, but the desire is there. Although many overt cases of incest turn up daily in our society for treatment, it is often these silent kinds of seductions that never get acknowledged. These mixed messages about our sexuality often lie below the surface of our consciousness—vague, inarticulate, and just out of reach. We are out of touch with these roots of our sexual self-concepts. Consequently these messages play havoc with our fears, our anxieties, and our misconceptions about sexual expression. Such impressions become like silent taboos that condemn healthy sexuality.

My own father's mother was a stern little woman from the

Midwest with a modest view toward life and a flagrant taste for Victorianism. My mother says it is amazing I was even conceived. For years I had a built-in fear of my own sexuality. I do not say this was solely the fault of the ancestors on my father's side of the family. My mother had a great deal to do with this too, capricious but frightened at the same time. My own experience of sexuality was a combination of both mentalities— something like limbo must be, suspended and not going anywhere. Consciously, I thought to myself, "Sexuality is a wonderful mystery. It's natural, it's healthy, and I enjoy it—I think." Unconsciously, I thought to myself, "This is truly disgusting, I can live without it, I should have been a nun, there must be a better way to communicate." The point is that between our conscious and unconscious attitudes about sexuality there is a lot of ground that most of us need to come to terms with, ways we need to bridge what we "know" and what we may feel at the less conscious level. It is our task to put together some of these double messages and to sort them through, to clean out the ghosts of our parents' sexual attitudes, and to acknowledge how these old forms of limbo still serve to bind us.

Many more examples of unconscious influence affect us as daughters. Just as we may act out the denied and split off parts of our parental psyche, we may also act out the failed mission of our parents—trying to take up where father left off, attempting to set right what he never could, to do what he failed to do. A great many women, for instance, seem to be bent on trying to compensate for a father who was a failure. According to author Linda Leonard in *The Wounded Woman*, many daughters live out their father's life more than they live out their own.[2] This woman looks to find meaning and satisfaction through completing her father's scripts, living in an unfinished landscape he began long ago. Without conscious awareness she goes about the impossible dual task of trying to be her own person and her father's daughter at the same time.

RECLAIMING THE FATHER WITHIN

The work that we do on our parental relationships is vital in our healing process as adult women. Locating where we are most wounded and incomplete as the child of either parent is both a painful and a freeing experience. It takes time and patience to allow these deeply buried parts of our past childhood and its blocks to authenticity and autonomy to emerge. It takes time to be able to train ourselves to spot the ways that our mother or father knowingly or unknowingly took something from us that needs to be reclaimed.

All of us live out of the past. As adults we are still effectively bound by many of the molds of our early parenting. I still am working to integrate the cold dispassion of my father's aloof Victorianism and the clandestine capriciousness of my mother's repressed Latin nature. This sort of duality, whether it is present in the psyche consciously or unconsciously, can erupt in a variety of emotional or physical ways.

A few years ago I began to experience some increasingly annoying indigestion and stomach upsets. Eventually it grew worse, and I thought maybe I was beginning an ulcer. Before seeing the doctor, however, I went to see a friend of mine who does acupressure. I threw myself on her table with my usual "fix this one" challenge. The moment she began to work on my body, I began to drift into my unconscious, and I suddenly recalled the following dream:

I am standing in the center of a crowd of strangers. My name is written on my shirt in big bold letters; the letters are strong and well spaced and innately seem to spell out clearly who I am. My name tag is obviously different than the others, as though I am risking to show myself without a mask to this group, without my usual persona. But the group seems to disdain that I am wearing who I am right out front, and they stare distantly at me in silent condemnation. The woman I am working with suggests I talk to this crowd. Addressing what seems to be a kind of patriarchal collective, I say, "All of you look alike. You're all tall, aloof, distant. All of you are the same height, you have the same clothes on, dark blue suits, conventional wear. You're all proper and stiff. You're stuck in your heads, and you all walk too far above the ground. Watch out you don't fall and break your faces." I begin to feel my stomach tighten and hurt again, but I go on with the dialogue:

"Somehow I get that none of you like it that I'm standing apart from you. But listen here, I'm going to do it anyway. I'm not going to look

like the rest of you. I'm not going to walk around tall and distant and aloof and out of touch with my feelings. I have feelings and I'm not going to deny them. I'm not going to pretend to be just like you because I'm not. I have a right to be myself."

Later, drifting from that dialogue, my unconscious produced a picture from my earliest childhood which I hadn't remembered for years. My father used to come home at night and have a drink before dinner. My mother and he used to dance together in a little celebration of their own cocktail hour. But eventually she stopped dancing with him. So he used to pick me up in his arms and we'd dance. I would sing happily and we'd dance around the living room. I couldn't wait for him to come home so I could be lifted up in his arms and serenaded. I think we used to dance to Benny Goodman.

Opening and yielding more memories by this time, my unconscious next produced a picture of my father a few months before his death. By then I was already married and was working on co-creating our second son. Hy had come from Las Vegas to visit us in our little farmhouse, and because space was limited, he had to sleep on the couch. One day he didn't feel like getting up, and so I went to sit with him. He winced in pain and I asked him what was wrong. Then he showed me his stomach, which was hard and distended, and I suddenly felt afraid. He must have known it was something fatal, but so far the doctors hadn't found anything. A few months later the doctors finally got it together enough to announce that he had cirrhosis of the liver and that he was dying. When I remembered this during my bodywork session, I began to get the connection to this thing in my stomach.

When I was little my father had become increasingly unhappy. I think he knew early on that my mother would leave him. All those times he danced with me, it was mother he should have been dancing with. But the man was brave. He rarely complained, and in fact he was always rather stoic about his problems. He used to laugh about them and dismiss them in humorous but cynical ways. But he kept his feelings covered.

It began to dawn on me that my father had picked me up for the dance in more than one way. Even at three I must have guessed what was going on between the two of them; and because we were so close, I unconsciously took on his sadness and long-ing. The melancholy I had carried for so many years (probably up until my late twenties) had not been mine, but his. My strange moods and inability to access feeling, his; my passive way of not saying the truth and not speaking out my needs, his; my fear of breaking with the crowd and risking to be myself, his. Clearly, my mother's problem with low self-esteem was also shared by my father, but I hadn't seen it until now—it hid behind an air of denial and he never overtly came off as fright-ened or insecure. It dawned on me that he too had frequently had stomach complaints, little upsets and indigestion, not quite ulcers but close. Yet he joked and laughed and intellectualized and stayed above his hurts. And when he died, it was his liver and his stomach that was holding and manifesting all his unex-pressed pain: a painful longing for the life he never fully led.

I started to weep uncontrollably. My friend just went on being present and gently poking acu-points, and I went on weeping and yelling and falling apart and letting my stomach agonize over all the ways I too had been holding myself in and not being in touch with my feelings. I remember distinctly feeling my father's presence there in the room amidst my grieving. I re-member crying out loud to his spirit, "Daddy I love you, but I don't want to die like you. I don't want to live in compromises and I'm not going to be afraid of saying who I am and what I feel." And I cried for a long time, big tears, hot tears, baby tears, grown woman's tears, tears a long time in building up. As this dialogue drew to a close, I went back to the group of tall look-alike strangers and made peace with them. Clearly, these were my own collective attitudes of disdain towards a side of myself that risks to stand alone. Somewhere in the course of this process work, my stomachache disappeared.

I am still trying to sort through the different parent sides of my personality and to stay with the steady descent into my own truer nature. It is the same work that my clients and friends and that the other significant women in my life are about doing. All of us are about this work of reclaiming the lost child and finding the kind of life for her that unequivocably expresses the truth of who she is.

Not long ago one of my friends told me that she had dreamed she was falling into an endless hole. When she awakened she realized this had been an important dream. As she worked on it she recalled a similar childhood dream she repeatedly had of trying over and over again to pull her father out of a deep grave. *"I had worked at this childhood dream many times as an adult, and what came to me was that I seemed caught trying not only to pull my father out of the grave, but that I had also been trying to pull men out of the grave of their own unconsciousness. Twice in my life I nearly lost my life trying to do this. Once I had cancer—I'm sure it was from staying in an unbearable situation with a man; then some years later I risked my life by trying to stay in a relationship I had no business being in either. Towards the end of that relationship this man's outbreaks of violence really could have killed me. I knew, finally, that since these men were not committed to pulling themselves out of their own unconsciousness, that neither could I."*

As she reflected on the events of her more recent dream she realized that it was her own grave she was now having to deal with. Commenting on the meaning of the symbols for her, she said, *"For me this deep hole I was falling into was like a sense of despair because it meant that somehow I was still locked into this process of saving others."* The dream meant that she was still falling into a pattern of pleasing and rescuing behaviors that she felt were pulling her into unconsciousness. She realized that she had spent years trying to help humanity but that, in spite of her successes, she now needed unequivocally to turn her attention toward herself. In analyzing the dream, she said, *"For me it meant that I had to close the door on my ancestral past (my need to pull my father out of the grave), and to move on with my life; it meant I had to stand up and say my own truth. It was time to stop smuggling donkeys, in a word. And I knew I was going to have to be like a soldier in order to do it."* She roared jokingly and flexed her muscles as she spoke, but I knew she meant it.

Like many women I know—myself included—often the truth we have within ourselves is not our first priority, and we find ourselves "waffling through life" because of it. If we are caught serving patriarchal ideals from the wounds of a father complex, often we quietly come and go through the back door of life— giving too much of ourselves to others, and not honoring our own inner needs, not roaring enough, not flexing our muscles. This woman, one of the most profoundly spiritual women I know, had been still connected at some level to the wounds of her childhood. No matter how accomplished we become at any level, many of us still carry vestiges of our parents until finally the soul says, "Keep this stuff up and you'll soon be slipping into your own grave." The soul in this case was forcefully coming up for air. Jolting her into taking a stand for herself and throwing off her pattern of serving her father's ideals, the dream insisted that she firmly get a sense of her own strength and purpose, that she fight, if necessary, for the expression of who she really is, and for the heritage of her own feminine self.

Thus primary to our work at a personal level is a focus on the early father-daughter relationship, and a sifting through to where we have been most wounded. When we get in touch with the memories in that relationship that have been the least life giving, or those that have been obstacles to our own personal growth and power, then we can begin to heal. We can begin to see what needs work, what needs airing, expression, and acknowledgment. As our father's daughters we can sense what wants to come out into light, and what wants consciousness out of the darker waters of the child's unconscious. Most important, we can see what needs forgiveness, because this ingredient is like hyssop over any wound at the personal level. Without it, we cannot be authentically free.

In time, as we acknowledge and heal over these old wounds and incompletions, we have more room to experience some of the positive memories that we need to refuel ourselves with. As the wounded daughter is allowed to weep, to mourn, to lament, to rage, and to ponder what still remains painful and unresolved, then we open to the truth. And when we open to the truth about what we feel and who we are, then the lies about who we are and who we aren't can be exposed. When the hero and the adversary are confronted—not only as the father models they were for us, but also as the archetypal energies they still command in us—then the positive father power can be released more effectively in our lives.

7. The Woman Beyond the Mask

THE OLD TAILOR

A young woman went to see the village tailor so that he might make her a coat. At one time he was reputed to be the best tailor in the land, and people came from far away seeking his fine work. Now, however, he was an old man and his sight had grown dim in the passing of the winters. In the course of making the measurements for the coat, all seemed to go well. But when it came time for the first fitting, a strange thing happened. Unable to see what he was doing clearly, and not thinking as well as he once did, the old tailor cut the woman to fit the coat instead!

Adolescence is the time that young women struggle for personal and social identity. As in the story of the tailor, young girls are frequently tailored to fit the "coat" of societal and parental values. With the alluring pull she may feel from parents, peers, social and religious institutions, popular myth, and the media, it is no wonder that a young woman is often more a product of cultural stereotypes than a product of her own inner woman.

To heal our self-esteem, many women have found it is useful to go back into our childhood memories and retrace where the roads to womanhood first became confusing and obscure. A major part of this work involves breaking the myths that do not speak honestly of womanhood.

PASSAGES FROM CHILDHOOD

I recently saw a late-nineteenth-century oil painting of a young girl of about eleven. She was standing in an apple orchard, her long white apron filled with apples, and the shadows from the late afternoon sun falling across her shoulders. She had a faraway look in her eyes that caught my attention. For a moment

she seemed caught between the carefree world of her childhood and the inevitable coming of her womanhood. Something
deep within me began to stir in recognition. I too had paused
in that orchard. I could identify with her desire to cling to the
youth of the past, her fear of embracing the unknown. As a
child entering puberty part of me wondered about tomorrow
with excitement and anticipation; part of me felt a sharp
ambivalence toward stepping into young womanhood, unsure
about what the future might bring. The painting filled me with
a deep melancholy.

The power of the image spontaneously released a flood of
memories. As I continued to dwell on it, I found myself getting
more and more in touch with old feelings I had long repressed—sadness about my parents' divorce when I was eleven,
a vague feeling that I had been abandoned at an important
crossroad. I recalled the longing I felt for many of the familiar
comforts of my childhood, and the security of knowing my
parents would raise me together. At a time when I needed my
father as an important role model and companion for my adolescence, he was suddenly out of the picture.

Another part of my dilemma at the time was that I was
decidedly mistrustful of the changes that seemed to be happening all at once in my body. The last vestiges of the child and the
tenuous new expressions of the young woman were often in
bold contrast to one another. Sometimes the child and the young
woman, unsure about what to do to accommodate each other,
would compete for expression. One side could be graceful and
attractive, while another side might suddenly humiliate me by
stumbling and falling headlong over something, some strange
snag in the ground that shouldn't have been there. At times I
was like an elegant racehorse who suddenly developed a peg
leg. Because the passages from childhood into adolescence are
so unclearly marked, many young women have lacked the confidence needed to navigate these important crossings.

If we are lucky, our ambivalence toward growing up is tolerated. If parents can allow the child to linger in a longer-than-
usual tomboy phase, or to hang around the meadow places of
childhood until it feels safe to emerge, then a child feels more
grounded. A ten-year-old boy I used to work with surprised his
mother one day by announcing to her that he wanted a Cabbage

Patch doll. I tried to assure her that this was normal, that the boy needed a companion, a friend to talk to at night; but she never went for it. She said she thought it would keep him from "growing up." If parents will trust that often kids do sense intuitively what they need, odd as it may seem, the result is often fruitful. I am indebted to my mother for not teasing me about playing with paper dolls until I was thirteen, because at some level I was playing out an inner world of interior drama and I needed this pretend world a little longer. It was one of the many places I quite spontaneously worked out my separation from my father (if one ever completely does).

Entering adolescence is more difficult for girls than boys because the passage is more abrupt. Major physical and emotional transitions are much more pronounced for the girl than they are for the boy. Puberty for the male child is a significant step into young manhood, but for a girl it is often more of an abrupt leap. The onset of menstruation involves a profound physical and psychological change. Many young girls are overwhelmed by the fears, uncertainties, and new responsibilities surrounding menses. This is a young woman's first major rite of passage. And it is one for which she is often only minimally prepared, and enters with only the greatest ambivalence.

When I was just fresh off the baseball field of grade school, my breasts were already on their way. By the following year, still trying to figure out how to hide them, I started to menstruate. I think I went into a state of shock. The thought of having to sit on the sidelines on some days, separated from the things other people were doing or from the sports I loved to play, was hardly tolerable. The days at Camp Galilee when everybody else went swimming but me convinced me that I stood out like a sore thumb.

It was a time of estrangement from the old world of the body and its child I once knew. Along with the tenuousness of the sudden onset of physical changes at puberty, there came a whole host of new emotions as well. My changing body chemistry often precipitated the emergence of the strangest moods; inexplicable thoughts and feelings went through my head. Erratic moods, little anxieties and sadnesses, sudden outbursts of temper, wild fantasies, all made their dramatic appearance from time to time. That period of latency which precedes adolescence, and which harbors the child's still sleeping sexual body, was drawing to a close.

One of the biggest gaps in our feminine adolescence, is that there are no rites of passage for a young woman as she leaves her youth and begins the initiative passage through puberty into young womanhood. In primitive cultures menstruation was an event of major social and personal significance. At the onset of menses young women were segregated for a specified length of time from the tribe; a time of ritual purification and waiting ensured. The idea that such an event marked an important passage into womanhood was common among primitive peoples. Such changes in the young girl were a sign that she was now becoming a woman. Clearly, the onset of menstruation served to ascribe to the girl certain sacred powers which she could not possess as a child. She understood that the taboos surrounding this event were a preparation for her future. For her, fertility meant an assurance of status. This passing of blood was not just a natural event, but a social and psychological one as well; one which was ultimately welcomed by the community.

During a recent trip to Alaska I met Katie John, an old woman from the AHTNA (or Copper River) tribe in the lower central part of the state. We sat together one afternoon in a little patch of moss beneath some white birch and shared a meal of steak and beans. I asked Katie, a woman with forty-four grandchildren and an incredible smile, to tell me about some of the old customs for women in her tribe. Although no such customs exist now, when she was a girl there were definite puberty rites for the women of the tribe. *"When I was a little girl, long time ago, the women used to come together when a young girl first got her time. They stay together a long time, many days, and teach the young girl all kinda things. Things about cooking, about herself, about life. It was a time to learn all these things."* Katie adjusted the long grey hair that hung gathered down her back, flashed me a beautiful grin, and went on eating while I sat in awe of her. She was remarkably agile and strong for her seventy-three years of weathering Alaska winters.

This is a vastly important time emotionally and psychologically. The young women who performed tribal rituals that followed their movement into puberty were being prepared for their role in society. They were also being prepared to experience themselves as women, as beings close to nature, and to the cyclic rhythms of the earth in their own blood. Esther Harding points out in *Women's Mysteries* that seclusion provided primitive woman the necessary sacred space for her to draw apart from the world and to enter the unknown mystery within her own body and spirit. To withdraw during this time was to afford one the opportunity to reconnect with a deeper side of the self, a side of one's nature that the busy occupations of the day often obscured.[1]

But our society does not define a young woman's role as clearly. Our social customs, according to Harding, place little value on fertility; and the extended span of adolescence in contemporary society marks a long period of ambiguity. Nowadays, although we prepare young girls technically for what to expect and what to do when the time comes, often we seem not to prepare them emotionally. Perhaps the reason we have not taken the time with our young women to teach them how to revere this process is that many of us have misunderstood it ourselves. Penelope Washburn, in *Becoming Woman,* cites this transition time as one of the most difficult simply because it constitutes a woman's first real identity crisis. If we are not prepared adequately for the fears, uncertainties, and ambiguities surrounding menstruation as young women, then most likely we will learn to devalue our sexual identity as women.[2]

Many of the women clients I see do not value their feminine identity; they tolerate it in much the same way as many of us tolerated the onset of menstruation. In the process of healing and re-creating our feminine self-esteem, many of us have to go back and reenter the moment we began to bleed; to uncover the ways we were not prepared, the times we felt humiliated or ashamed; the times we felt devalued because of our body's autonomous and impersonal entry into womanhood. At the psychological level (that is, at the level of feeling) we need to heal the alienation many of us experience between thinking and feeling—and our bodies. Ultimately, we must welcome our body. We need to allow the old women of the tribe who dwell within us to come to us, to take our hand and walk with us into the roads of our womanhood. We need to hear them counsel us to withdraw into the spaces of our own hearts during the time of our bleeding, because there is a wisdom in getting out of the fast lane during this time. When a woman will hold herself in reverence in this way, then the quiet spaces of silent pondering can be a profound healing force. All of us as women need to hear the voices of the old Grandmothers welcoming us, reaffirming us, chanting and singing about the goodness of our womanhood, our sexuality, about the goodness of our blood, about the beauty of the transition along the age-old trail of the Mother that only a woman can walk.

THE BEGINNING OF THE MASK: THE GOOD DAUGHTER OF THE MOTHER

The word *persona* is a Jungian concept that means mask or covering. It is the outermost layer of the personality; the face or image we most easily present to others. From the time we are small we are busy adapting to our environment. We try on different styles of being-in-the-world, and experiment with various ways of seeing and experiencing the things and people around us. While the personality is still in its formative years, children try on a variety of different behavioral styles. From these various adaptive experiments the persona eventually emerges. The trouble is that some of us forget that this mask is only a covering, and not the real person underneath.

Now that I am a middle-aged woman who has done some amount of digging around into the layers of my personality, I can tell you that I have masks. I have outer faces and inner faces; images and roles I take up and play out from time to time. I know now, for instance, that I am not just a mother or a therapist or a wife or a painter, but that beneath those roles I am many selves. I have a variety of hidden sides to my nature which I have been in the course of meeting over the years.

But when I was a child passing into young womanhood I would not have been able to tell you that. When the people and institutions in my environment began to tailor me to fit their own patterns, no one told me that these little adaptations were only things I was free to try on and sift through. Playing dress-up is something all children do naturally. But as we get older and try out new roles and behaviors and group identities, no one remembers to tell us that there is a real self beneath this myriad of masks. Sooner or later, as adults, many women find a real need to trace some of the ways the persona is still playing dress-up.

In her book *Kiss Sleeping Beauty Goodbye,* Madonna Kolbenschlag gives eloquent reference to the fact that a young girl can be lured into an unconscious sleep, not unlike the fairy tale of Sleeping Beauty. If parents and educators encourage young women to adopt a cultural mind-set about feminine behavior, for instance, and fail to validate their individuality, then we participate in a collective kind of thinking process; one that ultimately distorts self-image, inhibits autonomy, and keeps our feminine identity unconscious.

Instead of schooling young girls to think for themselves and to seek out their own path as individuals, to take risks, or to initiate independent behaviors, culturally little girls are still fairly stereotyped. Young girls are often taught to hold themselves in reserve, to remain attentive and sensitive to the expectations of others. When a young girl is rewarded for conformity and pleasing behaviors, the masks and roles she adopts will eventually hinder her integrity as a woman; in time the role itself will promote dependence on approval for her sense of well being. A young woman who is coached in stereotypic behaviors that hinder her full autonomy will have a difficult time trying to locate her own authentic self. Not uncommonly, many young girls lose themselves to these false sides of convention.

According to Kolbenschlag, there are a number of persona types that young girls commonly get seduced by. Some of these roles personify an aspect of what we know as the "traditional feminine," and are learned behaviors that society popularizes for women. "One persona is the *desirable object.* This role will school her in the art of cosmetic allurement, seductive mannerism, and the sublimation of straightforward assertion."[3] This first type of stylized feminine role has several effects. The most disastrous effect is that a young woman's creative and self-actualizing potentials are always short-circuited.

THE DESIRABLE OBJECT

The Performer

During a discussion of how our parents had affected us as children, one woman in our workshop group said, *"When I was a little girl my mother and dad thought I was wonderful. So wonderful, in fact, that my mother prided in showing me off a lot. On Sundays there was church, during the week there were family outings and shopping and teas, and on the weekends my parents entertained. My mother loved it when I would dress up in her long black gloves and her high heels and then come in and sing for their company. I was the center of attention. Saturday nights it was Mother on the piano and me in my dress-up costume, and I sang,*

"My Momma done tole me, a man is a two-face, a worrisome thing, that leaves you to sing, the blues in the night."

Then I'd pull off the gloves that came all the way up to my shoulders and swing them around and I'd do this little dance before I left the room." This is the Performer persona; the little girl mother coaches to be entertaining and politely seductive.

Many mothers take special pride in dressing and grooming their young daughters to be attractive, often coaching them to prioritize manners and appearance in favor of other potential qualities they might have. Other mothers seem to live vicariously through the daughter, and it is here that the will of the mother to be one with her offspring takes over. It is as if the two personas merge and suddenly we have a shared mask. My daughter in high school has friends whose mothers insist on picking out their wardrobes daily and who coach their daughters to work seriously at competitions to be yell leaders and homecoming queens. When a mother not only encourages but impels her daughter to go out for the social scene, whether cheerleading, student government, or fashions, she is saying, "Be like I need you to be, but don't be yourself." These models of feminine behavior are the very antithesis of autonomy.

The Temptress

Some mothers not only encourage their daughters to dress stylishly or glamorously, but permit them to dress seductively, perhaps unconsciously using the daughter to act out their own repressed sexuality. One of my clients said to me about her mother, *"When I was in my mid-teens, on some occasions I was permitted to dress somewhat in the same style as my mother. For evenings out, for proms and special parties, she made certain I was going to be a 'knockout.' She dressed me in flattering but seductive styles of evening wear that never failed to draw a lot of attention. I always felt furious and insulted if I happened to be propositioned when I was growing up, but I never got the connection that I looked provocative and I must have turned a lot of men on. It wasn't until years later that I understood that mother had been unconsciously living through how I looked. My parents were always proud of showing me off."*

Exploitations of this kind between mother and daughter, although denied by many mothers as intentional, serve to make the daughter merely an extension of the mother ego. Clothes, fashion, and looks have long been an area of unconscious enmeshment between mother and daughter. Using the daughter as a covert expression of her own need for increased esteem has long been a way that many women have unconsciously functioned. Undeniably, many young girls are more vulnerable to the sleep of self-image because many mothers model these "sleeping" behaviors themselves.

Scarlett O'Hara

Another aspect of this overly stylized feminine model gives the message that little girls do not ask openly for things; that straightforward talk and assertiveness are not sanctioned behaviors. Another client says, *"I clearly remember mother controlling my attempts at assertiveness. She wasn't rude, of course, but she consistently reminded me not to say certain things, not to ask certain questions, not to be candid or verbal with my perceptions; that 'ladies didn't do that sort of thing.'"* Another maternal injunction that seems to have left an indelible mark on many young girls is the insistence that the daughter conform to the indomitable mother-will, no matter what. "Don't you say no to *me!*" is a one-liner with a lot of prohibitive power to it.

When we do this over time to our children, it isn't long before they learn that what they experience or see is in some way invalid or unacceptable. In some families, such as the alcoholic family or the family in conflict, children's perceptions are repeatedly invalidated and hushed. For the child of the alcoholic and for the child of the southern belle, the model is: "Don't say what you *see* or what you *want;* sublimate your feelings and be indirect." And here comes the child that learns the art of covert manipulation; the discreet little Scarlett O'Hara personality who masks her heart, pinches into her social corset, and is a master at seduction.

The China Doll

The China Doll persona is the child who is coached in conforming behaviors. Dependent on others for direction, she is never shown how to take the initiative or how to do things on her own. In fact, very little is required of her except to fit into the family and not make waves. Someone else takes care of things for her, thinks for her, speaks for her. She is expected to behave well and to look nice, expected to do well in all her endeavors; but her feelings, thoughts, and observations are never directly encouraged. She is in some ways almost ornamental to her family. She appears to be there physically, but emotionally she has been encouraged to fade into the woodwork. Enter the child whose constant smile is a cover-up for a fragile heart and an enormous sense of personal inferiority.

One of my friends recently told me that she herself had been coached to be "seen and not heard," and she was acutely sensitive to how this had crippled her self-confidence. Something of an over-achiever, this woman had begun to become aware of how she was running to please the status quo, as though to make up for her long childhood silence where she felt like a doll on a shelf. She told me recently that a friend came to visit with her little girl. Each time my friend asked the little girl a question, however, the child's mother would answer for her. Every time the child opened her mouth, the mother filled it. As my friend was telling the story I could see her face begin to tighten. *"I was furious. It was like the whole thing was happening to me all over again. Just as though my mother and I were talking—her talking and me fading into the woodwork. I never knew who I was."*

THE GIVER

According to Kolbenschlag, the next commonly idealized mask a young girl is expected to wear for society is the one that teaches her to live for others.

This role will school her in the self forgetfulness, service and sacrifice, in nurturing rather than initiating behaviors. Above all it will teach her to "sleep"—to wait forever if necessary, for the expected other who will make her life meaningful and fulfilled. She will give up everything when the expected one comes, even the right of creating her own self. Whether it be a husband, a religion or a revolution, she is ready to live outside herself, to abdicate from responsibility for herself in favor of something for someone else.[4]

Enter the Giver persona, the child who lives waiting to fill others' shoes but who has trouble standing squarely in her own.

The woman who has been taught as a child to be self-effacing is taught literally to remove her face; to put on the social garment that someone else gives her to wear. *"When I was a child I watched my mother play a dozen different roles. She was really something. She had incredible energy and was endlessly giving herself to us, to her career. But the older I got the more I began to see that she wasn't really her own person. Sometimes I saw her really exasperated or tired and I thought surely she'd quit or get mad or blow up. But she never did. She just squared her shoulders and went right back to her causes. But when it came to herself she was almost ascetic. I mean she had trouble just letting others help her in any way, like it was hard for her not to be constantly giving."* When pleasing and serving others becomes gratifying to a woman to the extent that she has no clear personal boundary of her own, she is like a garden without walls.

A young girl whose mother has consistently modeled self-effacing behaviors begins to interpret that fulfillment means serving and getting approval from others. Here the girl's personal boundary is muddled because her self-esteem depends on what she can invest in outside herself. Here too are the makings for enmeshment, because a young girl's sense of initiative cannot form under these conditions. It remains forever tangled up in what other people expect of her. When children pick up toys in my office for the first time, invariably there are some who hesitate, who withhold themselves cautiously until they are doubly sure of a direction from me. Many of the kids who fail to initiate behaviors in play are candidates for waiting behaviors as adults. When they cannot confidently create their own world in play, without constantly deferring to me for my approval, then I worry. Teenage girls do this waiting sort of thing frequently—waiting for boyfriends to call, waiting to be noticed, waiting to be asked for a date, waiting for approval from the group. It may be common for some women in today's more feminist world to initiate their own personal and social actions, but so far I know very few teenage girls who do.

One of the hazards of adopting too much mask is that one can get lost in it. The persona, although necessary for some sort of covering, can effectively inhibit movement. Gradually, it takes up more and more space and crowds our vital growth potential. By the time we are teenagers we have already begun to learn the ropes of either self-sacrifice or self-promotion. Adapting to a whole host of social roles early on, we are increasingly influenced by parents, peers, boyfriends, fashions, institutions, and causes of all kinds. Coached to try to give a little of ourselves to everybody, and unaware of the danger of over-identifying with the role, a young woman can stay relatively unconscious. Of the many roads a young woman meets during adolescence, the road to the self is the most obscured.

THE MOOSE HEAD GANG OF RENO

When feelings are suppressed for long periods of time, and when there is a continual distancing between one's inner and outer self, trouble is always brewing. My own mask in my teen years was very heavy. Because my mother had remarried a prominent doctor soon after her divorce, my sister and I suddenly found ourselves in another world. One year I had been running through the Nevada desert sagebrush like a wild jackrabbit, rubbing elbows with country folks, and just getting into the rural life I had always dreamed of. And the next year, to accommodate my new father's Mississippi roots, I was suddenly expected to be a southern belle. Just as I was throwing off my childhood script of being the child everyone else expected me to be, I was met with another task. Suddenly there was a new father to adjust to, a new role to play, and no more sagebrush outside my window. Now, for the sake of appeasing custom, I was coached in the art of being a lady. My emancipation into nature and the rural life did not last long.

My mother had no trouble with this personality shift. She loved being Scarlett, being taken care of, being his woman, settling down into a lifestyle that she had always wanted. The trouble came when she insisted my sister and I do the same; at that point my identity began to take a nosedive. The persona of the good little southern girl was wearing thin; in fact, it masked a wild thing.

There were times as a teenager that I looked like everybody else; socially I excelled in good manners, polite behaviors, and knew a variety of social graces. But inside I was sometimes angry and sad. Because I repressed these fleeting moods so effectively, I was often unaware of what feelings lay hidden. Not unsurprisingly, the energy I used up containing these feelings sometimes leaked out in compulsive behavior, and in time I became an enigma to myself. During the long weeks of my adolescence I went along with whatever the program was, and during the weekend I went on automatic release.

A few friends of mine and I often pooled our leftover lunch money from the week, bought a few dozen eggs, and ventured out to practice the art of egg throwing. I usually sat in the passenger seat because I was the best shot. Eventually, I was able to perfect the long-distance toss; this feat consisted of a right hook, over the top of the car, aimed at the oncoming cars three lanes away. The good nights were the ones where we were able to score a direct hit through an open window of the enemy car. The father of one of my friends owned a large moose head trophy, which one of us occasionally wore while on our rounds, and in time we jokingly referred to ourselves as the Moose Head Gang.

Although there were many times my delinquency deviated from the egg toss, I somehow miraculously managed to stay out of the soup, at least legally. Now that I look back on these escapades I am certain that I was inwardly struggling against the pressures to be the person everyone else wanted me to be. Because there was little validation for being an individual in my household, I suppose I was throwing eggs at my parents and at a myriad of social and academic scenarios that required me to perform, when all I wanted to do was simply follow my own paths.

THE MYTH OF THE GOOD DAUGHTER OF THE PATRIARCHY

As a child I chose to identify with my father's world for a variety of different reasons. His life was vastly more exciting. He traveled, he loved the outdoors, the woods and streams and mountains. It was he that brought home all the exciting books and magazines about African safaris and the stories of wild adventure. I simply loved what he loved, and I shared his wanderlust. My mother's world was fashion, bridge, parties, and she had a flair for the romantic. I suppose I shared her penchant for the romantic too, but for me adventure and the call of the unknown was my romance. Betrayed by my body for its autonomous act of growing up, and afraid to trust the uncertainty of my feelings, I was even more attached to my father's values. Where things got vague and hazy for me throughout the remainder of adolescence was where I continued to seek his world rather than finding my own path.

THE LITTLE TROOPER

In my family of origin we did not discuss feelings. We discussed *things*. If people in my family got angry or upset about something they simply left the room. On some occasions my father would yell or storm about some issue, but it was always in passing; no one stayed around to resolve the conflict or to deal with the more delicate issues involved in family communications. If my father got into a roar, my mother became quietly distant and aloof. We adapted instead to the dysfunctional way in which emotions could be eruptive, but to talk about feelings or offer any feedback was taboo.

At about ten, as a result of the way my family repressed matters of the heart, I can remember gradually learning to withhold myself. When my parents divorced the following year, my mother expressed almost no emotion. She simply told my father over the phone that she was leaving him and marrying another man, and that was that. He had been away in another town on location for work at the time, and he never came home after that call. My sister and I were told one night before going to bed, and that's the last we ever discussed it. The following year, when I saw my father over the holidays, I choked back my tears and told him that everything was really all right with me. I may not even have known they weren't. Enter the Little Trooper persona—the child who, above all, learns to keep a stiff upper lip and gradually loses the feel of her tears.

At about thirteen I became increasingly melancholy. Certainly I had no lack of emotions, but generally I kept them hidden. If I was sad about my father's absence or angry at my mother because she had drastically altered our environment, I kept it inside. During the rare times I wept for my father or raged within at my mother for insisting that I become pleasing to my new southern stepfather, I never let anyone know. There were times too that, although I felt some powerful mood sweeping through me, I could not really identify my experience. Sometimes at night, after my parents were asleep, I would crawl out my window, cross the street to the golf course, and simply run at high speed across the green. Pitch dark or not, no matter what the hour, I just ran until I collapsed somewhere on the lawn and lay beneath the stars. I suppose that was my therapy.

Academically, I was never a good student throughout most of high school. Studies were not interesting to me until college, when I seemed more capable of making academics creative. But until then, I was like a lost person. All I wanted to do throughout most of high school was be outdoors, ride horses, and play sports. I could not bear the confinement of classes and I thought the things I had to study were nearly useless. It was clear that I wasn't fitting into the system. Somehow I managed to graduate after four years, but not until after having flunked algebra twice, chemistry once, and being expelled from at least one Catholic convent along the way. It was a trying time.

THE RED KNIGHT

If feelings were repressed in my own family of origin, in the academic and social world they were even more so. Although I had nature to quieten and console me, the world I walked into seemed to offer no place which felt either welcome or familiar to me. Gradually the enigma of my feeling world was replaced by the certainty of the known world, but not without substantial loss to my inner nature.

As a young woman ventures into the academic, social, and professional world, she has to give up substantial parts of her natural feminine energies. Most social, academic, and institutional settings are geared toward the masculine: toward the harnessing of reason, toward what is linear, productive, and measurable. Basically there is nothing wrong with this aspect of the mind or with many of the generative powers that involve the "doing" side of our nature. It's just that when the environment increases its demands upon us for performance, and for intellectual excellence, another split in our nature can begin to occur.

The Red Knight persona is the one that lures both men and women into competition, into games of achievement and a life of relentless knightly deeds. In the myth of Parsifal, the Red Knight is the hero figure young Parsifal must wrestle with and conquer in order to be able to venture forth on the hero's quest. In the myth the Red Knight represents a young man's need to differentiate and to conquer; to move out of the nest toward manhood. This figure is actually an important fellow. All of us need a little of the Red Knight for autonomy, because to follow the path of questing eventually will lead us to separate from our past and move into the future; we need it further for walking an individual path. It is only when we follow it too far that we can get into trouble.[5]

The Red Knight is supposed to inspire us to seek, to quest, to be powerful and capable. But if we do not access these deeper masculine strengths as energies and potentials in the psyche rather than merely acting them out, or taking them on as roles we play, then the Red Knight can become the Red Herring. When women make the mistake of becoming too closely identified with goals, with causes, with intellectual questing, with power, the negative side of the hero's quest takes over. Then we become fixed on chasing after power, after the material world, and after things of the mind, all of which can misguide the heart side of the feminine.

When a woman conforms to play by the necessary rules, her whole personality is affected. To play the masculine game of the Red Knight or the Little Trooper radically changes the way she relates to others and to herself. If she is not completely awake and attentive to herself and to what is being asked of her, she may walk into this adaptation unconsciously. Here then is the making of another fork in the road of her identity, a path that leads away from the river, because her thoughts will go one way with her and her feelings another. Reason, no matter how alluring, is never of itself complete without the balance of the feeling side of our nature. But most of Western culture endorses this dichotomy.

THE CORPORATE PERSONA:
WHEN THE MASK TAKES OVER

Just before my senior year in high school, some friends of mine and I made a plan to go away to a private school together. Conjointly we decided on St. Mary's, a Catholic high school for girls in Salt Lake City. Although my mother wisely expressed grave doubts about the place as we pulled up, I insisted that this was a whole new adventure and I would not be talked out of it. It was my attempt, I suppose, at autonomy and I needed to get out of the house for a while.

But life at St. Mary's was complicated by the fact that there was a new girls' prefect; having seen the angry Red Queen in Alice in Wonderland as a child, I should have been forewarned when I met this nun. But enthusiasm overrode the strange sensation I felt in the pit of my stomach, and I decided to stay. Within a few weeks, however, this woman had singled me out as the class incorrigible. Whenever anything went wrong in the senior class or whenever there was mischief, she immediately called me into her office. Although quite capable of mischief myself (and probably because the moose head would not have fit into my suitcase anyway), I had so far resisted my old bag of tricks. Yet, strangely enough, I kept getting called into her office. With each mounting accusation her face got more and more like the mad Queen and she grew increasingly morose and stern. The singling out continued and became an obsession. Presiding over the senior table at mealtime, this prefect sat in her usual manner, stern, unlaughing, and alert to the possibility of some deviation from the norm. In time dinner became for me an almost certain appointment with indigestion.

Not long afterward, for comic relief, I began borrowing the newly laundered underwear from the girls' college bathroom in the next dorm and decorating the religious statuary that adorned our halls with it. Whatever impish amusements I allowed myself, however, were no match for the oppression in the environment. I volunteered for off-campus activities more, took extra-long hikes, stayed in chapel longer, and prayed for sanctuary from the mad Queen.

It took me years to feel even the slightest compassion for this woman, and for many members of her staff as well. I did not fully understand the nature of neurosis in my late teens, and therefore my perception of these nuns was rather harsh. I bring them up here because these women corporately seemed to be an example of the sort of misfortune women incur as a result of too much repression and too close an identification with the institution. Once we put on the mask of the persona and do not question its fit, its rightness, its role in our lives, then we come dangerously near sacrificing the real person underneath. I am unsure whether in their case it was too much mask that caused neurosis, or too much neurosis that caused the mask; perhaps it worked both ways. But it is clear that these women were absolutely identified with a masculine stereotype, with the masks and roles of the institution, and with values that had long since abandoned heart and feeling.

The little nun who was my voice teacher at St. Marys was different. I loved being near her because she smelled like my grandmother and she had not forgotten how to smile. Yet most of the rest of the staff were not only like men in their movements and mannerisms, they also acted out the most negative side of the masculine. Hard, unyielding, accusing, brusque, and as unpredictable as the figure of Heathcliff in Brontë's *Wuthering Heights,* their corporate persona was a disaster. At what point some of these women sacrificed their feminine nature to become policemen for the church I can only guess, but the reality of it was a tragedy.

Now that I have done some inner work and acknowledged

some of my own masks and inner shadow figures, I have more understanding and compassion for these women. But any way you cut it, women who are alienated from their own feminine model act out of a distorted image of woman. The institutions of the world, be they religious, political, or social containers, seem to be especially dangerous to the feminine spirit because they are corporately programmed by the patriarchy. Harmful to women at any level, the institution is not geared for things of human compassion and for matters of the heart. To survive these systems a woman needs tremendous internal strength, the kind that comes from knowing herself authentically as a woman. Until she does the institution is going to swallow her without the slightest twinge of conscience.

SOCIAL CHANGE: IS IT OR ISN'T IT?

Periodically, the traditional image of woman is challenged, given a face lift, reupholstered to meet the times more incisively. Sometimes, individual or collective voices arise in an attempt to bring some enlightenment and change to the status of women. This last century has witnessed a social and personal pendulum swing for raised consciousness that began with an impressive show of intention for change. According to historian Jane Sochen, the spiral upward for change tends to descend back down over time and there is an eventual return to the powerful hold of the status quo. Woman's image has made some change over the last few decades, but there is some speculation that the suffragette eventually returns home.

For instance, during World War II much of American society rallied to present to the world a new image of woman, presumably to bolster the American image of strength and as a cheer for our soldiers' morale abroad. According to Sochen, American filmmakers portrayed a new feminist image of woman as equal to men—strong, self-sufficient, and self-actualizing. Actresses like Joan Crawford, Bette Davis, and Katharine Hepburn endorsed and gave life to the new image. Women's roles did expand during the war, with more women working outside the home and taking positions of responsibility, but it was a short-lived change. Ironically, when the war ended, "women resumed their old image—as wife and mother in reality and sex goddess in fantasy. Men and women alike wanted to believe that all women were alluring, attractive, and seductive, and every woman wanted to be a combination of wife, mother, Eve, and the Virgin Mary."[6]

Sochen goes on to note that during the 1950s, following the tremendous war efforts made to create and maintain a strong image, women's self-actualizing potentials went back into dormancy. Movie makers deep-sixed the war image of the strong woman in favor of a new postwar woman. Although less heroic and certainly more traditional, the ancient appeal of the sex goddess, personified by such actresses as Marilyn Monroe and a rash of Italian beauties, was back in effect. As a counterpoint to the sex-goddess image on screen during the 1950s emerged another classic feminine stereotype, the All-American girl next door. This traditional but naive image portrayed woman as rather innocent in comparison to the sex goddess. Using all her feminine wiles she sets out to entice and capture the boy next door. But innocent or not, the role still portrays woman as an object of allurement, incomplete without a man; her sole work is the work of landing a partner. Whether devious and sexually enticing or innocent and apple cheeked, women were portrayed as seeking wholeness through men. The status quo of the stereotypical woman had resurfaced.

Statistics in the 1960s shifted again and another rise in women's consciousness emerged. More women were enrolled in college and a greater number had entered business and professional fields. Equally more participated in political activism, social rights, and women's rights. As a student at the University of California at Berkeley I remember any number of social and political reforms being demonstrated, beginning with the Peace and Freedom initiative, and later the birthing of the feminist movement. It appeared that significant progressive changes were taking place within the lives of women in the late middle of the century. But such changes were often short-lived.

Although many young women initially broke from both parental and traditional molds by acting, dressing, and thinking differently from the norm, eventually the status quo was reestablished. Historians like Sochen noticed that these apparent differences in values between one generation and the next were superficial and did not constitute any significant or lasting social changes. In other words, daughters may appear different from their mothers outwardly, but statistics show that eventually the younger generation settles down, gets married, has children, eventually rejoins the old camp, and often reflects values not unlike the culture in which they grew up and rebelled against. Added to that, those women who did speak out in behalf of reforms, liberation, and raised consciousness, although highly visible, were a minority voice.

There is no doubt that the recent women's movement has brought about changes for women. Pioneers like Betty Friedan, author of the *Feminine Mystique* and organizer of the National Organization for Women, as well as many other contributors to women's rights, clearly set up platforms toward social and political change. Whether organic or militant in strategy, whether based on the idea of revolution or the slower reforms of evolution of women's rights, the indictment made against women's myths remains clear. Yet however slow these reforms are, these social gains themselves are not in question. What is in question is why they seem to affect so few women. I think the answer to that lies in part in the fact that although social change can liberate some women, it does not free those who are still bound by problems at the personal level. It seems to me that if women attach themselves to causes, no matter how noble, that unless there is a concurrent awakening of the self beneath the role or status we have achieved collectively, then there is no lasting change. To be liberated socially is no guarantee of personal inner freedom.

Since most women eventually go back home and settle into the generational milieu, it is no wonder that change is impeded. It is, after all, at the personal level where the greatest battle against the myths of womanhood will be fought. Collectively, we can say we support women's rights; in chorus we can speak and work for greater equalities socially and economically. We can band together in women's support groups and identify with the emancipating energies that flow from the chemistry of our sisterhood. In agreement we can stand together and demonstrate action, initiative, and assertive behaviors. We can continue to confront the old myths of woman as an object for men, as Sleeping Beauty, eternal martyr, sex goddess, or Florence Nightingale. But isn't that just the beginning? And isn't that just simply changing the mask? From time to time we may have chosen a better, more powerful image; but whether we have changed the wearer or not remains to be seen.

THE WORK OF INTEGRATION

It is precisely because the feminine is undervalued in our society that a woman gravitates toward fulfilling herself according to the standards of men. Yet the more she strives to achieve by patriarchal standards of perfection, the more she finds herself encased in an ideal mold that counterfeits her feminine spirit. As the subjective world of nature, spirit, and feeling gives way to the objective world of law and principle, the feminine stands to lose itself on several accounts. Jungian analyst Marion Woodman comments, "We are living in an age that puts faith in the perfection of the computer. Human beings tend to become like the god they worship, but unfortunately for us, our agony does not allow us to become perfect robots. However hard we try to eradicate nature it eventually exerts its own value system and its own painful price."[8] If we become preoccupied with a lifestyle, no matter how convenient, cost-effective, or materially impressive, what is the cost to the human soul? If in our striving for personal perfection, technical efficiency, and a status quo equal to that of men, we lose the natural woman, then what have we gained? The farther we get from the earth and elements of our nature that admit that we are still fleshy bodies disposed to our humanity and liable to error and paradox, the farther we get from what's true about our nature.

Recalling again that masculine and feminine here refer not to biology or gender but instead to a difference in the energies of the psyche, it is the feminine *yin* principle that we have forsaken when we chase the status quo. Performance, an obsession with an ideal self, a striving toward worldly goods, and an overidentification with masculine cultural values all adds up to an estrangement from feminine roots. When a woman who is unfamiliar with the gift of her natural feminine ventures forth into a man's world, she is like a ship without a rudder. Without the resources of her own inner woman, the recesses of the natural instincts, intuition, feeling and sensing, woman becomes a parody of cultural stereotypes. Without the acceptance of the mystery of her womanhood she is constantly bent on appearing to be some version of worldly beauty, professional success, or the ideal mate and mother. She lives under her mask until she breaks either the mask or the woman underneath it.

Whatever the causes, when women awaken to find themselves too caught up in a social persona, it is often a shock. Since we have often "chosen" this mask or covering as an adaptive response to our early environment, we have generally worn it for a long time. Many of us are never even remotely aware of the divorce between this outer and inner woman. Often the adaptation happens without conscious awareness. Most of us fail to notice it at all until somewhere in our midlife we begin to sense a split between our thoughts and feelings; between the roles we play and the fantasies we may entertain; between the person others see in us and the one we see inside; between the mind we value and the body we negate. Whether we choose the traditional feminine role or the traditional masculine, we must name the mask. In the naming process the silence is broken and the unconscious spell over us is severed and brought to light.

Beginning with the passages of her childhood, woman consistently moves away from her own center and outward toward the things and people that make up her world. From the orchard of her youth she encounters a profusion of tradespeople who make her the fine garment of her persona. Granted, some of the roles we assume and the things we are taught are of some value, yet we seldom possess real autonomy and identity in the end if we do not question the path we're on. Somewhere along the way it is important to reevaluate what substance our feminine identity actually has that is authentic. We must ask ourselves who the real woman is beneath the masks we have worn and the roles we have played. Re-creating the myths of our personhood and breaking free of the deadness of what we have struggled to conceal about ourselves can be another painful stage of the journey, but ultimately it is a major key in our healing process. Not uncommonly, women on this precarious part of the journey will ask, "How can I do this inner work unless I know who I am or where I am going?" But the truth is, knowing who we are *not* is often the first step in the process. Naming the mask is a major key toward change.

OF MOOSE AND MEN

This sort of work is not just a painful recognition of what is out of balance and inauthentic within us, it is also an uncovering of the finer potentials lost in the sacrifice a woman makes when she sells out to the collective. The more each of us takes the trouble to meet and greet the inner figures that populate our past and consequently hold us a prisoner to the present, the more this work begins to unearth the real heroine.

For example, some of my own cultural masks have been mainly associated with the patriarchy. One character in my psyche was a controlling inner figure I learned to call Herr Captain. I met him head-on at an intensive training group I attended in process psychotherapy work. Parallel to this rigid fellow, I discovered another personality, a sort of mooselike character that played an important role in my own unmasking process.

The leader of the workshop was a man from Zurich named Arnie. In spite of the fact that I trusted his work and liked him immediately as a person, I felt slightly apprehensive when we started to work. There were about twenty-five other therapists and some teachers in the room and we were all doing this work together. I began the session without clearly knowing what I wanted to work on. Then it occurred to me that I had a pain in my upper shoulder, so we went for that as part of my therapy work.

As many process-oriented therapists often do, Arnie began to simply follow the body and see what it was saying. With my permission he began to press on the pain in my shoulder and to ask me for feedback as he did so. But the only feedback I gave him was that he could keep pressing more. And more. "You can press even harder, I can take it," I said. I was surprised that I had said that, because by now my shoulder was really painful.

"Oh really?" Arnie said. Sensing I had a controlling side to my nature and no doubt hoping we might eventually flush it out, he went on with his elbow in my back. I am certain that had I said, "Ouch! That's enough of that! I can't take it!" he would have stopped, but I didn't say it. Then there were more hands pressing on my back and I went on enduring it magnificently. Bravely. At one point he asked me if I thought maybe I could even stand up under the weight of all these hands pressing on me. I said I thought I could do that and, after some additional hard work to get my body up off the floor, I managed to struggle up underneath the full weight of all six hands. It was a great show of strength. Somewhere in the midst of my own gasping and groaning sounds, I imagined that once or twice I heard certain members of the group gasp themselves. Finally standing, I stood looking at Arnie, a little unbelieving at what I had just done.

"Well, so who is this strong guy in there?" he said, gazing back at me. I said I thought it was this Herr Captain, one of my German ancestors who liked a lot of control and wasn't going to let me feel too much. He was part of my mask, part of the enduring role I had always played. He was my father, who never showed much feeling and who had remained stoic to the end. He was my psychic policeman, who kept me profoundly out of touch with the feminine, with instinct and feeling, with the fuller expression of my passions. I had known of him for a long time, of course. I had worked on him somewhat and caused him to loosen around the edges, but apparently he was still firmly in control at center. He had gotten to be habitual over the years.

"Let's ask him if he'll just let this little girl come out and play for a while," Arnie suggested. We went on working in the group, trying to open up the way for my inner child to spring loose from this character's tight grasp. As playful as I wanted to be in response to the prompting from the group leader (always ready to play himself), I could not let myself go into the child. After a while it became clear that the Captain was still in control. He was going to protect her from making a fool of herself and appearing weak or fragile. He had great investment, of course, in her welfare, and he loved a stiff upper lip. He also had a conscious aversion to any mooseplay.

At some point we went back to resume work with the Captain,

since obviously he was calling the shots. But he just wouldn't release the child, or the inner woman either for that matter. After a bit Arnie gave up and went over to sit down. "I can't work with you any more," he said. All along I had stood by, giving this stoic inner figure full power and ignoring my deeper feelings, and Arnie was simply giving up. He was clearly saying that my strength was too much and could not yield anything productive. Because this has happened to me before in group process work, I knew immediately that he had my number. I also knew I was the only one who could pull myself out of hiding. The only one who could break the mask of control I wore.

"Nope," I said. "I hate it when this happens, and it's not going to happen to me again." I scooted across the floor and announced I wanted to confront that thing inside myself that had been so enduring, so withholding and powerful. Arnie said, "It's like there is this thick glass covering over you. I felt it in your back. I can see in all right, but I said to myself, 'This is impenetrable,' so I gave up."

The thick glass barrier he spoke of suddenly reminded me of a dream I'd had a few days before and I began to re-create it for the group. *I am standing in a log cabin with huge, plate glass windows. Outside, a dark brown cow moose charges the glass and keeps trying to break through. I am afraid the windows will break, but somehow they do not. Then suddenly this charging moose disappears and in her place stand seven white moose. All of them placidly stand there, looking in, peacefully peering in at me behind the glass. It is clear to me they wish me to come out. But in the dream I put my hands on my hips and defiantly say, "I won't come out and you can't make me!"*

It became increasingly clear to me that the thick glass walls I had erected as a child were no longer either necessary or useful. When we are children there is often a need for these defenses, for rigid coverings. Sometimes children desperately need plate glass windows, brick walls, towers and fortresses; they are part of a survival kit. But I was not a child, I was a woman; and these protective defenses had no more need to be there. The glass was my stiff exterior reserve, the ways I held myself from an honest and gutsy exchange with life. My Herr Captain mask was a transparent but entirely fortified resistance against the world.

Arnie stood up then and faced me squarely. "Be a moose. Show me what mooses do."

"What?" I said. "You want me to be a moose?"

"Yes. Why are you afraid of moose?" he said.

"Because sometimes they attack you. When we were in Alaska I was told to forget about grizzlies and to worry about moose. They're even more dangerous. That's why."

"Well," he enjoined with the raised eyebrows of a man who is about to be charged by a moose, "show me what they do."

"You want me to attack you?" I said, beginning to like the creativity in my desperation.

"C'mon," he said, leaning into what was about to come.

Unwilling not to break outside of myself, I leaped across the room like a charging moose. I wrestled him until we fell right down to the ground. I don't remember much about it except that I wasn't conscious of the members of the group anymore or the skirt I had on or the way I might have looked with my mask breaking right out in public. We just wrestled and it felt wonderful. This moose was not violent, she simply wanted to play. She wanted to come out, to feel her fullness and her animal instincts, to feel her sexual and creative energies and to experience them as a transpersonal power, as a natural extension of herself. As long as I was hiding behind the mask that culture had pressed over me, I was going to hide from my nature, to lock it outside myself. And certainly it is true that if we do not respectfully acknowledge our animal nature and take care to honor it, it will attack us in some ways until we pay attention to what we may be constricting. In short, we will always be "charged" by what we have pent up.

In that moment I understood that I needed to come out and experience these moose for what they really were: beautiful, mystical creatures that transcended the oldest of my fears. My stoic and reserved captain and I had begun to part company, and it was clear that I needed to let him go. Further, I would have to have a talk with the old nearsighted tailor because it was time for a new coat. Not one that I would be forced to cut myself to fit, but one that was genuinely altered to fit the emerging woman within.

Eventually, we learn that the masks we wear or the roles we play are never worth the betrayal of our own inherent nature.

Thank God for the people who are brave enough to call us out to be who we really are, who are courageous enough not to let a little charging moose bother them.

8. Awakening Relationships

Out of the many roads to enlightenment, surely the paths of relationship are among the most direct. Some of the most painful moments of my life have been spent in relationship, and some of the best. But it takes time to awaken at any level, and like the woman Kabir is calling out of her long night's sleep, most of us are initially not awake in relationship:

> Friends wake up. Why do you go on sleeping
> The night is over—do you want to lose the day
> the same way?
> Other women who managed to get up early have
> already found an elephant or a jewel . . .
> So much was lost already while you slept . . .
> and that was so unnecessary.
>
> The one who loves you understood, but you did not.
> You forgot to make a place in your bed next to you.
> Instead you spent your life playing.
> In your twenties you did not grow
> because you did not know who your Lord was.
> Wake up. Wake up. There's no one in your bed—
> He left you during the long night.
>
> Kabir says: The only woman awake is the woman
> who has heard the flute.[1]

Most partnering behaviors women exhibit in relationship are unconscious because the personal level of inner work has not yet been tapped.

THREE ANCIENT ENERGIES

Ancient forces at work in the deep recesses of both the body and the psyche magnetically draw a woman toward partnering.

Most of these unconscious energies that impel us toward partnering are simply unrefined powers within us that were originally nature's insurance policy that life would continue on this planet. These instinctual energies range across three primary fields: creative, sexual, and psychological.

CREATIVE ENERGIES

Creative energy in the unconscious is constantly moving us toward life-giving activities. This energy is a deep pulse of power that we feel when we rhythmically move toward making something work for us. Creation is present when we write poetry, paint, play music, make bread, or touch the inner fibers of uniqueness within ourselves. This energy can be a tremendously vital substance for our life, when it is understood and used consciously.

Yet, since this creative energy is initially undifferentiated when we are younger, its pulse can also compel us toward behaviors which are in themselves destructive. All of us can remember times in our childhood when we were in touch with the winds of our youth; sometimes there would be currents of anger or sadness, sometimes vague melancholy or blank spaces. Particularly during adolescence I recall feeling incredible amounts of energy wanting to come through me in some way; there are times I would run, or sing, or dance wildly, times I could either be deeply mystical or do incredibly dangerous things. It was as if some great primitive magnet outside myself drew me into the expression of this wind I felt inside. Once on a dare I swam across the Truckee River in early spring, when the snow runoff from the Sierra was dangerously high. It was a purely stupid but incredibly exhilarating thing to do, and it must have squarely punched my creative energy stores because I felt high for hours afterward.

Some of my all-time favorite people, who are really dynamite in their own field of work and who seem to be innately powerful human beings, frequently have amazing stories to tell about their childhood. Their stories range from accounts of fighting in gangs on the streets of New York City, to pasts of drugs, delinquent escapades, and amorous adventures of all kinds. Some of these adolescent sagas are hilariously funny, others are tragic. The point is, if we have not yet found a workable place for these energies within us that want to be creative, to be doing something vital and meaningful, then they may continue to dissipate or to be misdirected throughout most of our lives.

For some people, the neglect of these creative energies can have overtly chronic results, as with people who seem to be caught in a perpetual state of crisis or unrest. When a woman finds herself chronically tired, tense, moody, or petulant, she clearly needs to pay attention to how she is using her creative energies—if at all. Something inside is wildly signaling her to get moving; something instinctively wants life to be lived instead of contained. Illness and disease are often the direct result of some chronic imprisonment of feelings, emotions, creative energies. In many cases this creative force is simply longing for release and direction, and we're sitting on it and saying "no" to that energy. If we are not aware of the potency of the creative force and its need for conscious expression, we may find it aimlessly wandering down all sorts of avenues that are out of control.

SEXUAL ENERGIES

Undifferentiated instinctual energy can manifest as a sexual force. Not unlike the creative energies, this magnetic force within us innately knows it wants to make life happen—in this case by a spontaneous emergence of energies at the biological level.

A woman may at first tend to partner out of this field of primitive energy. Something in her unconsciously seems to want to complete another side of her instinctual destiny—the ancient story of her physical body. Whether in actuality or in metaphor, the implantation of man's seed is for some women the force that connects her with her own life-giving energies within. And deeply rooted in her psyche is an unconscious movement toward that merging. "Whether it is the seed of physical, emotional, or spiritual life that she will carry for the man in her life," he becomes the symbol she moves toward in order to bring herself to completion and to purpose.[2] Yet it is also true that instinctual energies, when they are not consciously directed, can wind up as undifferentiated outlets for sexual acting out. Anxious to find a home for this drive, men and women alike go searching for love in often restless and promiscuous ways that generally leave the lover unrequited, uncommitted, and often unhappy.

PSYCHOLOGICAL ENERGIES

The instinctual energies can also manifest themselves at the psychological level. For instance, at the emotional level a woman merges toward finding her self-worth and a sense of personal meaning in relationship to a partner. Her ego, still in its primitive stage of development, gravitates toward union in order to find some strength, stability, and meaning. The pull in this case is toward a sense of completion, a sense of joining the two distinctly different energies of male and female. Often a woman instinctively merges toward partnering because she is basically attracted to her opposite; that which is feminine in her instinctively moves to speak to her masculine counterpart.

MAKING THE UNCONSCIOUS CONSCIOUS

All these energies, however, whether they are creative, sexual, or psychological, may still be operating out of the unconscious. Powerful and life giving as these energies may be, until they are made conscious they do little more for women than to keep us in the soup.

If I fail to understand what the dynamics of my own merging behaviors are about, and to know what parts are conscious and what parts are unconscious, then I am asleep—pure and simple. Those of us who blindly follow relationship without questioning the intention of these instinctual powers are potentially victims rather than full participants in life. Not surprisingly, life just seems to happen to some women as though they themselves have absolutely no idea how to dream up their own personal or relational destiny.

LEVELS OF RELATING

Most couples in contemporary society do not seem to reach significantly far into conscious relationship. Failed partnerships seem to be the norm in about half of all marriages, and one out of every two relationships ends in divorce. In fact, most couples I see in therapy for marital problems spend major portions of their time relating in basically unproductive ways. Many continue to act from unconscious personal scripts that limit both individual expression and conscious awareness. With such facts before us, one wonders just how consciousness *does* begin to evolve in partnering?

To answer this question, it may help to divide relational patterns into three categories: unconscious, more conscious, and awakened transpersonal states of relationship.

Eventually, if we're able to be honest with ourselves and our partners, we begin to see that our relational problems are often due to the flaws in our own personal and cultural myths. Often the primary work we must do is to confront the unconscious spaces of our personal past; it means healing the wounds of the inner child. Ultimately, being in right relationship to a partner means that we have begun to recognize and deal with the family ghosts that have previously permeated many of the current spaces in our relationships. The social masks we wear and the roles we play must also be examined carefully, because often we relate to one another not from the real person, but from the social scripts we have adopted. The goal of any awakened relationship is one that passes through any of these unconscious phases. However, awakening doesn't happen overnight. Most of us need a fair chunk of our lifetime to be able to relate genuinely to one another. We need to be able to make plenty of mistakes and then to possess the humility to learn from them.

At the spiritual level of relationship a woman has begun to descend the spiral of an inner life. She has begun to drop down a level, beyond the outer masks and the ego image she has developed; she begins to move more deeply into instinct, heart and mind, to go deeper within to the soul. This level of relating is more like a communion between a woman and her mate(s). It is this level that reflects the "transpersonal" element of the spirit, or a higher purpose between a couple. Union at this level has transcended ego, but in an integrative sense. When relationship operates at the transpersonal or spiritual level, the level of instincts and ego are not left behind nor polarized as some might imagine. Instead they function holistically, as parts of a whole.

UNCONSCIOUS RELATIONSHIP: THE TWO MERMAIDS

In the first phase a woman remains psychologically unrelated to others. Esther Harding, in *Women's Mysteries,* calls this unconscious aspect of modern woman the Mermaid phase. The mermaid in myth and folklore is depicted as half-woman and half-fish. While one-half of her may be relating at what appears to be a more human feeling level, the other half resides in a watery and primordial domain that lacks genuine human warmth and awareness. "These are the women who play the role of anima to men, as a game . . . deliberately repressing their own reactions so that they may more surely get what they want." In a sense, although desire has been awakened in the Mermaid, love itself remains yet unawakened; because at this level the heart is asleep.[3]

Young women in the Mermaid phase of relationship may move either in conventional modes toward singular relationships with men, or in unconventional acting-out modes where promiscuity is the rule. This pattern of relationship represents a primordial sea of energies that, unless directed, can cause all sorts of chaos between a couple. Unaware of the unrefined power of these primitive instincts toward partnering, a woman can often act impulsively or in ways she later questions or feels embarrassed about. She can either express herself in overtly emotional ways or remain distant and aloof. She can be pleasing and condescending, or competitive and dominant. She can appear independent and strong, with a mind of her own, or dependent or passive, looking to a man for direction. She can play the role of the saint or the seductress, the perfect wife or the siren, but her primitive ego may all along only be struggling to fill its own emptiness.

When a woman feels empty inside she often gravitates towards a man as though he were a kind of insurance policy. When her self-esteem is low and her self-concept is not yet firmly grounded her relational behaviors are exacted as a means to preserve her sense of personal meaning. She is like a child who is emotionally stranded and without an identity of her own. One woman, looking back at her own unconscious relationship patterns, told me, *"Back then I had no idea of how to be myself. I depended on my husband for everything. Even if I didn't like something he did or said, I often kept it to myself. I was always so attuned to his moods and his needs, I don't even know if I had a sense of my own feelings at the time. Now that I can see how things really were, I think I was really like a little girl with him."*

Unconscious relational patterns like these are a decided disadvantage for a woman. If her primary needs from a mate are to be taken care of, made secure, attended to, and continually reassured, she effectively prevents the relationship from maturity. In other cases a woman who carries an unconscious process towards her mate may not act so much as a child, but may play a caretaking role instead; she may be something like a mother to her partner. She may be the good wife or mistress who seems attentive to all his needs. The catch to her nurturing is that she may also want to get his attention (and his devotion) by making him dependent upon her. She does this unconsciously by endlessly giving, providing, and taking responsibility for many of his personal affairs. She is probably not in touch with her need for securing her self-esteem in this way, so she is unable to see that her "devotions" are really contracts. This is the woman who is often said to be living for others; but the truth is she is caretaking because otherwise she feels void of personal meaning. But whether she is the submissive child or the caretaking mother in the relationship, the relationship is dysfunctional because there is little room for individuality.

A woman who plays this role with a man is often possessive, overly protective, or intrusive. In some cases she may feel a primitive kind of psychological identification with her mate that does not allow for any healthy separateness for either of them. I knew a woman once whose giving behaviors were associated with a feeling of safety. As long as she was giving something of herself to others, she felt relieved. As long as she complied and pleased and acquiesced and went along with other people's needs, she was sure all of that giving would come back to her. Whatever she gave away, in other words, became like an unconscious extension of herself. She imagined that her giving behaviors were an insurance that she would be "carried" by others and thus not separated from them; that by doing things for them she insured their return to her. The token of her offerings had become some sort of magical talisman of personal power over the unknown of being alone with herself.

The woman who is at the more submissive end of the Mermaid spectrum often chooses to avoid conflict. Many women at this level of relationship live in exclusive denial because denial is the easiest way to deal with any dysfunction, personal or relational. If she enters it at all she invariably sees herself as the victim. If she has been wronged, hurt, or left without means, her pretence is that she is helpless; generally, she is unable to see her own part in the problem. Her resources for relationship are minimal, because most of her energy is bound up in the rigorous task of holding everything together, no matter how bad it is. Many women caught in this pattern have given up on any real relationship. Instead, some women often contain their deeper desires by holding them in a sort of psychic reserve, where things will always remain safe and unchallenged. Growing means facing fear; and a woman caught in a survival contract is unlikely to take any initiative.

Many such women put up with a poor existing relationship, and survive by pretending they are not in the relationship at all. Here women relate not to the partner but to some idealized internal figure, like the "ghostly lover" figure Harding describes.[4] Many women relate superficially to their real mates but "live" in a pretend world of fantasy and romance, or in a memory of some other significant person in their past. The internal figure may be a hero, a movie star, a lost lover, or a man with whom a woman has never had any contact except in her daydreams.

Other women ignore the problems of a dysfunctional relationship through a life of busy agendas. Yet when we are running to fix other things and people, to change other people's misfortunes and not our own, we are stuck in another kind of denial. When the dead spaces in relationship become too painful or chaotic to hide or deny any longer, this is where crisis usually erupts. A woman generally emerges from an unconscious process when her relationship suddenly becomes so conflictual that she either has to wake up or die to get out of it.

Another unconscious relating process is exemplified by the

sort of woman who is anything but submissive. She is the aggressive Mermaid, with a mind of her own and a will to have her own way with men. She does not make herself subject to men, but endeavors to make men subject to her. This woman is instinctively centered on herself and her own goals. She models her life according to her own needs and looks upon any hint of dependency with disdain.

This woman's self-esteem does not depend solely on her relationships. Her identity appears to stem from what she can accomplish and what she can do to prove herself on her own. She looks more independent than the submissive type, but emotionally she may not be at all. In most cases she would like to be strong, assertive, in control of herself, her own boss. But she may often act out a facade of independence—not because she has it, but because deep down she can't risk relationship.

Generally, a woman at the more aggressive end of an unconscious process is not without some sense of what she wants. But whether her assertions are more vocal demands for equal footing, or polite manipulative ploys to get attention, her assertiveness does not always come from a solid place of self-confidence.

Whether a woman's relational behaviors at this level are aggressive or subdued, her issues are often those of control. When she gets demanding or withdrawn with her partner, she is most likely in touch with a deeper, less conscious emotion underneath her show of fight. Inside she intuits an emptiness; she's hungry for something she never got, and therefore can't quite trust. Beneath her warrior-like cover she is afraid and beyond her show of being big on control is a little girl who's terrified to be small. Afraid of the thought of losing control and often wary of being humiliated or put-down, she has learned as a child not to trust intimacy. Being open, vulnerable, or willing to risk feelings may be an unspoken taboo in her book.

Once trust has been broken in consistent and sometimes traumatic ways, a woman may go to great lengths not to become vulnerable again. Women who have been abandoned by men tend to become overtly "independent"—sometimes competitive and not to be outdone, other times condescending and noticeably aloof. Such a woman's proud manner with men can become obsessive. The anger in some feminist voices echoes this clearly:

"I've never trusted men really. It always feels like the minute I do, something goes wrong. I can't pretend I'm some helpless little girl with men, because I'm not. Ultimately, if I want something, I go for it. I don't care what people think. I'm not sitting around waiting for a knight on a white horse, because in my family there never were any illusions about men. I mean, dependable and trustworthy they were not! My mother's 'white horse' came in one door and went out the next just after I was born. And I'm not about to be used in the same way." This woman's hatred and mistrust of men stems from her initial loss of the first significant man in her life. When women who take a challenging stance towards men begin to face their pain around loss and betrayal, a host of such childhood hurts begin to surface.

Another example of this kind of relational pattern is the woman who, because she fears the loss of her independence, moves through relationship like an Italian family goes through garlic. Unconscious of her distrust of men, she allows them to come close outwardly, but inwardly she remains distanced and always on reserve. Unable to form any attachments or to trust intimacy, this woman views commitment as a kind of personal loss. For her, attachment to someone means the same as a loss of her freedom and her right to exist. She pursues many men (either sequentially or collectively), and quite unconsciously finds none of them suitable for her. She pursues until one of them turns around and looks genuinely interested or asks for a commitment, then she invariably takes flight. Her role reverses and she then becomes the distancer, fearing that the relationship will somehow swallow her identity. Outwardly, she may seem assertive, confident, friendly, but inwardly she fears getting close.

"I've come to the conclusion that I have a problem relating to men. It's not the romance part that's the problem; it's the getting serious part where I start fading. The man I'm with now is basically warm and sensitive and we share a lot of common interests. We like all the same things, we have a lot of fun together, everything seems fine really. Lately, though, he's begun to let me know that he's serious and interested in settling down. On one hand he has all the qualifications I've ever wanted in a man, but on the other hand I'm feeling ambivalent. I mean I like being with him, but the closer he comes the more distracted I get. Basically, I don't feel safe being close."

Other women may be in committed relationships and yet have

trouble with intimacy. They may appear more steady, but often the bottom line is the same. One of my clients, married three times and working through a third divorce, says, *"I want to find out exactly what's going on here. Something is not working, and I realize it's not always the fault of my partners. I'm beginning to see a pattern in myself that bothers me. It's as though I enter these relationships with one foot in the front door, and one foot already out the back. I allow some shared life to happen, I let some growth and opening develop between us, and then that's it. I won't let anyone really come all the way in. It's like wanting my space and feeling isolated in the midst of it."*

Because a woman's partnering motives at this level can still be fairly unconscious, to her men are either objects to be used or enigmas to be avoided. Whereas an overly submissive woman is more or less dominated by others, the more assertive type feels fearful that she will be used or taken advantage of. Her mistrust and fear of men stems from a basic mistrust of life itself, and for good reason—she has been betrayed in significant ways in her childhood. Because of a genuine lack of emotional validation as a child, she has never learned how to give of herself. Instead she clings to her rights, her possessions, her privacy, and her fortresses as though they were life itself. And, of course, in many cases, they have been.

A child only learns to substitute things for feelings when she herself has been used or taken advantage of. When parents use a child for their own interests, the child likewise learns to use others. Her relational behaviors are what Joseph C. Pearce calls "attachment behaviors"; she relates to others in an emotionally impoverished or dependent way because she has not fully developed her own emotional channels. According to Pearce, when infants consistently fail to receive genuine bonding with the mother, the channels for healthy emotional response remain blocked in all subsequent relationships. For all practical purposes, such a woman relates to men and significant others not out of love, but out of need or attachment. When eventually a woman at this level begins to awaken to herself and to what she is doing, she is often amazed at her inability to feel genuine involvement. Of course, this sort of uncovering is often painful and takes a lot of courage to face, because it means grappling with one's core issues of fear, abandonment, and a lack of trust. Yet once a woman begins to break this denial of unconscious behavior and can admit the way she armors herself against trust, she has at least one foot in the door toward change.[5]

Clearly, the different styles of relating we have covered so far range across a fairly broad continuum. Not uncommonly, some women find themselves a blend of several partnering styles. Often one overlaps another to some degree, and in some cases we can exhibit several tendencies at once. For that reason I want to emphasize that the categories which I use are only a paradigm to be applied in the widest sense. My intention here is simply to imply that awakening has its growth phases, and psychological transformation comes by degrees.

MORE CONSCIOUS RELATIONSHIP: THE AWAKENING

In the next level of relationship a woman begins to awaken and to experience more of her own authenticity in partnering. She moves toward relationship with much more of her basic ego intact, and she forms bonds with others which are rooted in healthier ground. The good news here is that a woman who has begun to relate to others from this wider place of consciousness is not just self-serving, nor is she coming at relationship out of a survival mode. She is doing so because she has a certain sense of awareness towards others. A woman who is moving toward a more conscious process is beginning the task of waking up to herself.

While relationships at this level are generally more conscious and personable, they are not always free of areas of entanglement. But the lack of awareness is not so much because of a childhood of emotional deprivation as in the unconscious process. Instead, these behaviors stem from the relational dilemmas that mark later childhood. They result more because the relational models a woman experienced in her childhood, although not always overtly dysfunctional, were incomplete or lacking in some way. These difficulties, left unresolved, become the reasons why some women fall prey to the kinds of social stereotypes mentioned earlier. Whereas the unconscious style of relationship exemplified the woman who played out the whims of her partner, this sort of heroine role plays out a more collective figure: She dons the role society wants her to play.

THE "TRADITIONAL FEMININE" IN RELATIONSHIP: THE GIVER

One socially sanctioned relating style for women is the Giver. She is the stereotype of the woman who has been groomed by convention to serve others. Often available to a dozen causes and sensitive to her environment, she is a clear support to the people and the projects most important to her. This woman belongs to society at large and may be nurturing, giving, and generous with her efforts. When her relational behaviors are self-effacing, however, it is because they are part and parcel of the expected behaviors with which she has been culturally molded, and as such she is identified with her persona or mask. True, her consciousness is wider; yet if her ego is hooked into her social role, she may still lack authentic personal awareness.

This woman may be modeling her behavior directly after her mother and may be acting out of a sort of positive mother complex. Or she may be acting out a broader social script which reflects her socio-religious values, or the values of her childhood environment; in this case these behaviors are culturally learned behaviors. They are part of her ascribed role of the "traditional feminine." Or she may be motivated in her giving behaviors because of some stress-related problems in later childhood. In some cases, she may have had to assume a rescuing or caretaking role in order to survive a later family dysfunction.

Many women I know who have had relatively healthy mother-daughter relationships remain, for all practical purposes, fairly connected to the mother archetype. The recall of a warm lap, a comforting word, the smell of hot cookies coming out of the oven on a cold day, a sense of understanding—are all reasons why some women still feel close to their maternal roots. The Giver daughter will adopt something of the same sort of nurturing behaviors. She will be part and parcel of a collective mother model, and her relational behaviors will reflect that. At one level it is a real temptation to want to model after such a mother. To nurture is an admirable and needed function in a world that is so hurt by a collective negative father; yet to give compulsively, as some women do, is where many of us seem to end up walking the social plank.

To carry the collective mother, however, doesn't always imply that we have to have strong personal bonds to our natural mother. Sometimes a woman adopts a giving role because of what her religious upbringing has stressed. As one woman said, *"I think my own giving comes from the fact that I learned that that's what I was supposed to do. My mother did it, my grandmother did it. My Rabbi definitely saw women in the prescribed role of nurturer. In a way he was right, but in another way, he wasn't addressing the woman who gives too much of herself away."*

Many of the women who are Cosmic Mother types are devoted wives and mothers as well as dedicated professionals. Quite a number of them are the fabric of our helping and healing professions. They are our professional rescuers, and society probably needs many more. They have kept our social programs alive and are the heroic backbone of most of our volunteer programs. They are the indispensable secretary in every office and the great Earth Mother to many lost souls. But if the giving is out of balance so that a woman becomes cut off from her own inner woman, then crisis is surely brewing.

In partnering styles many women carry the collective mother right into their personal relationships with men. For years in my own marriage I repeatedly gave up not only my agenda but also my own identity for whatever the marriage program seemed to require. Often I gave priority to what my husband wanted because I was anxious to please him and to make things work for us. The nest I created was my refuge, and I was going to make it as comfortable and predictable as possible.

Like the Greek myth of Psyche, who sacrifices herself to the god Eros for love, a woman caught in the collective mother often releases herself with abandon to become her mate's counterpart. To begin with, she sacrifices her maidenhood to the man. She relinquishes her singleness and her freedom to merge with her chosen one, and like Hera, the goddess of hearth and home, she pleasures "in making her mate or husband the center of her life."[6] Many feminine types view this kind of sacrifice and giving as a woman's rightful role. In a traditional sense she becomes the heart of the home and the willing keeper of the hearth. She will generally want to nourish, protect, and support her mate's emotional and physical needs.

For a time this woman experiences gratification in her need to be important to her mate. But when a woman relates to others out of a social script, she does so because her self-esteem is locked into performing a role she feels obliged to play. While the woman who acts out the unconscious process clearly expects a man to fill all her needs and to be her source of self-esteem, the woman who identifies with a social role does so primarily out of a sense of duty. And, not uncommonly, her giving feats in relationship are heroic. Yet often the bottom line is that she is unable to be real with her mate because her own authenticity may yet be buried. In a sense, although she has invested a great deal in the relationship and has sacrificed some of her best years in some cases, she still has not brought her real self into the picture. Her sacrifice has never allowed her to explore who she really is.

Some relationships seem to do well for a while on this menu. But trouble commonly arises when a woman awakens to find her identity lost in a mass of entanglements. Eventually, she may find her self so closely aligned with her mate that she becomes unable to distinguish his needs from her own. This is where the "I" of the relationship has become lost in the "we." Whereas at the Mermaid level of relationship there is very little "I" to begin with, the problem for the Giver is that the "I" gets spread too thin.

A woman in this case acts as if her identity is completely dependent on how others see her. Her feeling of self-worth is measured by her "goodness" and giving behaviors. Refusing anyone a favor often transforms itself into a feeling of guilt. Thus the rightful "no" a woman must sometimes say has in this case become a compulsive "yes." Instead of standing apart from the things and people around her, she throws herself, willingly or unwillingly, into the midst of the needs and demands of others. When the Giver was growing up, someone in her environment convinced her that in order to receive any sort of affirmation she must be complying: Saying "no" brought disdain, punishment, alienation, and shame. Conformity brought recognition, smiles of approval, and reward. Who would want to say "no" under those conditions?

Children of alcoholics are prime targets for giving behaviors. Many kids are aware that the family drinking problem is out of control. If father drinks and mother covertly agrees to be the co-alcoholic, and is passive and ineffectual as a parent, it is not uncommon for the child to take charge of the family. A great many women learned their giving behaviors early in life, out of a need to patch up and rescue the family dysfunction. Care-taking children are eventually going to become caretaking adults. A child who grows up with chaos often finds that taking the helm of the family ship is the only way to keep it from sinking. When this little rescuer grows up, she will similarly want to control and organize everybody else. Giving simply helps her run a tight ship.

Before one can be genuinely self-sacrificing in a healthy sense, however, one must know that self completely. In other words, we can't give away what we don't really have. Yet many women relate out of learned behaviors or out of a sanctioned role rather than from a place of authentic partnering. It is this kind of caretaking that many women need to question. Furthermore, this level of relational behavior is mainly using energy associated with the heart—except in this case, the heart channel is perhaps being used without full consciousness. In fact, when a woman gives out of this exaggerated sense of caring, she counterfeits the feminine heart because she uses it without wisdom. It's as if the heart were flooded either with sentimentality or at least some degree of ego need, and therefore is prey to a feminine stereotype. In this case the Giver is wedged into yet another false identity. For the woman whose identity becomes lost in a tangle of caretaking behaviors, the road to the self will become increasingly muddled. Until we learn to deal honestly with the past that has locked us into the role of the false heroine, life will continue to be a duty rather than a choice.

THE "TRADITIONAL MASCULINE" IN RELATIONSHIP: THE ACHIEVER

A girl whose father was absent or somehow did not match her needs as a model for a "significant other" is not immune to cultural stereotyping either. Because of what we have lacked as our fathers' daughters, many women have turned to some of the masculine models that society offers. This is the reason why the male persona or mask is so firmly entrenched in some women. If we have not had our biological father to model after, we always have the collective father—the patriarchy itself. Although seemingly autonomous and in some ways more individual, the woman who plays out the masculine stereotype has the voice of the father archetype still speaking through her. At the other end of the relational spectrum from the Giver, this woman is the Achiever.

Further along than her younger sisters in her individuating work, she can be competent, clear headed, insightful, assertive in a healthy sense, and in possession of many relating skills. She is no one's woman, nor does she wait for the directives of any of the men in her life. She makes her own rules, sets her own goals, and generally creates her own agendas. Although she enjoys relationship, this is by no means her first goal in life. She may enjoy working alone or with others, but work is where she aims her creative energies; it is toward this that most of her incentive flows. With a mind and a will of her own, the more autonomous woman prefers leading to following. Her personal power is fairly well developed because she keeps it consciously focused and directed and does not simply give it away.

Like the Athena personality in Greek myth, whose mind is her greatest asset, the Achiever is stimulated by intellectual pursuits and roused by the challenge of creative tension. Generally, this woman has often struggled to develop her own life, and because of this she is much more independent. In matters of work she is generally bright, competitive, assertive, and often loyal to whatever cause she has chosen to support. In the midst of some crisis at work she can keep her head and find a workable solution. She is the strategist in the business world, and the diplomat in political circles. Hard working, sensible, and pragmatic, she is often at home wherever the action is. She is a good person to have on your team if you're trying to get something done, because she usually accomplishes what she sets out to do.

"I have always been an independent sort. I've always had to be. It became clear to me very early on that life wasn't just going to make

itself happen for me. I had to take charge of it for myself. Dad and Mom divorced when I was in grade school, and shortly after that Dad was killed in a car accident. All of us had to go to work just to pay the bills. I'm married now and have kids, but I still enjoy my profession. Somehow it always makes me feel grounded. I think I need life in the fast lane. Otherwise I might be tempted to feel a bit bored or edgy. I've got to be doing something."

A woman at this more conscious level may put the emphasis on making a successful career of either her work or her marriage, but she generally has some goal in mind. Although she relates well to others and to her choice of a mate, relationship for her is generally secondary. While her more stylized feminine counterpart is focused on other people's worlds, this daughter of the patriarchy is off in her own. With clear agendas that characterize her desire for independence, her relational style often reflects strength, purposefulness, and some degree of individuality. She can become a pleasant companion to her man, supporting him intellectually and giving him good counsel in many of his own undertakings. She is often a responsible mother and a loyal wife. Ultimately, her partnerships are processed and run with some efficiency, and things can go along well for some time this way. Trouble may come, however, when the couple finds themselves stuck at some of the outer limits of the contract.

When difficulties arise at this level, it may be because each partner is competing with the other for power and control. The woman who identifies with the masculine side of her nature does not act out any hint of dependence toward the man in her life, nor is she his caretaker. She may treat her mate fairly and with respect, or she may be competitive and like control; but either way she will endeavor to be her own woman.

In terms of relationship this may mean that her feeling life is put on hold; her ability to be intimate, vulnerable, and trusting toward a man can be covertly inhibited. A woman may be competent and lively, but in the end she will do anything to keep from being found wanting in anything. For the woman who wishes to remain loyal to her own principles, to surrender often seems tantamount to a loss of face. Often she will go to great lengths to deny most characteristics associated with any kind of stylized feminine. Even the thought of it makes her somewhat distrustful. *"Bill is beginning to drive me nuts. He's been doing some sort of sensitivity training or something, and now he's trying to drag me into it. I told him I thought it was fine for him if he wants to learn how to explore intimacy, or whatever. But to me it seems like a waste of time. We seem to argue a lot more now. He wants me to 'open up' and be a more 'feeling' person, and all I want is to be left alone with a good science-fiction novel."*

When a woman's energy has been invested in accomplishments and performance, she has very likely developed an armoring against her feelings that undermines a fully authentic relating style. Thus feelings for her are either a rarity or a nuisance. She has them naturally, but she expresses them more in terms of something she's "thinking" about, rather than in terms of something she "feels." One woman said, *"I think my emotions are definitely enigmas. I mean, I have little patience with them, and little trust. People talk about 'going with the flow' of things and frankly I have a hard time with that. 'Go with the flow' in my book means I let go and slip into limbo. I don't do limbo well because I need to know what's going on. Given the choice, I trust my thoughts but not my feelings. They're too unpredictable."*

This retreat into reason often works well in the professional world or in the marketplace, where careful diplomacy is called for; but it is a source of frustration in a relationship. When one prefers to stay within reason and in some safe intellectual retreat, one cuts off a good deal of spontaneity and passion. And a life without passion may also be robbed of intensity and fullness.

While it is true that many women have become more conscious through their intellectual and social accomplishments, the danger is that women will not complete the feminine journey if they remain locked within a predominantly generative framework. When a woman rejects the stereotypical feminine (and what woman in her right mind doesn't?) she must be equally careful not to dive into collective masculine values, into a place where there is more power than compassion, more control than sensitivity toward oneself and others. When women invest in the material rather than in the relational world, without some degree of integration between giving and achieving, then there is bound to be an imbalance. When the Achiever prioritizes a personal or social agenda over unmasking her deeper identity, then she is unconsciously seduced by the father because she is still lying in his corporate bed.

One of my clients, who was right on the edge of her own interior work, commented reflectively, *"I think for years I have done well in business. I know I am successful and that I've made it on my own. During the feminist movement I was very active locally and got very involved in many of the issues facing women socially and professionally. I must say I'm glad I did. All of that has made me both a better businesswoman and a more assertive person with my family. But this next year or so is for me. I've really felt clear about needing something for myself. Something to do with my own soul, my real self. I've given notice at work that I will be taking this next year on sabbatical so I can take some time to allow this inner side of me to develop. The feminine side of myself needs to know who she is. This dream I'm going to tell you was one of the real waker-uppers for me, the thing that caused me to know something more needs to happen in my life.*

"I'm in the bedroom with my husband, Ralph, and we're trying to make love but for one reason or another we keep being interrupted. The phone rings and it's somebody at work. Then one or two of the women's groups I belong to calls. Then my editor calls, wanting that article I'd promised. Anyway, I really want to make love; it feels good to be close; it feels very erotic and I'm aroused. But the phone keeps ringing and the door to the bedroom keeps opening; once my secretary walks through and wants to conduct a press review of some kind. It is insane! We never do make love. In the next scene our bed is in the middle of a merry-go-round and we are at the state fair, like an exhibit of some sort. The whole dream is nuts, like my life is on exhibit—as though I have no personal identity, no privacy, and hardly any intimacy. I can't even make love without interruptions from my professional life. So it's true I've accomplished a lot; but on the other hand I'm feeling a need to get out of this rat race and into my self."

This woman is somehow without real relationship. Life on a merry-go-round gives her little or no intimacy and consequently her whole life seems far too public. Realizing that she has sold out to values that she now questions, she makes herself ready ultimately to face the next level of her search.

FOCUSING ON INNER WORK IN RELATIONSHIP

We can participate in our own healing work in relationship a number of ways, but the best way is by being centered in relationship to ourselves. Awakened relationships happen because at least one partner is awakened. When a woman honestly levels with herself about who she is and what she wants as a person in her own right, she can begin to change. When she changes, the people around her are also free to change. Therefore, whether we have only patches of fog to clear up or a whole fog bank to penetrate, the surest way toward the healing process is the inner journey.

Sometimes a crisis notifies us that we have some work to do at the personal or relational levels. Other times we may know we're in need of growth and change simply because voices from the unconscious signal us to get going. No matter what makes us begin, this inner work is what makes the difference at all levels. Sooner or later, all of us have to get into honest communion with ourselves. Most people I know are often both delighted and terrified to open up a deeper inner dialogue; it's always a shock to discover we are not who we might have imagined. A sense of humor helps.

As we begin to create more space for some of these unconscious sides of the personality to emerge, eventually a more honest interior dialogue begins to happen. The two main participants in this dialogue are generally the mask we have become too closely identified with, and the real feelings beneath that mask. As we do this we begin to open up and make honest the tension that already exists within us. We become aware of two movements happening at once, two energy fields meeting and perhaps pushing against each other.

This is the phenomenon that sometimes makes us feel a little crazy, like we're "losing it." Our agitation and restlessness, depression or anxiety, result from the confrontation of these two fields. The outer mask is holding us in, the old role and the ego want dominion as always; but new voices are emerging from below. So there is a struggle between our mask and what we have repressed unconsciously, or may be feeling but not acknowledging. The wall of defenses with which we have so carefully protected ourselves over the years may be breaking, melting down, allowing the real woman license.

The more we allow these inner voices to talk to us, the more old hurts, suppressed conflicts, and new awarenesses begin to come up. A whole host of subpersonalities begin to reach upward in their struggle to make themselves known. When we engage in this sort of dialogue we discover who else may be voicing their archaic opinions in us; we shed the outer garment of the personality so that more of the authentic self can emerge. These other voices within may be personifications of the Mermaid, the Giver, the Achiever, or the shadow side of our personality that we meet when we begin to break the crust of our persona. They can be mothers, fathers, grandmothers, the collective voices of the past. They can be feelings long suppressed, anger that we're out of touch with, sadness we've not acknowledged, or heroic potentials we've never uncovered.

HEALING THE GIVER

When I began my own inner work one of my best guides to these inner figures were my dreams. For a while I worked off and on with others in dream analysis, and that was helpful; yet my real insight about dreams and their meaning only came when I took the dream inside myself to process. I did this by playing out the dream actively, by inviting the dream figures to speak to me and then allowing them to lead me to some deeper truth they wanted to show me. To amplify the characters in the dreamscape by giving them a voice (as in some of the previous examples of therapy work) is one way we can get more closely connected to the unconscious. The dialogue that ensues is often insightful and of real help to one's inner process.

Let me give you an example. The following dream sequence speaks of what can happen to us if we have neglected our inner work over a period of years. Eventually, when we have endured a situation long enough, the body begins to take on the conflict. This dreamer, an inveterate Giver unable to make the connection between her compulsive goodness and her asthma, finally began to get the message. She told me the following recurrent dream:

"I am lying underneath a great weight. It's like some evil force that

lies on top of me and I can't seem to shake it. First it's on my chest, causing me to panic because I can't breathe. I wrestle with it and manage to turn over, trying to crawl away on my hands and knees. I try to stand, but the force of this monster sits even more squarely on my shoulders. And now this evil thing is hissing and the weight of it is so great I lose consciousness and faint. My last thought before waking up is the awful terror of dying like this. When I awaken I can hardly breathe and I feel terrified."

As we process through the dream I ask her to imagine that she is reentering the dream, reliving each part. When it comes to playing the evil force she balks, feeling frightened and beginning to wheeze. We wait for a moment and then eventually continue, with her as the victim who is being squashed and me filling in as the evil thing that sits on her and won't let her get up. *"You can't come out,"* I said.

"Why won't you let me stand up and walk?" she moaned. *"I want to come out!"*

"I'm not going to let you live. I'm going to cut you off. You've had it. I'll win this match, and there'll be nothing left of you," I enjoined. *"I'm getting heavier and heavier, and you're getting weaker and weaker. Just give up."*

"You're crushing me!" she cried. *"Get off! I don't want to fight you any more. Who are you?"*

"You know who I am. Your chest knows me. You just say you don't know who I am, but you've known me for years. C'mon, give up. Give me everything. The last drop."

"I don't want to give you any more!" she shouted.

"Of course you do," I said. *"You've always been so faithful. Besides, you're only saying that so I'll get off your back. So stop playing games and give up. Just hand your last breath over."*

In a serious moment of insight she said to this thing on her chest, "I have nothing left to give you. You've drained me. I've given enough. I've given everything of myself and now I'm angry." I step out of the role of the evil weight and she continues. "Now I'm seeing something. I think I know who you are. You're the weight of some neediness I have. Like a need to give myself away. To make myself small before the needs of others is always what I've done, but now it's crushing me. I've been giving, but I've been resentful. Feeling less and less space for myself. All of this doing things for others is hemming me in." She looks surprised. "Maybe that's why I have trouble breathing. There's nothing left over for me anymore. No room inside. I'm literally suffocating in here."

Recurrent dreams are warning signals that something is very off balance inside. Fortunately, this dreamer took her dream seriously, and the threat of her asthma made her sit up and take note. The character that was underneath the evil force was her victim self, the helpless frozen self that somehow gets to be the common victim of circumstance in our lives. After years of identifying with our social script or mask we get dangerously near sacrificing the real self. This woman's charitable attitudes and giving behaviors were masking something inside her that was literally being crushed: her own right to life as an authentic person. In this case, her asthma was the effect of her incessant need to cover her real feelings, and the evil force was her own anger at holding herself at a boundary that was not productive. This overwhelming negative force could have also been an unconscious inner attitude of low self-esteem that effectively kept saying, "You've got to keep sacrificing and giving because you're just not good enough yet."

The moral of many stories like these is that if a woman hopes to understand the nature of relationship to others, she must first be in balance herself. If being in communion with others is a natural outgrowth of her relational nature, as it seems to be, then she most always has some inner work to do. Because only when a woman is able to separate herself from her roles, her collective identities, and limiting self-concepts is she able to be there for others. Her own autonomy and secure identity is the major key to balanced and integrated communion with others. But, as with any other worthwhile task, it takes patience and courage to find our own autonomy.

Caught at one time in a marriage that completely stifled her spirit and kept her out of touch with herself, another woman had one of those epic dreams that gave her an absolute conviction that her relational life needed a clean sweep. Speaking of the dream, she said, *"There is a beautiful, circular Roman pool. In its waters several young maidens are bathing. I know they are virgins and that I am their matron, their chaperone. It is my responsibility to see that they arrive at a wedding. They are full of joy and there is an air of celebration in our midst.*

"Once we are dressed we load ourselves into a small boat to continue our journey from the pool up the river to the wedding. Suddenly, huge dark soldiers stand blocking our way. One of them tells us we don't have to die as long as we are willing to go back and not go to the wedding. The young girls look at me terrified, not knowing what to do. In that moment I am aware of a complete lack of fear; never in my life have I had such a feeling of determination. I tell the soldiers that we have to go to the celebration or die; we have no other choice. We are all willing to die for this purpose."

In the dreamer's growth process it has become absolutely vital for her to move past these formidable men and continue with her mission of bringing these young women (the undifferentiated side of herself) to consciousness; even if it meant a certain kind of death. For many women there are stages in the journey that are like death. In this woman's case she needed to leave a man who was keeping her in bondage. *"But I was afraid many times that I couldn't make it on my own. I had depended on my husband for everything. Yet to stay behind was killing my spirit; I had no choice but to leave. I knew that welfare was just around the corner, and I knew I would have to work hard to support myself, but I had to go. It's like these young virgins were that weaker side of me, rather innocent and dependent; but it was clearly up to me to get them where they had to go. I think those men were not just my husband (who wanted to hold me back), but they were also my fear that I wouldn't make it."* As this woman spoke with the figures in her dream, it became clear to her that to stay in such a marriage would be completely counterproductive.

Like this woman, many of us on the road by the river have to pause from time to time and ask ourselves where we are going, and if in fact we are living life out of choice or out of compromise. Sometimes, too, we must ask ourselves difficult questions about what collective values as well as what securities we must sacrifice in order to get all the way up the river.

HEALING THE ACHIEVER

Whereas the woman who has been locked into the traditional role of the Giver may need to reexamine or relinquish certain unhealthy aspects of relationship in order to find her self, the Achiever may temporarily need to relinquish her own preoccupation with work and causes and to find relationship. One

woman was a professional in her early thirties with three children. While in the process of establishing a new relationship
after her recent divorce, she once said to me, "*I am attempting to
start relationship all over again. I've dated this new man in my life
about six months now and we both want to go deeper. We're talking
marriage and I'm noticing how afraid I am of another failure in
partnering. It's becoming painfully clear to me that I have trouble
letting anyone see my feelings. I know now that I want to show them
and let myself be known, but I'm sometimes unable to let go of myself
enough to even know my own feelings. They're there, but they're vague.
I cover them somehow.*"

I asked her how she sometimes masked her feelings, and she
admitted that she often immediately went into her head when
feelings came up. In the course of our conversation we began
to speak playfully to the dominant more rational side of her
personality; I asked her to give this "other" person inside her a
voice. Not unsurprisingly, these inner voices that spoke of maintaining control and disdaining feelings soon began to manifest
as her father's voice, the one she had unconsciously identified
with as a young girl. We had the following dialogue:

"*What do you want?*" she asked this inner father figure.

*After a pause during which she tried to imagine how this inner
figure might respond, she said in a somewhat paternal way,* "*I want
your attention. I want you to give yourself to me. To be like me. Oh
well, you don't have to look like me, you just have to uphold my values.
To excel. I like it best when you excel.*" *Her voice tone began to pick up
here, and I sensed she'd suddenly found herself squarely in the role of
the corporate father. She went on in this patriarchal voice,* "*Remember
now, I want you to stay in line. When you stay in line then you're safe.*"

"*That's right,*" *I joined in, playing the collective father.* "*Control
yourself and you'll be safe.*" *She began to laugh and then to wince as
our dialogue went on.*

*Amazed at how much control this inner character seemed to exert
over her life, she commented,* "*It is astounding to think that he has had
this much power all these years.*" *I asked her how she thought this inner
father figure had exercised his strengths.* "*I think he's got hold of my
mind,*" *she said.* "*It's as though when I'm safe and rational, when I'm
in control, when I'm doing my work and tending to what I can do well,
then everything is OK. Then I'm self-assured. But when I get into*

relationship, being in my heart is not my territory and I don't feel sure of myself at all. I suppose I retreat then."

Thinking out loud I said, "Why do you suppose it's so tempting to retreat?"

"I guess I use my head because that's what my father would have done. I suppose I feel loyal to him. A way to get his approval. He never trusted feelings because he said they made one open to ridicule. If I expressed feelings around him he didn't exactly disapprove, he just sort of withdrew. He made it hard for me to be small in some ways, because his expectations for me were always so big."

As with many other professional women, this woman was highly competent and articulate. But at some interior level this corporate character wasn't going to let go of her. Driving his hard bargains and watching over her like a hawk from some dusty corner in her psyche, he made it virtually impossible for her to experience her feeling side or to be herself. She was a beautiful, passionate woman, but this father figure was taking up too much space, and her loyalty to him included keeping herself strong and virtually unassailable. She was being seduced by the strength of her devotion to his values.

Our strengths, so vital to our early survival, can also become our greatest enemies. Yet ironically, in order to really come alive in the feeling world and to awaken the heart, some of these strengths have to be released. The task for women is to honestly own where we *are* weak or vulnerable. Where we get sidetracked and inflated because of what our defenses have programmed in us. In the realm of relationship some strengths are inhibitors. This woman had to let go of the corporate voice and embrace her own unaffirmed inner child, to admit her weakness and her need for love and closeness. In a sense her task was to allow her lover to not only be her lover, but also to enable him to occasionally act as a father presence—not in a dependent way (as the child does), but from a more vulnerable place. The Mermaid child needs to grow up and become independent, in some cases to let go of relationships for a while until she finds her own identity. But the Achiever (or whatever other mask this energy has become for us) needs to get down to the ground of the feelings; to offer herself to relationship without the strongholds of the past so firmly covering her heart.

A friend of mine had a dream that seems to echo a similar kind of dilemma. Although frightening at one level, it has clearly a certain soul quality about it. *"I am being shown an overview of a Nazi concentration camp. Babies are being separated from their mothers and there is terror and sadness everywhere. One of the few men who tries to stand up for his family, for his wife and child, is smashed by the soldiers. The rest of the men seem powerless. I am aware that I am missing my mother too and I'm grieving for her. Suddenly, a young man—not a Nazi, but a rebel—comes in with some other young men. He has a gun and he is going to shoot me. I tell him there has already been enough killing here but he doesn't listen and it appears he will shoot me anyway. But just then another person kills him. Somewhere in the back of this compound there is a door. When I look through, I see a Native American celebration going on. A dance. Men and women in colorful costumes dance rhythmically around in a great circle. Stamping the ground in unison, each of them dances and chants together in a powerful and beautiful synchronism."*

Working through the dream, she spontaneously recalled a time at thirteen when she went on a group date with some friends. They had gone to an island in the Carolinas called Kiawah, and were walking together on the beach. She remembers walking there feeling the ground under her feet. *"I used to pay attention to where I was walking on the sand, to my feet on the ground, to walking connected to the earth. Suddenly, out of nowhere, a volley of bullets began to hit the sand around us. My girlfriend was hit by two gunshots and she screamed. I turned suddenly around to see her and I was hit too. The boys we were with started screaming that we were being attacked, but no one could see where the fire was coming from. We were both bleeding, but I knew I shouldn't fall down. In the midst of the panic and confusion I knew I had to take charge of myself, that I had to be strong or I would die. I imagined this rod of lightning inside me, and I centered myself around it so I wouldn't collapse. I remember it took tremendous will to stand, but I did it.*

When we were taken to the hospital I was told by the doctors and by my father that I wasn't going to die, so I should stop making such a commotion. They said it was only a flesh wound. I had been hit in the breast. It was humiliating to be exposed, to be shamed because I was crying too much, to be told to shape up. All I knew was that I had gone on my first date and had been shot, and that there was nobody there for me, not even the comfort of my own father. Not only that, the investigation the sheriff's department did after that was minimal. I begun to know that the world was an unsafe place. Yet at the same time I began to see things like life and death much more intently; I became much more introspective and independent. I remember I kept this lightning rod for a long time afterward. It was part of the strength in my own will; especially at times when there was no one else to rely on but myself."

The will, so central to our survival, is an important tool in our early life. In truth, it *is* a lightning rod around which we can position ourselves for strength. But it is an ego strength, nonetheless, and can become like the enemy itself, if we are not careful about how we use it. Once we begin an inner journey we are going to be accountable for our whole internal ecosystem, and if something is out of balance, if it is *koyaanisqatsi*, we will be called right into the core of the trouble. This woman, now in the midst of a spiritual journey, had begun to feel how the Native American in her self (her natural, earthy feminine) had become somehow prisoner inside a concentration camp. The dream itself was strangely reminiscent of the dichotomy between the island where she used to walk so connected to the earth as a young woman and the violence of the men who shot randomly at her and her friends. There was a timeless parallel between the events of that moment in her adolescence and her own current psychological process.

Perhaps these soldiers may represent a collective masculine that has never been there for her except in a negative sense, like the ruthless men on the island, the doctors who had no compassion, and her father who insisted she negate her anguish and be stoic, like himself. Yet in another way the violence of the Nazis in her dream may be her own compelling side; the side that will tolerate no weakness in herself nor allow much vulnerability. Perhaps it is the side that masks feeling or judges it in some way; the side that collectively tells her to shape up and take it "like a man." In some way her "dream body" is urging her to look at the split between the soldiers within herself and her own inner woman; to embrace the schism between her masculine and feminine nature.[7]

Undoubtedly, power, when it lodges in idealism, *is* a dangerous concentration camp. Inside such a place there is no room for caring, for nurturing, for the feminine relational self. The classic will-to-power that the Nazi movement became so intoxicated with was in fact germinated by the ideal of perfectionism. This distorted patriarchal ideal crushes the feminine at any level. And when any of us as women are driven by a collective patriarchy that imposes its values and ideals on us as women (personally, socially, or religiously), we are in trouble. Our own will to serve ideals, to be stoic, to be so strong that we are effectively cut off from feeling or from our feminine instincts, may be the very thing that brings us violence. Yet behind all of this "concentration" of negative masculine energy in the dream, there is a dance; men and women in perfect unison, in perfect synchronism dance and sing together, and another reality emerges.

The Nazi scenario in women's dreams is common whenever the masculine and feminine is out of balance. It is common especially for professional women, or women who have penetrated far into patriarchal strongholds. It simply comments that the feminine is repressed and wants life; that it wants the freedom of the dance. That it wants to honor its earthy nature and to show reverence for a far simpler communion with life.

AWAKENED CONSCIOUSNESS: THE SPIRITUAL LEVEL OF RELATIONSHIP

The idea of a spiritual relationship implies that as an individual moves toward psychological liberation, there is a parallel movement toward the authentic self. In effect the journey moves from the unconscious realms of the self to the conscious and then to the transpersonal—that which transcends the personal. If we go beyond the personal or the human level, we suddenly enter the inner realm of the spirit. Cultivating the meaning and the use of a spiritual presence within is what makes a relationship transpersonal; it's when one or both partners can move through all the outer levels of relating and come to the essence of what is within each of them, to the source of life inside. Some people call this "soul making."

When an individual begins to develop self-awareness, to move through the layers of the personality, the false selves and masks, one begins to meet one's authentic nature. The closer we come to a fully human nature, however, the closer we come to our divine inner nature. A spiritual relationship is simply one that reflects our deepest self, or that is in touch with the spiritual substance within each of us. Kabir describes this part of trans-personal love in the following poem:

> The darkness of night is coming along fast,
> and the shadows of love
> close in the body and the mind.
> Open the window to the west and disappear
> into the air inside you.
> Near your breastbone is an open flower.
> Drink the honey that is all around that flower
> Waves are coming in:
> There is so much magnificence near the ocean.
> Listen: Sound of immense seashells! Sound of bells!
>
> Kabir says: "Friend, listen, this is what I have to say:
>   The Guest I love is inside me."[8]

How do we enter into a transpersonal relationship? In the first place, we have to be willing to acknowledge that there are resources greater than we are. Most people I know who bear some testimony to this have accepted their own human limitations. Thinking that there must be more than just myself in the scale of the universe, I went seeking for answers to the soul somewhere in my early twenties. But my search was not inspired because I wanted to make my relationships right. Rather, I was prompted out of a hunger for answers to the paradox that continually stared at me from within and without, and from a sense that there had to be more meaning to life. I went seeking for the inner life out of pain and fury, out of sheer desperation, and out of an intuition that the Native Americans and the saints whom I loved could not all be wrong. In time, the spiritual discipline I found and adopted for myself began to bear fruit, and the prayer and meditation I learned became a source of guidance for me. The formula was fairly simple: The closer I came to knowing myself, the closer I came to meeting God within.

The Hebrew word *ruah* means "breath of God." The spiritual questing we do, either as individuals or as a couple, opens up the possibility for this breath of God to happen in the relationship itself. To share this breath between a couple is somehow to draw in more life. In relationship, the transpersonal means that we can bring something to partnering other than just ego, or self-interest, other than just a mask or role. Ultimately, it means we bring our whole selves to the relationship and that we open ourselves to a greater reality.

At some point in my quest I realized there was no difference between the psychological and the spiritual path: To follow one was to follow the other. To be lacking in one was to lack in the other, and to gain in one was to gain in both. I found that the realm of the unconscious began to become familiar territory, a ground from which alternately my self emerged and my soul quickened its own work. By the time one comes into the deeper ground of the psyche, one begins to find there a tremendous resource of knowledge, insight, and wisdom. It is at these deeper intuitive levels that the transpersonal manifests itself. There is another presence in the well to draw from.

The actual uses of this transpersonal resource between a couple are rich and varied. Whenever my husband, Arthur, and I have called this breath of life into our midst, asking for guidance, clarity, or wisdom, we've always been heard. Something always happens to turn our impasses and differences into productive places in the relationship. We have used prayer and meditation for all manner of guidance: conflict resolution, problem solving, personal and family direction. The Navajo and Sioux believe that the breath they draw in the dawn of each new day is always holy; it always represents a new beginning. Whenever my partner and I have asked to receive this holy breath between us, we have never walked away empty.

Here is an example of how we put a question forth and waited for an answer from the deeper well of the Spirit. At one time in our marriage we weren't getting along and were experiencing some heavy stresses, and I was thinking of leaving. At the time I was teaching pottery to kids in high school. During my classes there were often free times when I could turn to my own work. During one of these times I picked up a wad of clay and began to form a small pot with two spouts and something of a bridge handle in between the spouts. I had seen such a pot years ago

on one of our family trips to the Southwest. When it was finished I felt satisfied that I had worked hard on it, and so I set
it aside for a while. Later that week some friends of ours came
over for dinner. They were aware that we were on the verge of
a separation and suggested that we find some time in the evening to meditate and pray for a direction. I remember feeling
very resistant to this at the time. Feeling too angry with my
husband to allow myself any vulnerability in front of him, I
asked my woman friend to meditate with me in a separate room
from the men. I also felt this was a time for my own private
space.

At first I was only aware of my anger and skepticism. Then
slowly I began to descend within and to let go. After a while
the small clay pot I had been working on came to mind. In my
meditation I stood up and became the pot, lifting my arms
upward like the two water spouts. I felt aware of a need to be
empty like this water jug, empty so that I could receive from
beyond the place of my anger and resentment. I began to feel
lighter, more in tune with something deeper than just my feelings. I entered into a kind of spontaneous dance that went on
for some time. The more I followed this movement the lighter I
felt and the more the oppressive hostility that had settled over
me began to fade. When the dance stopped I sat down and
tried to listen for some sort of inner guidance.

The woman who was with me in this prayer experience asked
me quietly if I thought I could image my husband as a kind of
prince. She made it clear that I did not have to try and love
him or even like him just at the time, but that I might try
visualizing him differently. She asked if I could see him not so
much based on what he was currently showing me, but on his
inner potentials. Supposedly, my imaging him in this way might
help him to release his own blocks in our relationship; or in
any case I might concurrently be freeing him of my furious
projections. In spite of my intellectual reservations and the
emotional arsenal I felt, I agreed to give it a try. Whether it
worked or not I had nothing to lose.

Later on that night, after our company had left, my husband
and I shared what we had each experienced. For the first time
in weeks we felt a strong sense of inner connection. Some

obstacle in the way we were seeing one another finally broke loose, and on that night we saw each other clearly and without any judgment. Our angry stalemate had given way to a deeper reality. It must have been the intervention of divine beings, because suddenly I was seeing him in a different light entirely. The following week we flew off to Kauai, where we reconsecrated the gift of our marriage by devoting a whole week to ourselves. Reflecting on the remarkable events and breakthrough of the previous week, we hiked through the countryside, picking wild fruits and flowers, taking long hikes into hidden lagoons, and making love in the warm island sun.

Some weeks later I saw a show of pottery from the Southwest. Among the collection of fine pots I saw a larger version of the same pot I had absentmindedly fashioned earlier and then danced in my meditation. Surprisingly—or perhaps not so surprisingly—it turned out to be a Hopi wedding pot. Over the years this pot has become for me the symbol of the way we have transcended many of our stretching experiences as a couple. This is something of the way we plug into the spiritual or transpersonal element of our life together.

Not unlike most relationships, there have been plenty of misunderstandings, rivalries, hurt feelings, and high-spirited squabbles over the years. There were times I felt overwhelmed, hopeless, sad, furious—in other words, ready to fly the coop. However, once I finally learned to express myself openly, to express my feelings, my needs, and to stand up for myself, we had some incredibly healthy rows. Sometimes there's just nothing that takes the place of a good Spanish-Armenian free-for-all. It was always a puzzle to experience how beautifully the air was suddenly cleared after a particularly good fight. The more we learned about fair fighting, the more creative our fights became. In the beginning of a fight both of us used to shake and feel scared and vulnerable; but the more at ease we got with our feelings and assertions, and the more we practiced saying the truth, the more productive our disagreements got. It generally always opened the way for an open and level communication, deeper understanding, and more passionate lovemaking.

Sometimes, when there were other kinds of ongoing disputes between us, we found we could simply come to an agreement through honestly talking through the problem. And sometimes we could get creative solutions even if that meant agreeing to disagree for a while. But at other times I simply had to find myself a desert space—be that a closet, bathroom, or basement—where I could get away with my annoyances, hurts, or questions. In my better moments I managed to be able to pray or be silent, and to attempt to let go of the thing until I felt some inner peace. Sometimes I was too mad to pray or be contemplative. But I took my refuge anyway, and used that time to speak with the thing or person that was offending me. Of course there were times I came away from my basement desert feeling drained and still slightly warm under the collar. But at other times, through that dialogue or that solitude, both a personal and a spiritual strength began to emerge.

If the matter was a relational crisis or impasse to which there seemed no immediate solution, then I began to visualize taking that person (husband or other) into an imaginary inner altar. I began to practice letting go of the person or the issue, and turning inward, to myself and to this inner breath of God, for some needed renewal. During some of these times it was only my own soul that could quieten and direct me; times when the practice of leveling and confrontation needed to be withdrawn from others and made an interior exercise.

Undoubtedly, however, some of these inner confrontations and moments of dialogue were not just a matter of coming into silence and letting go. Some of these moments were instead a vigorous exercise of loud verbal protest, holy obscenities, and a restaging of the Wailing Wall in Jerusalem. This act of crying out to the Holy Mystery within us is an act of prayer, even if it does sometimes resemble a wrestling match or the dance of a village idiot. But the point is that this dialogue, which we have begun with ourselves earlier at the personal level, is also one which can lead us through relational impasses—especially when we bring the transpersonal element into that relationship.

Both my husband and I value private individual prayer, but there are times that coming together for shared prayer has been a vital substance in our relationship. Although the ways of prayer and meditation are rich and varied from individual to individual, there are many ways that a couple can share meditative experience. Whether we are sitting contemplatively or dancing spontaneously to some inner rhythm, or even about some form of a vision quest, the results of shared prayer have often been powerful.

Sometimes what the mind cannot understand nor the heart encompass, the spirit finds a way to enlighten. Out of the depth of our own unconscious sanctuary an answer often emerges. Often it is a real temptation to take matters into our own hands and try to force a solution. Our society seems obsessed with instant solutions and immediate answers to our slightest problems. We have prescriptions ready to ward off just about any discomfort, paradox, and pain. Yet in spite of all these sometimes useless shortcuts, one still does well to remember the ancient way of the vision quest. The road by the river is basically an experimental one. Sometimes in the midst of an impasse in relationship there is nothing to do but to wait and see where the next bend of the river takes us; and it is often out of a space of quiet pondering or meditation that an answer spontaneously yields itself.

LIVED BY LIFE

Much is left to be said about how a woman relates to a man at this spiritual level in ordinary day-to-day events. Outside these moments of spiritual insight and deep inner wisdom, life goes on. We are not just divine creatures, we're also human. There will be moments when everything we aim for at the spiritual level seems to suddenly fall apart or to be just beyond our grasp. There will be times when all our insights and spiritual capacities fail us. As high as I've been from the ether of our two souls touching at certain points in our relationship, there have also been plenty of dark moments. These are the ups and downs of the partnerships we find ourselves in. Suffering and difficulty and the trials that accompany us through life are simply there to be an ongoing grist for the mill.

Yet when I am talking about ways a woman relates to a man at the spiritual level, I am talking about a quality in her being. I am not interested in a count of the actual times that she has been able to effect a spiritual presence in relationship to a man. I am talking about a general path she walks, her ability to touch into her own feminine essence, and the ways she can commune with the Spirit in her. If we are in touch with these keys to the deeper life within us, then we are naturally in communion with our spiritual feminine nature.

This feminine principle within us as women is not one which stems from any of the roles we assume; it is not because we are wife, mother, partner, caretaker, or lover; it does not describe our sex or how we do things. Neither does it describe what we do or say about our own religious beliefs to our mates. It is, moreover, a quality of being that the feminine nature reflects. Irene de Castillejo views a woman's relational nature as one which, among other things, can be "a mediator to man of his own creative inspirations, a channel whereby the riches of the unconscious can flow to him more easily than if she were not there. . . . to do this she must never lose contact with the living springs of the unconscious."[9] She says that as a woman nurtures and enlivens her own self by the inner work that she does, that she also nurtures and enlivens her partner as well. Because she travels this inner path to the wells of her own nature, she also has the power to take others to the same depths within themselves.

When a woman who is in touch with her self becomes a bridge for someone else, she is simply a pathway that spans from one point to another. "To do so is an attitude of mind. It is the readiness for relationship in whatever field, whether it be with God, another human being, a work of art, a blackbird's song, or with one's own masculine counterpart. It is the readiness of the feminine soul for the meeting with another, though that other may be her own creative spirit."[10] Should a woman cultivate this communion with her unconscious, with her own deeper self, she would understand something more of her inner nature and the potential power she holds.

Native American teacher Marilyn Youngbird says that women are the givers, "the nurturers of life." If this nature is *rightly* understood, and if the spiritual force within her is touched in reverence, then everything a woman touches can receive this life. When women are in communion with the inner soul, then that life flows out to all who need it. In terms of relationship to her mate or partner, the same is true; if a woman remains true to who she is and speaks from the ground of her own inner being, then the man can likewise receive his own truth more deeply. Grounded in her own wholeness and close to the earth of her own nature, she is both authentic and powerful. But it is not ego power she holds relationship together with, it is the power of surrender to the spirit of truth within her.

In the recognition that man does not live for himself alone even in his most individual and personal acts—not even in his relation to the one person in all the world he most loves—in this recognition the truly religious spirit is born. The most precious things of life do not belong to us personally. In our most intimate acts, our most secret moments, we are lived by life. Again and again we are reminded that in the daily contact with the one we love, our little personal egos must be surpassed; only so can we take our place in the stream of life and submit ourselves to that suprapersonal value which alone can give significance and dignity to the individual . . . [11]

When we allow ourselves to be "lived by life," we have come to the fullness of our strength; and it is from that place that we can turn and let go of ourselves. Authentic love does this. This story of a Jewish man and his family speaks poignantly of this kind of transcendent love:

Near the end of World War II, a man and his wife, his two sons, and his parents were incarcerated in a Nazi concentration camp. Everyone had to work daily, and when one could no longer work, that person was put to death. The man and his wife were concerned about his parents because they were old and daily they were growing weaker. Then one day, it happened. The old grandfather and his wife, unable to work any longer, were taken to the gas chamber. The family held one another and wept.

Time went on and the youngest son, David, became lame. Again the parents grew worried, fearful that the soldiers would take him too. Each night they all returned from their separate work assignments, anxiously looking for his return. One night the father came back, and unable to find his young son or his wife, ran about the camp asking for them; running and weeping he called for them. Then he saw his older son lying on the ground, sobbing. "Father," he said, "they came and took David. But he was unable to let go of us. He was afraid and began to call out for Mother. Then Mother took him in her arms and she said, 'No David, you won't be afraid. I will take your hand and

I will come with you.' " And the mother took hold of David's small hand and talked softly to him as they neared the gas chamber. When the war ended and the surviving prisoners in the camp were released, the older son and his father, along with only a small fragment of those who had entered the camp, returned home.

The goal of transpersonal love is to let go of oneself to the full experience of what life calls us to. Although most of us do not have such experiences of sacrifice to endure, it is the heart that knows itself securely enough that can risk dying to itself. This Jewish mother's heart moved spontaneously to give the full measure of herself to love. And regardless of what feat love calls us to, women who have begun the journey to the awakening of heart and soul will innately know what road to take when life asks its greatest questions.

9. Soul Making

The transpersonal force in a woman's life is a vital life-giving spring. Yet the crisis in Western spirituality is that most traditional religious forms obscure the spirit (and the feminine). The problem women face in attempting to adapt to a linear expression of faith is not new to this century. Historically most Western religious expression is based on an educational model. It is the experiential approach to the spiritual life, however, that invites true religious holism. Some women who follow a masculine program of religious expression seem to be able to transcend its limitations and come to a deeper awareness of spirit. But an increasing number of women (and men) have not found any authentic religious expression in these traditional containers.

If we engage in religious ritual without being awake to the significance of the ritual nor aware of the value of our direct participation in it, we lose the potency of the ritual—no matter how powerful the mediator is. If as Moslems we make our ritual washing of the feet and hands before prayer without consciousness of the sin we wish to cleanse, we are out of touch with the ritual. If as Catholics we make confession without the intention to change (but expecting the priest to expiate the sin instead), then we miss the power latent in the symbol of reconciliation. If as Protestants we look primarily to the minister to teach us about the subtleties of the Guest, then we miss the fire of direct experience, and God remains a belief system. In short, if we do not take responsibility for our own spiritual growth, we may be left holding onto no more than the door knocker of an inner Kingdom we have not personally experienced. It is only when we as women become actively present to our own spiritual life that significant personal change and transformation can happen.

We need to ask how we can genuinely access the spirit within us. We need to ask how we can remythologize religion in behalf of finding a true religious experience; how we can seek for the content of the soul rather than religious forms. Kabir says,

> The small ruby everyone wants had fallen out on the road
> Some think it is east of us, others west of us.
> Some say, "among primitive rocks," others,
> "in the deep waters."
> Kabir's instinct told him it was inside, and what it
> was worth,
> and he wrapped it up carefully in his heart cloth.[1]

The small ruby that lies on the road symbolizes the treasure of the spirit that many of us have lost. In many cases we have failed to develop the inner ritual of communion, the deeper relatedness that flows from the feminine side of the spirit. When we take the road that leads to religion, we will find something, but it will not be the ruby. Until we look for the treasures in the soul, we will not see God.

The feminine element of religious life has very little to do with its structures, rituals, or creeds, but comprises instead its whole inner content. It is not law but spirit; it is the contemplative and mystical counterpart to the masculine. Accordingly, throughout the history of religion, East or West, the mystics were and are those men and women who have endeavored to go past the mind and into the heart of religious experience. They are those who have gone beyond a rational approach to God and have transcended a legalistic interpretation of codes and rituals. They are the ones who, like the Sufi mystic Kabir, St. Francis of Assisi, and St. Theresa of Avila, have walked past the conventional and have plunged themselves into the heart of God whose spirit is so unpredictable. These men and women were in a deep sense the feminists of their time, because they separated from the strictly linear traditions of their faith and began to explore the depth of a more relational and consequently feminine approach to God. They are also the ones like Gandhi, Dorothy Day, and Mother Theresa of Calcutta, whose human works reflect what they know of the spirit. They are those whose acts of love and charity parallel how they personally experience the heart of God.

The feminine religious experience is to begin to see into the spiritual world with the eyes of the heart. It is to feel out our own unique inner needs and rhythms; to bring our authentic self before the Lord of life. A woman needs to rediscover the hidden language of her own feelings in the spiritual life, and to embrace more of the paradoxical side of her faith. Soul making has little to do with our understanding, our concepts, or with the dogmas that religion has created for some sense of direction. God is not just to be found in Scripture or in the words of holy books. These descriptions, as useful as they are, fail to say the whole truth about God to us; just as religion can do no more than open the door to the spiritual life. I am certain this more masculine sort of knowledge is essential to some people. But it is only a beginning. The deeper reality of who God is can only be experienced; God is flesh and must be lived out in each of us.

THE MANNEQUIN DREAM

A friend of mine recently related the following dream, which she had several years ago at the time of her own interior realization of a need to journey: *"I am in a church listening to a sermon on the power of the Spirit. It is being spoken by a pastor whom I can see understands the breadth of such a power; he is deeply inspirational, and his words fill me like a fire. Enraptured by the impact of the idea that God's love can actually empower us to transcend ourselves, I open my eyes to look around to see if others are also able to receive this important message; a message I feel their very lives depend upon. But to my horror the church is filled with mannequins. All of them are overdressed, just plied with clothing. Then I notice that I have on absolutely no clothes whatever. After the service we wait to walk out to shake the minister's hand. Finally able to greet him, I implore him to do something to wake these people up. They have to listen and to come around to life. I leave feeling that the whole matter is incredibly urgent."*

This woman was fortunate enough to be in touch with her interior life. She realized that she needed more than what was being offered in the context of a traditional religious process. Yet many women who are not in communion with their own inner soul, never awaken at all from their rigid, doll-like passivity, and the fire of spiritual awakening blows right over their heads. Like the mannequins in the dream, all nicely overdressed and unresponsive to the deeper wind of the spirit, there are women who populate religious traditions of all kinds but who have no sense of their own identity.

I find a number of ways in which women seem consistently blocked in an authentic expression of the feminine spirit. First, a great many women approach religion unconsciously. Some simply follow the cultural and historical religious script that's been handed down to them from their own families, going about the mechanics of "doing religion" just as their parents did. Or they follow a religious program in an unquestioning conformity to the law of the thing, and generally without any personal questing of their own. But it is not God they are bound to at all; it is the law which they have equated with God that binds them. Yet the woman who comes to God out of a need to serve the law is not coming out of love, but out of an unconscious seeking for approval and out of conformity to her traditions.

Generally, women tend to follow religious life in somewhat the same way they participate in the constellation of relationships. Thus a woman can repeat in her religious quest any or all of the patterns of human relationship we have discussed. A woman whose relationship to God is based on an unconscious projection reflects the same psychologically undifferentiated state as the Mermaid does toward men. Some women practice religious devotion as an investment toward self-esteem. In some cases a woman makes an unconscious bargain with the divine that insures her a sense of belonging, a feeling of safety among others who think like she does. It is as though her devotion, her good works, and her absolute conformity to the law will somehow ransom her from the unknown.

One woman, whose mother practiced her faith under such a contract, said, "*I used to think that I was more or less obliged to go to church, as though there were some unwritten contract in it. It was something my family always faithfully did, although I don't think our lives reflected much of the investment. Mother always insisted we sit in one particular place, as though the church would fall down if we didn't sit there. When services were over we'd go for coffee in the basement of the church and the parson's kids would have always gotten to the sweet rolls first. On the way home Mother invariably commented on what Mrs. Hall had on, and why it never seemed to match her shoes. After church we always had Sunday dinner precisely at two o'clock in the afternoon; and at two twenty Mother and Dad always had an argument about either the bills, or why my father shouldn't be so addicted to watching football games. I suppose I carried the whole thing on in my own life before I eventually saw how habitual and lifeless my rituals had actually become."*

Many women faithfully attend religious services in the same way this woman did for years. But at this level of awareness, God has not yet become a direct experience, and there is no deeper dialogue going on. When a woman is not awake and asking questions about her religious experience, she relates to the spiritual life unconsciously. She is without the self-knowledge she needs in order to make the descent to the inner woman. Consequently, many of us are without the divine madness that compels us to look beyond the programs and the words and to hunger for a real participation in the spirit. In any unconscious practice of religion, both programmatic structures and rituals are given priority over the simple act of soul making.

One of my Jewish friends once said, *"When I was a child I used to go with my parents every Friday night to temple because that's what we all did each week. To me as a child there was something special and mysterious that always happened on that night and I never questioned its rightness. There was a beauty and a holiness about it. My mother used to say she thought it was the glue that held us all together as a family. But somewhere around high school I began to feel the mystery had gone from service; as though its earlier magnetism had somehow gradually been reduced to words and rhetoric. At that point I had to begin to ask myself where I was going and what I wanted from the religious experience. I knew there was more than just this religious 'service' happening and I was determined to find it."*

THE ROLE OF PROJECTION

PROJECTION

Projection is nowhere happier than in a religious setting, where its works can be deceptively subtle. For some women the figure who may receive the most unconscious "attention" may be the head male in her religious setting. Whether he is minister, rabbi, or guru, he may not only receive a woman's negative projections, he may also play a variety of other roles. Often he may become the lost father, the spouse she has lacked, the son she never had, the authority figure she had issues with in the past. Many an unconscious relationship can and does get acted out in religious and spiritual settings. In some cases a woman may unconsciously project her need to be taken care of to the priest or minister; she may ask his advice about all manner of things, devote herself to him, or attend to him in "special" ways. She may feel an attraction towards him or be subtly seductive with him. At the very least she wants something back from him—affirmation, approval, to be special.

I have spoken to many women in such situations, and I have been there myself. A woman at this juncture of her life may awaken to find she has fallen in love with her guru or priest simply because he seems suddenly like the missing link in her life. In his robes, whatever color they are, he is something numinous and out of this world, magical and godlike. He represents her connection to the divine, and here he is in the flesh. He may represent everything extraordinary she's apparently never found in a man. Because her attraction to him must often be hidden and clandestine, in a way he may become even more exciting and desirable because he is "out of reach." Sometimes.

Although the head male authority is most often the target for these projections, others in the body may receive these unwanted feelings as well. It must not be forgotten that projection can go both ways. If the spiritual teacher is not clear about his own personal issues and has not looked at his relational needs, he may likewise put out unconscious (and sometimes conscious) messages that he wants these attentions himself. In some cases he too may act out the seductive role toward the women in his following—especially if he invites nurturing and caretaking, or is just plain lonely. Because the religious community must always play the role of the surrogate family, the individuals who enter that group are always going to come in with their own family ghosts. Whatever the issues of unfinished business were in the family of origin, they will all resurrect themselves in the larger body. Because these projections are both unconscious and subtle, they may go undetected at first. But the effect is always invalidating, because neither the one who makes the projection nor the one who has to carry it has any genuine freedom to be who they are.

A large part of what we do at the religious level is merely a repeat of our early childhood constellations. If our parental models have been ineffectual, abusive, or absent, we are also bound to project these same psychic contents upon our concept of God. If, for instance, a woman's father failed to be there for her in some way, she may project that same fear of abandonment upon God as father. If her father has been her adversary, she will be ambivalent toward a transpersonal father figure. To her God may be both desirable and unobtainable. Unconsciously, she may strive to please this cosmic father, but at the same time she may resent and distrust him. At best, her relationship to the divine will be clouded and insecure, and she will be prey to an innate sense of her own inferiority before a God she can never live up to.

One young woman, who was just beginning to work on her broken father-daughter trust, said, *"When I was about thirteen my stepfather molested me. It went on for about two years, until my mother found out and divorced him. He used to fondle me at first, but then later it got to be more. I was frightened and terribly guilty, but after a while I guess I went along with it; maybe I just gave in.*

"I've worked on this issue in therapy already, and I've let myself get into my rage—more deeply into my outrage at a person who would do that to a little girl. But now I want to work on why I seemed so passive at the time. More and more I'm becoming aware of how I've been passive not only toward others—men especially—but how I've carried that same passive feeling in relation to my experience of who God is. Maybe because I've always felt rather guilty about my relationship to my stepfather. That could be the reason I feel so insignificant before God, so afraid to do anything wrong. It's like a part of me wants to buy back the approval I lost when I was young; to gain it back by being obedient and conforming.

"The more I work on that, though, the more I struggle with myself. I mean, the more independent I feel like being, and the more willing to change this bind, the more scared I get that the moment I make a

mistake something terrible will happen. My frustration is that, intellec-
tually, I know that God is a God of love and not a punishing force, but
emotionally I can't believe it."

It is fairly common for women who have endured sexual
assaults (whether rape or incest) to feel unworthy, inferior, or
submissive to the men they serve, or alienated from God as
friend. More and more stories of sexual abuse are now being
heard, and we are seeing that even among religious groups
incest is not uncommon. The male, and the idea of a masculine
God thought of as "He," becomes an authority figure that must
be pleased, feared, sacrificed to, and served in ways that are
not wholesome. Another woman, who experienced sexual abuse
from her natural father, commented,

"I suppose in many ways God has felt unreal to me. I hoped he was
real, but another part of me didn't believe it. Since I've been a little
girl I have felt small and insignificant before men—or I've been angry
and removed. Since the time my father abused me, I have been unable
to trust in the absolute goodness of men the way some women seem to
do. A part of me is always on reserve; I never expect they're completely
trustworthy. In the same way the idea of God as father has always been
suspect to me. I'm either caught between feeling like I can't please him
enough or that I can't get far enough away from him; I am ambivalent
about whether or not to run towards him or to completely walk away.
Either way, I can't imagine he cares." The rage and mixed emotions
she felt toward the father who had betrayed her had become a
toxic chemistry that she projected on her concept of a divine
father. God was simply another man to mistrust.

The alcoholic parent is another prime contributor to feelings
of unworthiness, guilt, and wounded trust. As the adult child
of the alcoholic knows, the alcoholic family can model issues of
denial, an inability to be in touch with feelings, a basic distrust
of intimacy, and a strong need to overcompensate for the family
disease. All these issues restage themselves in the religious environment. *"For years I went to church faithfully. But I must have*
been half asleep. The sermons were never really much to speak of; the
program itself I never related to. The one saving grace was that the
choir was good and the music spoke to me in some ways. Still astound-
ing to me is that I went there for three whole years before I decided I
just couldn't take another one of this man's sermons! I suppose my kids

were happy in Sunday school classes; maybe it was a convenient church to go to because it was close by; maybe it was because I knew a lot of people there. But I was simply enduring this whole thing without really getting anything out of it for myself. After starting a women's support group last year it suddenly dawned on me that I was stuck. A pew casualty.

"Later, I realized that this innocuous pastor figure was sort of like my dad in a way—I responded to each of them in the same kind of way. That really woke me up! As a kid I never questioned my dad's drinking; I just lived with it. I adapted because that's what everybody else did. But then adapting got to be a way of life for me. I was definitely up for a change." Women who have been emotionally wounded as children will bring all of the same relational issues and defenses into the religious environment. They will be the eternal child—the Giver, the Pleaser, the Rescuer, the Endurer, and the Martyr—both before their concept of God and the male authority figures around them.

RELIGIOUS CARETAKERS

Unlike the saints and mystics, who seem to understand what real submission is about, some women relate to authority passively either because they are victims of abuse or daughters of parents with low self-esteem themselves. Similarly, many women I know in religious settings are subtly attached to a kind of martyr complex. In early Judeo-Christian history martyrdom was fairly common. Among the early writings of the church fathers, however, there was question and controversy about whether or not followers of the faith should actually seek it out as holy.

Nowadays, there are two distinctly different kinds of martyrdom: the kind that happens to us because we are defending the faith personally or politically, or the kind we assume voluntarily because of the acceptance of an inferior status. But most women I know who act out the martyr complex are not being called upon to defend the faith. They are taking up the role in unconscious ways. Their endless giving behaviors are not motivated from a healthy state, but flow from a neurotic sense of unworthiness. A woman who exercises healthy giving does not do so out of competitive striving or a need for approval; nor does she find satisfaction in criticism or gossip of others who don't think like she does. Her giving does not call attention to what she has done or how hard she has worked or how little she is appreciated.

One woman comments, *"I have a real problem saying 'no' in my parish. Whenever something comes up that needs doing, I seem to be the one who ends up doing it. Sometimes I take things on because I know I'm a good person for the job; but sometimes I take things on because I know I'm expected to. I grew up with this idea that being available and being a hard worker is what charity is all about. That living for God is like dying to myself."* Two things made me think that the giving this woman was engaged in was not authentic behavior for her. The first clue that something was amiss was her doctor's report of high blood pressure, and the second was a series of dreams in which she reported a highly repetitive theme. One of the dreams went like this: *"I am in one of the buildings of the church and fire breaks out. Out of nowhere it seems to take over everything. People are running to get buckets of water, to save furnishings and the like. I am trying to save an adolescent girl who is trapped and helpless."* The adolescent girl in the dream is this woman's own helpless victim within; the one who stands by and allows herself to be given away to others. The fire could certainly be her own unexpressed rage and resentment at the way she keeps submissively taking things on.

Many of us make the appearance of being good wives and mothers or strong supporters of religious community life, but this perpetual giving behavior can cancel out a woman's individuation process. Until we as women know ourselves and are genuinely able to know our own strengths and weaknesses, our continual acts of surrender are inevitably bound for disappointment. Because many of the caretaking women I know in religious settings are high in submissiveness and serving behaviors and low in self-esteem, it remains clear that the giving is often from personal need. It is my own bias that before we can understand what real selflessness actually means, we must look carefully at our issues of self-effacement. Otherwise, the giving becomes simply another burnt offering.

I don't know any women, no matter how sophisticated they are, who don't have at least some unconscious religious habits. No matter what level of consciousness we may be working with, most women I talk to are somewhat short on self-esteem, self-confidence, and a strong sense of inner direction. Many of us are still in need of healing the places in our early parenting where there was little validation for authenticity. This is why it's so necessary for most women to be careful about being seduced into roles, into blindly adopting religious principles that speak more of conformity than spiritual awakening. We simply cannot do these things productively without a firm sense of our own identity. Only when we build up the ego sufficiently and genuinely know who we are inside, can any of us afford to consider the greater acts of love and surrender that the great religions speak of. If we do any act unconsciously, we genuinely have to ask ourselves what our motives might be or what woundedness may need attention in the healing process.

THE RELIGIOUS ACHIEVER

An odd thing happens to most of us when we start to awaken from our unconscious states. Sometimes the more we mend and strengthen the ego and redeem ourselves, healing the wounds of the past and reconciling with our inner orphans, the more other sorts of orphans seem to appear for claiming. No sooner do we achieve an awakening at one level, than almost immediately there is another level to descend, another rung of the ladder inward to the self to climb down. One such orphan is the one I call the Religious Achiever.

One of the reasons some women in religious circles seem so wounded, in spite of their obvious accomplishments and abilities, is because few of us have really challenged our religious persona. We are, in many cases, still locked into a role or stereotype that parallels a kind of patriarchal thinking. I know several women who are bright, competent, definitely upwardly mobile in their own faith. They have made significant socio-religious changes within their own denominations and are awake to contemporary issues at many levels. They are involved in social justice, professional fields, peace initiatives; some have written books on feminist theology, helping and healing work, and contemplative life. Most of these women do not relate to God out of a collective sense of identity, nor as a parent to be feared and placated, but instead experience God as a friend. Their own religious process, in other words, stands on firmer ground and they have reached some degree of independence and self-direction.

The good news is that many of these women who enter the religious quest have attained some degree of personal and social awareness. The work they have done in many cases has coopted a broader level of consciousness. The bad news, however, is that in order to be able to be effective within the context of a well-entrenched patriarchy, they have sometimes sacrificed the authentic feminine.

One of my clients in her early forties, a devout Catholic in pastoral care work, walked into my office one day and said, *"Well, my life is great. Work is good, my kids are all staying out of trouble, Stan and I are enjoying ourselves. Everything outwardly seems to be running smoothly, but my body is having fits. For a little over a month now I've been experiencing some awful bouts with something like bursitis. I've been to the doctor but the tests are not exactly confirming that that's what it is. There's an inflammation of sorts but the doctor feels reluctant to diagnose it as bursitis. He gave me some muscle relaxants and told me to go home and learn how to relax. He said that I might try some stress reduction, but the whole thing is a bit of a puzzle."*

After a few weeks we began to get closer to the problem of her pain. The more we worked directly on her shoulder, doing both acupressure and process work, the more both of us began to sense that her shoulder seemed merely a symptom for some deeper problem brewing. During one bodywork session she said, *"I don't know what's going on, but the more you touch that spot on my shoulder the madder I get. Just a moment ago I wanted to punch you. But I know it's not you I'd like to hit. I just felt this rising anger coming out of nowhere. I don't get it."* I asked her whose face came to mind when she felt like punching me. After reflecting for some time she said, *"I see a stern old man in a white collar. A priest of some kind. But I don't recognize him."* As she got more deeply into the image I asked her if she could talk to him. *"Ask him what he wants from you,"* I suggested.

She was silent for a while. I noticed her face tighten and her brow began to wrinkle. "What's happening?" I asked.

"I find it hard to want to talk to him, his face is so stern and disapproving. It's like he's some old task master from my early childhood. He looks like he has a perpetual frown across his face; like he wants me to be perfect. I can just hear him saying, like Scrooge, 'Do a little more. You're not living up to your promise. You could be doing much more.' "

"What promise?" I asked.

"When I was a child in school, one of my confessors made me promise to be a good girl. I told him I had cheated on a spelling test. After he forgave me he told me I should try to be perfect, as perfect as my father in heaven. He said I would get to heaven if I could live up to that promise. My dad had died when I was young, and I thought he meant that if I wanted to see my father again that I'd have to be perfect, so I promised."

I said, taking the old man's part, *"Yes, you need to do much more then. Much much more. What you have accomplished is not enough, my child. It never has been, and never will be. There must be a few more things you need to accomplish today. Put off your rest just a little longer. Build up this ego thing a little more."*

"That's just about right," she said.

"Of course, it's right," I said. *"I'm always right. And never mind that pain in your shoulder either; it's only a little distraction from the evil one to keep you from doing all you can do. Just ignore it. Rise above it. Rebuke it. Now quit complaining and get back to work. Here's your list."*

She started to laugh. She laughed and laughed and then burst into tears and then came a deluge of furious rebuttals, most of which is better left out of print. The best part of her session, and certainly the most healing, was her acknowledgment of her anger toward the old man who had clearly, in the course of her religious education, gotten under her skin. Compelled by her own "should" behaviors and unable to let her anger out, this Scrooge figure had over the years lodged himself directly into her shoulder. As soon as she began to acquaint herself with the old man she had internalized and been so faithful to (but so furious with), she could give her anger some direction other than bottling it up in her arm.

Another woman, who seemed to experience a similar incongruence in her life, said, *"Actually, everything's fine with me. But I am having nightmares, repetitive ones, and since I know a little of dreams I think something's up. But I don't know what. Most of the dreams involve some sort of chase, and the frightening part is that I seem unable to run. I'm being attacked and I can't run away. I always wake up in a cold sweat."* This woman, active in her congregation, and considered to be an excellent Scripture teacher and a pillar in her church, was having nightmares because something was out of balance. Well known for her teaching capacity and talent as a public speaker, she was very much in demand. Her one apparent complaint was that she was on the road too much and it was interfering with her interior life. One common dream scenario was the following: *"I am trying to run away from a man who is trying to kill me. His attacks seem to be aimed at my face. In one sequence I am trying to run faster to get away, but I can't seem to run except in heavy, cumbersome steps. When I turn around to look at him I notice he is gaining on me quickly. Panicked, I glance down at my feet and notice I have on a pair of heavy men's boots which are slowing me down. In my arms I hold a small baby girl whom I am trying to protect. Eventually, I pull off the boots and am able to run away."*

In spite of the fact that this woman was highly visible and successful at what she did, something in her spirit was objecting. The appearance of the small baby in this dream is most likely the emergence of this woman's own spiritual life. Because she was just beginning to turn the corner of her busy life and get more deeply into her own interior journey, something of her still emerging soul life needed more care. Working on the dream further, she said, *"In several of these dreams it's always a dark sinister man that's chasing after me. But I can't run away because either I am stuck in some sort of mud or I am trying to run in heavy men's shoes. It's almost as though this masculine thing in me is so entrenched that it literally attacks the vulnerable side of me. Like there's a brand new baby inside, but there's also this relentless attacking side that won't leave me alone. I both attack myself and then I can't run away."*

Performance-oriented people are often driven by a need to excel in order to feel good about themselves. Often, no matter how outwardly together we may seem, some of us still feel an inner lack of confidence. As successful as some of us may be, we can still be caught up in a need to prove ourselves. Likewise, many women either consciously or unconsciously entertain a chronic sense of unworthiness. In this case the dreamer's lack of personal self-esteem has made her vulnerable to the attacks of this man. Because his attacks were aimed at her face, this tells me she may feel her reputation is at stake if she fails to keep up with her own demands for excellence. The social and professional role she plays somehow assures her some safety because it protects her from "losing face." This dreamer's task is to get out of these men's shoes which are neither designed for running or for nourishing her feminine spirit.

Unless we awaken more fully to the ways that we play out religious performance games that are devised by the masculine side of our nature, we may be in danger of harming the spirit within us. At the very least it will be constrained. When I was stuck in my own achieving phase, I had the following dream: *I am in a church filled with women. We have formed a large circle and are beginning a spontaneous experience of worship. The atmosphere is electric and powerful. Suddenly, a young priest enters and begins to orchestrate the service. He seems to intrude upon the spontaneity of the group with his own agenda. Although there is a joyful anticipation of this experience, the atmosphere begins to feel a little constipated. Soon afterward the women begin leaving the group, and I begin to mourn their loss, as though a part of me is missing. I begin to watch this fellow continue with his orchestrations. And the more I watch, the less I am directly able to participate in the actual ritual itself. It is as though what I had initially been able to receive on my own spiritually (by watching my own inner signals, needs, and transformations) he is now attempting to receive and transfer to me. I awaken furious with this man, and try to ponder about how I might be doing this sort of thing to myself.*

The sacred circle of worship, an ancient symbol of unity and wholeness in both myth and practice, represents a spiritual arena in which the feminine is in full play. If women are attuned to their inner life and are in communion with themselves and God within, profound transformations can occur. Yet in the dream, as often happens in real life, a mediator enters, and the full expression of the spirit is dampened. Sometimes the mediator is actually the man in robes, the minister or rabbi who endlessly tries to orchestrate the spirit. He is the man to whom we give over the power of mediation. Sometimes he is an inner figure like Herr Captain, the male side of our psyche who drives us toward performance and perfectionism. Yet this intrusion onto the holy ground of the soul continues to happen either when women fail to be awake to the potential of their own spiritual autonomy, or when they themselves are striving too much in the realm of ego work.

BEYOND SACRED

If women are going to venture inward past the old identities and scripts of the past into a fuller communion with soul and into a place of silence, the road is bound to get increasingly narrow. For most of us to venture past the pretence of who we are as spiritual creatures, we must face a lot more emotional healing. The more honest we become, the more we have to admit that prioritizing agendas and valuing performance in our religious life (no matter what our religious orientation), has not been without an ulterior motive. Many of these erstwhile religious activities have long seemed to be a cover up for the fact that many of us simply haven't done much inner work at all. In fact, many of us may have been afraid to get into these waters for fear of what profane or untoward aspect of ourselves we may find there.

Some of the most talented women I know—good at what they do and brilliant as scholars and teachers, effective as pastors and health-care professionals, active as both lay workers and clergy—seem the most invested in a strong religious persona. Many of us engaged in a spiritual quest often downplay our own emotions, have difficulty with intimate relationships, run from any sort of confrontation, and are blatantly uncomfortable expressing feelings. Smoothing over distresses, silently withdrawing from any apparent conflict, and often smiling in the midst of some chaos or hurt, many women unconsciously program themselves into emotional denial. Sometimes quick to fix problems, forgive wrongs, cover over unpleasantness, and quote religious platitudes, many of us often either hide in convention or underneath a mask. However, the feminine nature, when it's working correctly, is innately relational.

Yet whenever one honors a preoccupation with a religious

ideology that masks feeling and insists on a stiff upper lip, there is no relationship, no sensitivity toward real communion. Whenever women on a spiritual quest serve a masculine convention that loves control and "prudence" over a good old-fashioned heart-to-heart response between two or more people, we are again in danger of counterfeiting the feminine. When women of any faith hide in the more respectable sacristies of the mind and in the safety of a religious script, many of us do so because we are afraid to face the real woman within.

When I began to level with myself some years back about the false sides of my own religious persona, I found myself out of balance in a number of ways. I found that although I could meditate up a storm, often seemed particularly sensitive to the spirit, and might be in tune with certain spiritual gifts, certain things stayed the same in spite of these cosmic feats. I could still lose my temper just as quickly, slay someone with my tongue without remorse, or pass some quick judgment on unsuspecting bystanders. I could doubt myself, fear the unknown, hide out in a pleasant smile while masking some hurt or anger; I could still dislike and criticize myself and others for making mistakes. Although I displayed these little glitches only in my least-guarded moments or during particularly stressful times, I knew they were there waiting for some attention. In short, there were plenty of loose ends.

I knew also that in many places I was protected against facing these imperfections. In particular, I found myself often preferring to coast along comfortably with others who shared similar interests. I found that I was very dependent on others to be bridges for my self-esteem. I needed to be needed in the ministries in which I was engaged. I felt comforted by the fact that there were others who thought like I did, felt like I did, and padded my basic fear of facing God alone. Some sort of religious or spiritual community had always been there for me, and I never found myself very far from it. Community was a nest for me, an extended family, a refuge. But in some ways I also buried myself in it and hid from my shadows. Another favorite place to hide out from the need to get into my own inner work was in my agenda; busy with a multiplicity of things and people, I likewise managed to cover my own vague spaces

by my involvement in the needs and problems I found in others—a favorite smokescreen for many people in any sort of
ministry work.

For many of us, to turn and face our own silence means that
we will be faced with the wounds of our past; it means we will
be staring directly into our own excesses and neediness. It
means what we have relied upon from the group as security
and protection may now have to be set aside for a deeper
challenge. Sometimes, too, it is not the group or our activities
that seem to cover the dark side, it is simply a well-educated
and long-established line of defenses. Attitudes that we are too
busy, that the inner life is too demanding, or that it's someone
else's turn to change and not our own are certainly all effective
postponements.

The fear of actually seeing our own less-than-sacred side is a
major block among religious anywhere. The thought of pursuing an inward passage (one which interior silence amplifies) is
generally always a frightening one. But we simply cannot venture into the spiritual world without owning our dark side and
facing our incompletions as women. It is precisely this inner
work that is essential to soul making. No desert, no oasis.

Until we discover a need to shed ourselves of all of our
excesses, to strip down to what is unsuccessful, to face our
needs and explore our dependencies, we have not become fully
conscious. This is the idea of the desert, the place we go not
only to gain the vision of God, but to see our own frailties as
well. The spirituality of the Christian Desert Fathers, and the
Native Americans of the Southwst, is one which invites the
pilgrim into the bare bones of her own self; to be in the desert
is to meet the great interior silence that one needs in order to
be able to come to terms with one's weaknesses and illusions.
The desert stands as a symbol for meeting the essential self.
Here there are no usual conveniences or comforts, no distrac-
tions, no wedges between oneself and one's soul. It is essentially
a place where one becomes empty before the truth and must
reckon with the false self, to search out the places of one's own
interior desert.

Once, on a week-long silent retreat, I picked up a story about
the life of Gandhi which had a profound impact on me. The

story seemed to pierce something inside of me which I had been neglecting but needed to be reminded of. The story goes like this:

One evening at the Sevagram ashram hundreds of people had gathered for the nightly prayer meeting. The sun was about to set and it was the time when snakes begin to come out after the fierce heat of the Indian day. This evening a cobra was seen gliding toward the gathering. A cobra's bite is swift and deadly, and in the villages of India, where medical help is usually far away, such a snake strikes terror into everyone. A ripple of panic began to spread through the crowd, and there was danger that someone might be trampled if the terror spread. But Gandhi quietly showed a sign not to move.

Gandhi was seated on the platform. He wore only his dhoti or loincloth; legs, chest, and arms were bare. While the crowd held its breath and watched, the cobra made its way straight for Gandhi and slowly began to crawl up over his thighs.

There was a long moment of silence in which no one dared to move or make a sound. Gandhi must have been repeating his mantram, Rama, Rama, Rama. Even the cobra lost all traces of fear. In its own way it must have sensed it was in the presence of someone who would never cause it suffering. Slowly, quietly, it crawled away, leaving everyone unharmed.[2]

I wept when I read this story. I would have been terrified if this snake had crawled up on me. Most likely I would have jumped, leapt six feet up into the air, and been bitten by one equally terrified snake. When I collected myself I began to ponder the incident and why it had had such a powerful impact on me. On the other hand, I thought to myself, suppose I hadn't jumped? Suppose I might have pulled this thing off? After all, Gandhi did it, children do it, I can do it. But inside, most likely I would have been racing with fear, pumping up plenty of adrenaline. I'd have been salivating, needing to swallow or blink, or breathing like I had just run the fifty-yard dash. So even if I were able to reason with myself, the snake might sense my inner terror. A sudden insight hit me like a ton of bricks: If that had been me instead of Mahatma, I'd have been a dead woman.

I took some time to imagine what that black snake might represent within me that, metaphorically at least, I might have split off or separated from. It simply stood for at least a dozen ways in which I am still alienated from myself, not connected to my own wholeness. The more I played with the idea of giving this serpent a voice, the more it spoke out my fears and insecurities, my fantasies of rejection, disapproval, failure, my lack of feeling worthy. It spoke out my whole shadow and my personal evil which I have not yet come to terms with. It became anger, judgment, criticism, vindictiveness, self-righteousness, fear of sexuality. It became the tax collector, the client I dread seeing most, the guy who stole my hubcaps I haven't forgiven, all the people who are authority figures for me. The serpent is my own shadow side. The serpent also seemed to represent my whole instinctual, feeling side.

This story caused me to become aware of how alienated I am from my deepest self, how far I am from my inner soul. What was so remarkable about Gandhi sitting there calmly before the cobra was that he felt unafraid because he was at peace with himself; because he felt somehow connected to the serpent and did not separate himself from it. In spite of the obvious danger to himself, he stayed connected with his inner feeling of prayer; he was one with the cobra.

In the same way, children are rarely bitten by rattlesnakes. The snakes know that children mean them no harm. There have been several accounts of children playing with these creatures and not being bitten. They touch the serpent with a reverence, with an innocent curiosity of play, and the snake knows it. The snake knows the child is not to be feared. In assuming this childlike at-oneness with the snake, Gandhi was left unharmed. In communion with his own soul and the spirit that brought inner peace, he made no separation between himself and this snake.

Gandhi was always a model of holism for me. But his great political and social reforms, unparalleled in this century, emerged not so much as a result of his political genius, but because of the nature of his spiritual life. Gandhi, like Jesus, lived as he taught, and his theories became his practice. Whether he was at conference with political heads of state, walking among the Harijans, spinning cotton, or at prayer, Gandhi was seldom separate from his inner soul. Over and over again in the spiritual life, the universe patiently wants to remind us that the divine and the human go hand in hand.

I continued to reflect on the image of the snake for some days afterward, and came across another story of a different kind of spirituality from Thomas Merton's book *The Wisdom of the Desert:*

Abbot John said: A monk must be like a man who, sitting under a tree, looks up and perceives all kinds of snakes and wild beasts running at him. Since he cannot fight them all, he climbs the tree and gets away from them. The monk, at all times, should do the same. When evil thoughts are aroused by the enemy, he should fly, by prayer, to the Lord, and he will be saved.[3]

The lesson of this fourth-century desert spirituality stood somehow in bold contrast to the reality of the truth that was struggling to emerge in me. It is true that as children we are educated to flee evil; to take flight from it and to ascend into a higher place. In many cases following that advice has brought us through certain trials unharmed. It is also true that this negation of evil and running up a tree is a rather linear way to deal with the problem of evil or danger. It is simply avoided and cut out of our lives. Yet when we run from the snakes, we may be running from an opportunity to face something vital but frightening within us. This act of going away from what is unseemly or scary is essentially an act of separation.

Feminine spirituality, it would seem to me, is centered upon the act of merging, of going towards, of entering into; it is an act of taking in, of receiving the thing and sitting with it. From the feminine side of the spirit one would perhaps be willing to accept the strange appearance of the snake as some sort of task. It struck me that the feminine spirit, so present to children and to people like Gandhi, is a manifestation of the mysteries in life that will not gestate until we provide them a womb. In feminine spirituality the paradox is simply held patiently in the dark until the light comes again. So one prays and remembers God, but one does not always climb trees.

INTEGRATING THE SHADOW IN THE SPIRITUAL LIFE

Because of my work with women who have some investment in the spiritual life, I venture to think that it is precisely this fear of our own dark side that sends most women into a panic.

Self-esteem seems consistently low among many of us, and ultimately it is a major place where healing work needs to be focused. I am convinced that one reason self-esteem is so low among many women on a spiritual path is because we have been wounded deeply where we are most vulnerable, at the level of our sexuality. This is a primary reason why so many women remain stuck in the orderly harbor of the intellect and are not healed emotionally. Our work of wholism is not only to mend the split between heart and mind, but also to look squarely at the great chasm that spans flesh and spirit.

It is this earth element in women that is so important to retrieve and integrate if there is to be any healing of the feminine. The metaphor of the feminine force in mythology is commonly referred to as earth and flesh. The masculine nature, on the other hand, has been symbolized by the sky, which is spirit. During a visit to Alaska recently I fell in love with the colorful, intricate beadwork done by the Inuit artisans there. In one of the museums where several traditional Inuit costumes were preserved was an ancient poem describing the different symbols that adorn men and women's leathers. The poem says,

> Ornament is symbol
> Symbol is speech
> On the men's clothing, symbols speaking
> Of the sky, the sun and stars
> On the women's clothing, symbols speaking
> Of the earth, of the rolling living plains.

But in the West we resist the wedding of flesh and spirit, of earth and sky. Women in most religious settings disdain their earthiness. Frequently, the "ideal" woman as expounded by most religious traditions is not earthy at all. She is often equated with the virtues of meekness, mildness, chastity, purity, and obedience. This is the woman that many men revere and put on a pedestal, but it is not a real woman, because a real woman is also flesh and blood and she is in communion with the earth in her being. She is in touch with her feelings, her instincts, and her sexuality, with the rolling plains of her soul.

Since the West sees man as the dominant sex, and our theology has been basically masculine, it is not surprising that woman's religious esteem has suffered. It is not surprising that many women in religious life tend to ignore the fact of their sexuality, splitting off from the instinctual side of their nature altogether. Among many women there is either an overt or subtle identification with masculine spirituality, and herein lies the distortion of the feminine spirit. In the male exhortation to "rise above" and to "transcend" the flesh, women are subtly alienated from the Kingdom because women *are* earth and flesh. The bottom line is that in order to make it in the religious world, a woman has to conform to a program of transcendence; she should avoid the flesh and the earth and strive to remain in the spirit, with her head in the clouds and her body forgotten. Further, in most traditional religious settings, the qualities and elements of the earth, long-time symbols of the feminine related to feelings, instincts, and sexuality, go underground. According to traditional Western spirituality, salvation seems to lie in the head. And that which is nature and earth and flesh in a woman must consequently become shadow.

The shadow characterizes whatever we have consciously repressed. Some interesting characters turn up in the dreams of women who are alienated from themselves at the emotional and sexual levels. Since the religious persona is often portrayed as in control, obedient, kind, and giving, the shadow is often just the opposite. The shadow figure for most of us on the spiritual path (I include myself here) is often the woman in rags, the bag lady on the streets, the harlot or seductress who is wildly anti-Victorian in her dream scenarios. For those women who have the courage to face their dreams in their religious questing, it is the sexual side which is the most denied and split off from. Most of us have overachieved in the masculine side of religious life and have completely turned Eve out onto the dark streets of our own repressions. Redemption, however, calls for the full healing and integration of our sexuality. This raises the question of how a woman can begin to remythologize her sexual identity as a woman. How can she begin to respect her earthy womanhood as well as her spiritual womanhood?

Perhaps one of the most prevalent biblical myths responsible for the attitude that women are an inferior sex and should be thus subject to men is the myth of Adam and Eve.

"Eve—woman—because she incarnates inferior energies, becomes a stereotypical source of evil. The church fathers propagate a similar mythology: 'Women, do you not know that you are Eve? You are the devil's gateway . . . how easily you destroyed man, the image of God.' " In these and other church statements, systematized church law claimed that woman was not equal to man and not made in God's image.[4]

The debate about the validity of the story of Adam and Eve and the subjugation of women has raged in the church for centuries and continues to cause real confusion for women in the church today. However, whether or not the story of Adam and Eve is historical fact or Levite fiction is not the point I want to address here. It is the impression it has made on the status of women in the church that I want to speak to.

St. John Chrysostom bore the same indelible stamp of disapproval of the feminine when he wrote, "The woman taught once and ruined everything. On this account . . . let her not teach."[5] And St. Clement denied that women should "pleasure themselves" with health-building sports; instead they would do well to perform more domestic things like cooking, weaving, and spinning.[6] And last but not least, another early church father, Ambrose, says the following: "She who does not believe is a woman and should be designated by the same of her sex, whereas she who believes progresses to perfect manhood, to the measure of the adulthood of Christ."[7]

By nature of the fact that a woman was not a man, according to early church patristics, she could find salvation only by embracing all that which was male. This meant that she had to disavow her "inferior" feminine nature in order to become acceptable. In other words, to redeem herself meant that she had to take on the nature of the masculine, to become as a man. And because God was described predominantly in terms of the male sex, as "father," "son," and "he," woman's natural identity automatically fell out of sync. In a much more divergent way than the male, the woman was automatically different from God because she did not share in the same image. Woman in this sense is essentially alienated from her own inherent nature since her "wholeness" from a masculine perspective was only won providing she aspire to progress "to perfect manhood."

In traditional church theology, if Eve is equated with flesh and flesh is equated with original sin and man's ultimate down-fall, then it is no small wonder that flesh and spirit have long since parted company. Historically, woman has internalized the male myths that both consciously and unconsciously portray her as "temptress," as inferior, as different than a male God; as lacking in completion because she is not whole without a man. Because we have unthinkingly accepted our likeness to Eve, coupled with a masculine theology that fears a more primitive identification with the flesh, many religious women today are still wary of their own feminine nature. The duality of the split between male and female, mind and heart, spirit and flesh, has continued to alienate men and women over the centuries.

REDEEMING EVE

If women strive toward real consciousness and understand the deep feminine mysteries inherent in their own nature, there will be no cause to embrace themselves as second to men. There will be no need to be passive, submissive, to silently accept such a status quo. The more a woman genuinely opens herself to a real relationship to God, the more she will trust in her own innate goodness. The more she embraces her whole self and honestly seeks to be her own authority about her spiritual needs as a woman, the less she will need to feel inferior to men. She will know that there is really no "divine proof" that man must hold the authority over woman. Devoid of the myth of Eve, which has always run counter to her spirit, she is able to break the idea that there is something basically inferior about her sex and likewise her sexuality, her flesh.

> Eve, you are woman, I am woman, I am you
> I am the seedbed, the womb, the mother nourisher,
> the lover. This inner nature of mine
> dreams that I will awaken and find her out
> And when I know Her, I will know Him
> And when I know Him, I will know the One.
> And we will not sleep, but awaken
> No longer meeting as enemies
> This flesh of mine and I
> Coming to greet one another at last

All that with me that is Earth and Sky
Father and Mother, Male and Female,
Flesh and Spirit, You and I
Waiting to make the new canticle of Creation.

Women who are seeking a more authentic feminine are those who have come well along the road of their own autonomy and integration. For them there are no man-made "ideals" because they are true to themselves as individuals who uphold the authentic feminine. They are virgin in the sense that they adhere to the ancient meaning of virginity, "she who is one-in-herself." Helen Luke reports that "Philo of Alexandria said that when a virgin lay with a man she became a woman, but when God began to have intercourse with the soul, she who was a woman became a virgin again." The idea of virgin to Luke does not imply a woman who has not had intercourse, but speaks of the woman who is emotionally mature, who is in touch with her feelings and instincts; one who has found herself consciously.[8]

Healing the whole self is essentially a journey to reclaim both our psychological and spiritual wholeness. To be one-in-herself a woman must have begun to deal with the emotional bondage that holds her from expressing her authenticity as an individual and as a woman. Before we can come fully into the realm of soul we must acknowledge and work with the broken aspects of our personal life. If we experience poor self-image, a sense of inferiority, a fear of saying our feelings, or dependence on others for meaning, then we must work through all these incompletions. Whether we find ourselves the victim without any sense of assertiveness or the aggressor who gains esteem through competition, power struggles, and a will to succeed, our woundedness will continually bind us to inauthenticity. Whether we carry an unconscious process with our mother or father and are still caught behind the closed doors of our childhood, the task remains the same: to move beyond our parental psyche. Wherever Eve is most wounded in us, and feminine self-esteem lies unredeemed in our own inner attitudes, still in emotional bondage or still stereotyped by masks and roles, so will the spirit be in bondage.

As oppressive as the patriarchy has been, it remains part of our task as women on a healing journey to heal not only the feminine self, but also to heal and restore the wounded inner masculine self. This work is both an inner and an outer task. Outwardly, it means that we renounce the false masculine stereotypes we have swallowed, the status quo we have chased after, the corporate male values that have misled us. If these patriarchal foundations have wounded the feminine nature within us, then we must make more authentic ones. If we have strayed too far into the linear world and find no consolation in an overly rational approach to life, then we must seek out the healthier aspects of the masculine which are an anchor for us. The masculine, after all, is never an enemy until we allow it to either oppress or drive us in imbalanced ways.

Inwardly, it means we find the authentic male self within; that we put aside ways in which we have idealized those values or the men who uphold them. I know some women, for instance, who idolize priests, gurus, doctors, movie heroes, and just plain men, period; women who are still locked in the search for a father-lover. Healing at this level means that the quest for the hero power must move inside—to the place where a woman can genuinely find her own power, her own voice, her own beauty of and by itself. For many women, as the deep feminine is restored, there is often a more harmonious blend of these two polar energies and the masculine is freed to be the hero who complements and strengthens, rather than a force that divides and conquers.

Ultimately, too, spiritually questing women who have been hurt by an abusive or emotionally distant father, or by a significant man in their lives, are going to have to deal both with their anger toward men and with their anger toward being woman. Women who have been hurt by men or by some aspect of the patriarchy often feel a deep resentment. Such a woman may feel a need to justify herself, to chase after achievements, and to hunger for vindication. She may unconsciously develop some of the very same traits towards others that have wounded her in the first place. Undeniably, there is something to prove when one's self-esteem has been wounded. Yet if the work of justifying or proving oneself goes on too long, then the deeper nature of the feminine is invaded by a power imbalance; and instead of healthy reconciliation, a subtle vengeance may be at work. Yet the healing process asks us to embrace the shadow both in ourselves and in the men we disdain. Eventually we must begin to forgive these betrayals.

For a long time, when I was processing my own divorce from the patriarchy, from my father, from the masculine values which I had unconsciously adopted, I was angry. Sometimes petulant in my assertiveness, or at the least distant and critical of anything remotely masculine, I wanted no closeness or help from my partner, my male friends, from authority figures. I raged at all of them alike, either covertly or right up front. I and everyone else around me endured a period of fireworks as I moved through my wounds toward independence. Combining that with some historical hurts from the patriarchy, the institutions in my life, from the cold rationale of scientific technology which I saw as another aspect of the negative masculine, I was fairly volatile for some months. The healing for me began to happen when I could articulate and express the anger and resentment I felt; when I no longer repressed my feelings but allowed them to open and course through me. It happened when I could begin to feel my own impasses around control and performance; when I could level with myself about how I lived more ideals than flesh. Healing moved in me when I began to know which of my strengths and abilities were spawned out of defenses and which were a genuine accessing of internal energies. Reconciliation happened when I realized my brothers were just as hurt as I was in some ways, and just as confused about their own masculinity as I was about the feminine.

Once during a women's workshop a group of us spontaneously began to sing an impromptu blessing on all the men in our lives. Crying out a spontaneous song of prayer for the men of all countries, we called out a blessing on political leaders, on the nations in conflict, on the men who control atomic weapons, on the Pentagon, the President, the Soviets, the Shi-ites, on the men who have forgotten love and soul; and on all the men in our lives who have made no "garment of brightness." In the group there were women from different religions, different nations, and clearly different political persuasions. But in this prayer for unity among the nations, we were as one woman lamenting for the loss of her child. That experience clearly enabled me to feel how closely paralleled are both states of wounded masculine and feminine; how much we all need songs of forgiveness.

One of the major tasks for women who wish to pursue some sense of religious practice is to establish a genuine connectedness between themselves and God. Women must learn to relate to soul, to penetrate the endless forms and rituals we practice until we come all the way into our own sacred ground. But the sanctuary is always inside. The spiritual life is seldom anything we can receive through a mediator. Religion is transmitted in this way, it is true, but not spirit. Spirit is an energy which never conforms to ritual, to hierarchy, to conventional procedure. It is a wild wind that alights within those souls who are spiritually hungry for direct contact with God, and who are willing to be attentive to the subtleties of the Guest.

10. May All Your Roads Meet

A CELEBRATION OF ALIVENESS

A chorus line in the play *Zorba the Greek* left a lasting impression on me: "Life is what you do 'til the moment you die." As I sat watching Anthony Quinn's delightful portrayal of Zorba, I felt both exhilarated and sad. It struck me that there were a number of ways I seemed afraid to risk living my life fully; ways I still seemed on hold. Of course, I am aware I am not alone in this dilemma. Without the full commitment to life that is required of the lover, most of us are afraid of the unbridled passion of someone like Zorba. We laugh at his honest indecencies and his bravado delights us on stage; it's always nice to know someone else is passionate, gutsy, excruciatingly honest, and filled with the fire of a life uncompromised.

Another moment in the play is equally provocative. The young man whom Zorba has befriended has experienced a tragedy in his life. Unlike Zorba, he seems afraid of life. When the young widow he loves is murdered by a jealous mob of angry men from the village, he becomes frozen with fear and can only watch from the sidelines. In the final hour he has no courage to save her. Having failed himself and lost everything, he is ashamed and grieving. But in the last moment before his parting with the old man, he suddenly breaks free of himself and cries out, "Zorba! Teach me to dance!"

When we begin to touch our own inner springs and know who we are, when the healing begins, then the passionate heart for life begins to awaken and stir. The more we can break free, the more the heart can be healed. The shadow the young man carried in the play was fear. He was accomplished in a worldly sense and was adept with his mind. But he failed momentarily in his heart, when the darkness of his own fear kept him back from the full power of his manhood.

The power for transformation of the shadow side lies in

embracing it, loving it. The more we experience this transformation, the more authentic our lives will become. It doesn't matter how incomplete our past has been, what abuse or neglect we have experienced, or how powerful our shadow or unconscious our behaviors. When we fully accept and embrace our brokenness, then we can turn to work on our wholeness. In spite of our personal or relational tragedy, we can choose to say to God, "Teach me to dance!" Our awakening lies in the choice.

To choose the dance over the tragedy of our lives is to risk abandoning ourselves to a fuller measure of life. Soul making is a celebration of aliveness; and that's the transcendent call we hear when we begin to look for the empowerment that comes out of our struggles and for the kernel of truth that waits to grow from the trials we have endured. It is a life lived in passionate response to itself and to the soul within.

The dance itself is a powerful vehicle of holism in behalf of the actual celebration of our aliveness. The ritual of the dance is a movement of religious devotion that invites our whole being to move, not just our head. When we are finally involved in a more conscious relationship with God, our heart and body have to get into the rhythm of the music. When we enter the inner gates, and have come into the presence of God, we are being asked to *feel* the spirit, not just to 'know' about it. And sometimes allowing feeling may mean moving to accommodate that feeling. Francis of Assisi knew the powerful releasing and receiving aspects of the dance, and practiced it frequently as a part of his worship experience. The Indian Bhakti poet Mirabi often danced her recitation of praise, bringing the devotions of her body into resonance with her religious poems.

I have two Hasidic Jewish friends who are therapists. They often begin their therapeutic workshop with singing and dancing. Sometimes a whole room full of strangers dances together, and by the end of the dance we are without our little masks and pretences and fears. In the dance we have become one people, because in the celebration of the movement we have forgotten our differences.

Dancing has been a part of the celebration of the spirit for centuries. David dancing into the gates of Jerusalem when the Ark of the Covenant was returned to the city is another example of the passionate expression of the heart. David was so joyful, he danced in his skivvies right through the streets. In his heart he was responding to some prompting of the wind in his own spirit, and he resonated outwardly by dancing. Giving in to the ecstasy he felt before God, he simply followed without much thought about how he might look to others.

Good Jews like David and Jesus were passionate men; they simply lived what they felt. Young children do this sort of thing as well. Without thinking about how they look, they simply follow these inner signals. When they feel joyful, they show it; when they feel exuberant, they let everyone else know. Clearly, however, it is difficult to feel exuberant or to dance or celebrate spontaneously when we are relegated to the orderly seating arrangement of most religious congregations. Pews and ecstasy do not go together in feminine spirituality.

At a couples workshop my husband and I attended, we were drawn into a group experience involving dance. First we were asked to stand before one another in a silent gaze while music was played in the background. Then, after we felt fully present to the gaze we shared with one another, we were told to slowly begin to move, to begin to dance in whatever way the body led; to speak nonverbally through the motions and gestures of the dance. In this powerful event I experienced myself communicating with my eyes, through a gaze, through movement and body signals. It had been some time since I had entered this deeper way of being with someone else. It had been a long time since I had danced so consciously.

It is a great freedom to dance before the presence of God in this way, as though we were staring into the eyes of a lover and moving consciously to the sound of praise between the two of us. In my imagination I dream up the thought that sometimes God looks for this freedom in us and delights in the gutsy splendor of our risking.

CREATING FRIENDSHIPS THAT ENLIVEN SOUL

We are in an age of spiritual experimentation, and many women are looking for ways to open up the boundaries of their own religious experience. Women can increase their spiritual vocabulary by pursuing more intimate relationships with other women who are interested in the spiritual life. Over the last few years I have had the privilege to share some spiritual comradery with a small group of women who have been seeking more authentic ways to deepen the feminine spirit. All of us are from different faiths, and yet we share a common bonding in our devotions that seems to transcend ordinary boundaries. Some of the strongest expressions of the spirit have evolved from the group, not because of any ritual or specific practice, but from a mutual honoring of the sacredness of the moment. The form and content of worship is sometimes a song, a dance, or a silent meditation. Sometimes there is laughter or the spontaneous expression of tears, but always there is an inner ritual. And here the only mediator is the spirit that speaks to each one of us uniquely.

Even if only a few women come together to practice new prayer forms, it is essential that we know who we are with one another; that we take the time to share honestly about our own journey. The rituals we create as women need to come out of our trust for one another and our openness to the spirit, out of a place of spontaneity and freedom rather than from old structures. In this framework the heart is the ritual and its subtle leading is the program; the spirit, not the agenda, is in control.

One of the best ways to exercise the heart is to be in the kind of relationship that brings us right to the edge of our own personal boundaries. Risking to say who we are to someone else and to tell the truth about ourselves is an essential element of spiritual comradery. Women need to risk reaching out to one another without fear of rejection, without competition, without the false self, without the awful religious personas most of us wear. Historically, women have spent most of their time relating to their spouses, to their children, or to social causes. Yet few of the many women I have spoken with take the time to cultivate deep or intimate friendships outside their immediate family or work environments. They have friends, but not intimate ones. They are active in clubs, charities, religious study groups, fundraising activities, and promotional activities for the men in their lives, but few of us are intimately connected with other women.

Perhaps another reason for a lack of deep feminine intimacy

is that many of us have been hurt by other women—by mothers, sisters, grandmothers, aunts, peers; by teachers, friends, and acquaintances. Sometimes our greatest wounds are not from the men in our lives, but from the significant women with whom we have shared our lives. Many of us have never learned to cultivate deeply intimate relationships with one another, because few women have ever been vulnerable or open with us. Often, we don't risk showing our feelings, saying our hurts, and expressing our needs with one another. Rather than coming honestly and openly before one another with our real self, we present an ideal self, a mask that hides who we are. As a result too few of us actually relate to one another holistically, honestly, or from a genuine heart level.

Many women seem to judge one another more by standards of perfection and performance than with genuine compassion. Sometimes we are calculating and exacting with one another, demanding a standard from each other that even we ourselves can seldom measure up to. Some women, seemingly forgiving and nurturing toward men, can be incredibly rigid and uncaring toward other women. Some put men on a pedestal and unquestioningly support them, no matter what, but will not support a woman at that same level, and may even perceive her as a threat. Wounds at the personal level are often to blame for these often senseless rivalries; but equally to blame is the society that rewards the conforming woman (the good daughter of the patriarchy), and crucifies the Artemis personality (the woman who is one-in-herself). It is these deep wounds to feminine self-esteem that women need to redeem in themselves and to be sensitive to in other women.

Western society has, in its own protective paternal way, kept the feminine relational heart from developing full awareness of itself. Consequently, most of us need to explore a whole new territory in friendships. Women need to mother one another; to experiment with what it means to be able to trust one another and to nurture one another's gifts. We need to exercise the heart, to practice calling forth the relational giftedness that often lies dormant there, because there is no healing force like the human heart. When we are being loved and when we are loving, we are exercising the deepest instrument there is for channeling the energy of the spirit. But in this culture we have often prioritized only the upkeep of the physical heart. The most we hear about the heart is how to exercise it, feed it, keep it healthy. Yet when we are happy inside, the heart is healthy— because it's automatically being cared for and fed in ways that medical science or nutrition can never match. But to exercise the heart and open it for access, we have to use it. We have to be in love with life or in love with somebody or in love with God; we have to risk being lovers.

Not long ago I was talking to a friend of mine, an Italian Franciscan priest who loves garlic and folk dancing. He was talking about the art of "people making." That means when we see something special in someone, no matter what other personality problems they may have, we risk calling out the gift in that person. Even when there is no immediate evidence of the more redemptive side, the people maker suspects it's there and affirms it anyway. Women have been especially great affirmers of men and of men's causes, and no doubt men need women to call them forth. We all need that. Yet because feminine self-esteem seems disabled and frankly hurt, women need to turn this supportive tool of affirmation towards one another with more sensitivity.

I have a friend who has a passionate Irish heart. She doesn't always have the answers for some of the dark spaces in her life, but she can generally always see the bright side of things and has an uncanny ability to love all of humanity without reserve. No matter what I confess to her, she's affirming. She laughs nonjudgmentally, uproariously, and there is no end to her loving. All of us need this atmosphere of acceptance and nonjudgmentalism in order to grow inwardly; we need it in order to heal the wounds of our childhood when people around us were abusive or not affirming. If anything, women need to find one another now, and to begin to partner one another's emotional needs. Each of us needs at least one other person who knows how to console, to listen, to laugh with us, to accept our tears, who knows how to be there with a genuine mother's heart. Women like this are people makers.

DEEPENING THE MYSTERY OF THE WOMB

Meister Eckhart, a thirteenth-century mystic and writer, spoke of the need for all men to allow themselves to be pregnant with God. The inference in Eckhart's writings is clearly that God is to be celebrated beyond the limits of the mind. We are to embrace the whole creative element of birthing God within each of us; to gestate with the creative seed until we can birth it to full consciousness. This idea of becoming pregnant with God and letting that holy mystery fill us completely was an outrageous concept in Eckhart's day because it inferred that to receive God, we must be like a woman with an empty womb.

> I once had a dream
> I dreamt that I, even though a man, was pregnant,
> pregnant and full of Nothingness like a woman who
> is with child.
> And out of that Nothingness
> God was born.[1]

If we are to be soul makers, we must not reject the idea of the womb. A direct communion with God is more powerful than accomplishments and a life of services aimed toward others. Yet this communion requires an emptiness, a waiting, a silent pondering; it asks for the desert. In Hosea 2:16 it is said that God lures us into the desert so that he/she can speak to our hearts. And here is the most essential ingredient to the dance: our aloneness with God. This is the essence of *yin* in its most potent form. We often misunderstand the concept of the feminine and judge its posture of quiet reflection as passivity. But in the spiritual world, authentic life is born out of silence and waiting; out of the power of the surrender.

Ego life comes from our doing, soul life emanates from our being. We need to ask ourselves honestly where we stand here; how much of our time is spent directed outward toward the doing part of our lives; and how much time is spent directed inward. The masculine and feminine energies in the spiritual life need balance. This wholeness can only come together if we take the time to develop and nurture the womb of our feminine spirit.

The important thing is to be open to the spontaneity of the spirit and to cultivate a listening ear that connects directly to our own heart and soul. If we are interested in the inner life this means that we start searching for more silence in our lives, making more time in which to reflect, to ponder, or to do nothing. We make more space in the attic or along the seashore in which we can simply be alone with God. To do this is to remember to see ourselves as an empty vessel, through which the fire of life is always free to travel. To the degree that we remain busy and preoccupied, there won't be much room for the spirit to land. Likewise, if we are filled with thoughts, ideas, words, and petitions, we seldom leave much room for deeper awareness. Just as we initiate a dialogue with our deeper feelings and thoughts in the interest of self-awareness, we must come within in order to dialogue with soul. To be near a lover, a woman gives up whatever she is doing and makes herself ready. It is the same way with God.

The problem for many women at this juncture is that when we seek the contemplative life, the initial results are often intangible. Learning to pray without words for many of us is unthinkable, and relinquishing familiar forms is difficult. It is always a temptation to go with what we know. Yet the spiritual life, like the territory of the unconscious, is unknown. To journey there is to walk right into the midst of paradox; this is why contemplative prayer is often called the desert experience. Unlike the rewards that come from the results of our doing nature, the returns that flow from the being side will be much more subtle and initially more diffuse. Yet one can only judge one's inner spiritual work by direct experience; and eventually time yields its answers.

Sometimes, the more I experience God, the more I am faced with an undeniable sense of paradox. In my own prayer life, for instance, my dialogue with the Guest has not just been cultivating a deeper sense of intimacy and an inner knowing. Aside from the sometimes blessed and powerful ways in which I have connected with the spirit, there have been moments of real impasse and testing. On the rare occasions when I remember to let go of my concepts and expectations about how God will (or should) manifest next, I am freer to open myself to the mystery, to divine surprises. The trick is that when we can admit that we don't know all the answers, then we somehow get closer to the knowing.

Faced with a conflict, stuck in a place where I can't see a way out, when I don't feel anything holy, the feminine has been especially useful to me. Feminine spirituality is good at crossing the abyss: She simply allows herself to fall in and then waits it out. If part of our journey plunges us in to darkness and we can hold fast, without running to fix the dilemma, then the knowing eventually happens. But enlightenment dawns from the inside; it gradually begins to emerge intuitively, instinctively, from the feelings and from the unconscious.

There have been countless times in my inner life when I have had to simply drop my need for control and predictability; when I had to unlearn everything I had previously learned. These were times of letting go, giving up, admitting my inability to "know" the way. I have endured moments during a crisis, a personal or relational upheaval, when I had no direction, no sense of where I was going. Sometimes I felt discouraged, felt nothing divine at all; sometimes I only experienced my own humanity staring back at me. But when I abandoned my will and efforts and allowed my unconscious to lead me intuitively, I was regrounded. The whole universe was telling me to embrace the abyss.

One of my clients on a spiritual journey once said to me, *"It's all dark down here. I knew I was in for it after so many years of neglecting my soul life, but I had no idea it was going to be this difficult. The moment I parted company with rituals and words and all the stuff we used to do to keep ourselves occupied in church, that's when it started getting hairy. If I didn't know better I'd run back toward the old comfort of letting somebody else lead my prayer life. Sometimes, you know, when I close my eyes to meditate I feel absolutely empty. It's like the black hole of Calcutta inside. And although I can't see anything, I can feel this agitation.*

"But I read somewhere that things get better once we get over the fear of facing our silence. It's just that my particular silence brings up a sneaking suspicion that I'm not in control, that it's not me calling the shots. But I think I'm simply going to have to face this fear and smile at it. The only comfort I have is that something bigger than I am

is looking in on my dark spaces and I don't always feel alone. I'm learning that God is in my silence too."

Another woman said, *"I know what it is that's so unnerving. Temple for me used to be a container. Everything was clearly spelled out and all I had to do was to participate in someone else's program. But this inner work is much more demanding. When I sit to pray or meditate now, or when I drop into the silence inside, there's no more container and no one is in charge of making some sense out of the darkness but me. It's just me and God, and somehow that feels so immense. This new kind of spaciousness is somewhat overwhelming. At the same time I am aware that this dark abyss and I have to make friends. That eventually I'm going to be able to know myself—I mean really know myself. I'm going to have to be forgiving about what I see down there that I don't like."*

When we can embrace the abyss in ourselves we can embrace it in others. Said Rebbe Moshe-Leib of Sassov: "We are told that the holy spark exists in all things—even in evil."[2] When I was younger I was obsessed with confining God to good things, to goodness itself, to my kind of people, to "believers," to holy moments, and to the comfortable little ecstasies my limited prayer life offered me. It was hard for me to understand that God was beyond all that. Gradually, having made enough mistakes and wrong turns, I began to see something of God in everything. The more I experienced my own false self, my own darkness, the bag lady and the failure within myself, the more I could embrace these same things in others without judgment. The evil in others that used to frighten and alienate me slowly began to teach me that there was also something of their personal poverty within me. To the degree that I could see their helplessness and deprivation, and accept their weaknesses as a part of myself, I could also begin to embrace the dark side of my own soul. And God was never far from that poverty for me; somehow his face was always a part of the suffering I saw.

In downtown Berkeley one night I saw a man playing a guitar. Nobody was listening, so I stopped and put some change in his guitar case. He turned to me and asked me if I'd like a song and I told him to go ahead and sing whatever he'd like. So he started a song and suddenly he walked very close to me and stared into my eyes and sang into my face; I wanted to run, to back away. I was sorry I had ever stopped, because he was obviously loaded and his eyes looked crazy and he had crossed my boundary. The whole world walked by and I stood there, hating my naivete, wondering when I would ever grow out of it, hoping for the end of the song. But as I stood there I began to realize that beneath the glaze over his eyes there was only a man in pain; and in the dark vacancy of his eyes I saw my own abyss staring right back at me.

Whether we are learning to see God in the desert of our own poverty, in the abyss of our own silence, or to hear the holy sound in the winds of the desert, we must try to cultivate a continuous sense of that presence. The Guest is always ready to speak, to dance, to play, to experience, to console, to bring insight, to heal, to discomfort and pierce, to work side by side with us, to do nothing with us, to adorn us, to strip us, to add to us and to take away. God is a rhythm, a season, a movement, a celebration. Feminine spirituality is based on this total sense of God as an ongoing relationship with Mystery. One never knows where she will turn up next.

OPENING THE BOUNDARIES

Whether we choose traditional or nontraditional forms of religious expression, whether we go East or West, we need to seek God knowing our own identity. We must come before the Mystery not unconsciously, as Mermaids or Givers, but with some sense of our own direction. It is essential that women do not just simply follow men into the arms race, along stereotypic paths, domestic or social, or especially along the blind corridors of religious dogma. Neither should we enter the religious quest as Achievers, as competitors of men; as women who simply transcribe the Great Noun from He to She and go on with a celebration of the same rituals with a different gender attachment. Instead we need to come to a place where we can sense what the moment calls for; to be open to the divine process, whatever form it wants to take with us.

It is important that we hang onto our heritage as women with the potential to nurture and empower heart and soul. We cannot allow the "relocation" of the feminine spirit in a world that is impatient with the ancient ways of nature, or with authentic human and spiritual values. What is sacred is sacred. If we do not know who we are as women and where we come from, we will have no vision to survive the decay of the spirit in any major corporate social, political, or religious system we happen to find ourselves in; and neither will we have enough personal or spiritual insight to make any substantial impact on a world that is increasingly hostile to love.

Women need meaningful rituals, sacred spaces, holy ground from which to redefine and experience our meaning. When we get brave enough to begin to move beyond a literal approach to God, and can admit the Mystery, we are entering new ground. Often this involves the acceptance of an inner shift, both in our attitude about the transpersonal and in our prayer life as well. Sometimes this involves creating new prayer forms which may be more suitable to our own nature as women; perhaps it means exploring new rituals which are more meaningful to our celebration of the feminine; or maybe it involves scouting out how other religious devotees are experiencing God. Again, these other prayer forms may appear different from our own; but often learning how other people relate to God can be an important step towards expanding our own consciousness of prayer.

When anyone (male or female) becomes liberated at the soul level religious forms become increasingly questionable, and religious dogma becomes effectually shallow. Catholic, Jew, Moslem, Buddhist, Protestant, Hindu—what does it matter as long as there is love? Over the centuries devotees of all kinds have sprung into the dance that marks the lover's search for God. In this age all of us have to go past the runways of religion, its structures and belief systems, its demand that it of itself has answers. All humanity must be respected and welcomed into the pilgrimage for God. At the deepest level of soul, all devotees look alike. When a mother of any religious faith sees a hungry child, or one who has stepped on a land mine, there are no boundaries to her compassion. When a child disappears and is forced into the dark streets of prostitution, or another dies in the brutality of a concentration camp, the grief of any mother's heart knows no discrimination but weeps for all alike. This immediate and passionate response to the child of any faith is the essence of feminine spirituality; it is the feminine side of God, and all races deserve to be mothered. The closer any of us walks to soul, the more we see this truth: All of us are alike in the sight of God.

There are always other cultures and observances of the spiritual life we can learn from. The simple but powerful spirituality of the Native Americans is one that many women have been drawn to because of its inherent connection to the earth. The Navajo and the Hopi have a very earthy and holistic sense of the Great Spirit, and their own observance of God seems to infiltrate everything they do. When they are planting corn, they pray; when they are walking, they pray; when they are working, the older ones will sing. In the film *Broken Rainbow*, one old Navajo matriarch chants,

> We shake the pollen from the plant
> and offer it to the sun.
> The Holy Spirit protects us
> We pray for ourselves in this way.

The Navajo concept of a primary connectedness to the earth as mother stands as a powerful model for feminine spirituality. The sense that the Great Spirit is not confined to a set of religious principles, but spreads to all life, is another. Just as the Native Americans do not confine the Spirit to one dwelling, neither does the Spirit conform itself to a particular space. Although many people associate their religious experience solely with the place they congregate, like church or temple or some religious formal gathering, church is only an outer structure. It is merely the vessel for the possibility of communion with God, a place whose symbols remind us of a truth we already know within. In another sense, I am also the vessel for that communion. If I pause to pray with a friend, a client, someone I meet along the way, that's church: It is the act of our communion that makes it happen. Church is the whole multitude of religious gathered spiritually across the face of the earth. It is not something one does once a week to insure salvation; it is not solely a ritual obligatory act. It is the act of communion with God. It is an ongoing event that gathers up life and forms it into sounds of praise. The best of mystics, East and West, tell us that.

Elie Wiesel, in *Somewhere a Master,* says that the very substance of Hasidism is an absolute commitment to bring God to life on this earth, whatever form that might take. He says,

The holy man must not necessarily look holy; he may appear as a peasant, a wanderer, a worker, a merchant. He must not necessarily stay within the covers of the Talmud, the Zohar, or the prayer book; he may—and indeed should—leave his house, leave his shelter, leave his study and his work, and go into the forest, and perhaps chop wood in order to come closer to God.[3]

Wiesel tells a story about a Ukranian Rebbe (Rabbi) who disappeared every day during the early morning hours. No one among his Hasidic followers in Sassov could find him—not at the synagogue, nor in the houses of study, nor at home. Sometimes people were irked at his disappearances, especially during the high holy days when they needed his advice and help. One day a visiting Lithuanian Jew, an enemy of Hasidism, came to town. Hearing the story of the mysterious Rebbe, he resolved to spy on him. Climbing under the celebrated teacher's bed one night, and concentrating on the logic of the Talmud to keep him awake lest he should miss something, he thus spent the night. When morning came the Rebbe got up, washed his hands and face, and went to the closet. From the closet he withdrew a bundle of peasant clothing which he then put on. Next he went to the kitchen and, gathering up an ax into his belt, left the house. His adversary, although frightened by the mysterious doings of the Rebbe of Sassov, trailed him like a shadow.

The Rebbe walked along the streets of the town to a forest. He walked far into the dark trees, felled a young tree, split the logs, and made them into a bundle. As the morning light was filling the sky he turned again to the path that led to town. At the end of a narrow road at the edge of town stood a poor hut. The Rebbe knocked at the door and entered, leaving his curious follower to linger in the doorway. There lay a sick woman in bed under ragged blankets who had neither firewood nor money. Pretending his name was Vassili and that he was a peasant with some wood to sell, he set about talking with the old woman, building her a fire, and encouraging her to trust God. Whispering the morning prayers as he worked to make the poor old widow warm, the Rebbe seemed to light up the whole room with his devotions. Seeing the holiness of Moshe-Leib of Sassov, the Lithuanian Jew set aside his rigorous need for the letter of the law and became the Rebbe's most devout follower.

Wiesel concludes that the original version of this classic tale portrayed the old woman not as Jewish but Christian. He says, "If Reb Moshe-Leib takes care of a sick woman, it is not to attract her to the Hasidic movement, but to give her faith in her fellow man; if the Master disguises himself as a peasant, it is to impress upon her that one need not be a Rebbe to be charitable. In Sassov, what matters is compassion."[4] In the religious heart what matters is not the place or the form, but the devotion.

There is a cave in the desert of the Southwest that has been for me a profoundly holy place. I discovered it one day during a thunder shower, and as it was only a short distance up the cliff base I hustled up there to stay dry. Just as I was entering the cave, a loud thunderclap rumbled above. As I walked into the cave, the thunder continued to roll underneath me, as though the sound weren't coming from the sky at all, but from the belly of the earth beneath me. I stood still just inside the mouth of the cave as it continued to pulse with the sound. It was an auspicious entry inside Mother Earth, because it sounded on the inside as if the whole belly of the earth was singing bass. After the sound faded, I sat down to meditate and to pray as this thundersong had seemed to beckon me to do. Somewhere during my prayer I looked up to see a beautiful snow flurry sailing by outside, the snowflakes whipping sideways to the east in the strong air currents. Everything was a dance of white wind outside the cave. As I continued to watch God in this amazing handiwork, a bald eagle soared past the mouth of the cave, and the great bird cried out his blessing to me as he passed. In the spontaneity of the moment his cry seemed to echo the blessing, "The mass is ended, go in peace to love and serve the Lord."

When one begins to listen to the call of God outside the traditional dwelling places it can be a real revelation. God becomes wider, more encompassing, more real. I am baffled by people who carry their Scriptures around and constantly refer to "the Word." Some of us have forgotten that the word is flesh, and that God is an essential force that does far more than form words. He forms wind and sleet and luminous caves to shelter the pilgrim from the storm and to harbor the bag lady and the saint. She forms seas and storms and brilliant shells that echo the depth of the waters. He makes deserts, granite peaks, elk and bear, and covers the high places with snow. In the wind She is a holy sound, in the sunset a splash of crimson praise. In the clouds He forms great noises and pours out His rains over the earth. In the child She makes a heart that is open to receive itself and still believes in magic. In the eyes of the beggar He reflects our poverty and desolation back to us and still we are beautiful.

Feminine spirituality is the awareness that God is simply a mystery—uncontainable, unimaginable, and never without some degree of paradox, never without some bit of unpredictability. Often manifesting in a creative force, the transpersonal is always waiting to be tapped into. Yet few women avail themselves of the mystery or leap into the heart of that creativity. Most women who follow a specific religious program without consciousness may miss the inner content of the soul unless they are awake and listening for its message. What's more, many of us miss the level of communion that the soul hungers for if we restrict holiness to sanctuaries and books, theologies and little rituals, or worse, to our particular brand of religious experience. These masculine forms, important as they have been for the religious container, are not the essence of that container. Just as God freely pours the Spirit into devotees and sinners alike, into great mosques and temples, and along the worn trails of the holy land where Jesus walked, that same essential power congregates wherever life is happening. That holiness knows no boundaries.

In the midst of an ongoing religious identity crisis a few years back, I had the following dream. Its soul quality is unmistakable: *A tall Native American man with long dark braids and dark eyes stands before me. He leads me to a waterfall and asks me to strip off my clothes and to cleanse myself in the pool beneath the falls. After that he sprinkles sacred pollen over me and chants a blessing. Bright gold pollen swirls in a shimmering pattern of light as it falls over my body.*

Just as the chanting stops an eagle appears overhead and soars majestically above me. The man tells me that the great bird is my spirit bird, that wherever I walk in my life it will be my companion, never far away. Suddenly, I become the bird. I soar over the earth, over the hills, over the forests and the land. At some point I see a small, stark black-and-white church below me. The image is quite sharp and it bothers me somewhat; its austerity both pierces and releases something inside that I've been holding.

Then I hear a voice say, "My church spreads over the face of the whole earth, and it cannot be contained. My mass is a celebration of all life." I awaken with a sense that God is absolutely beyond anything I have ever imagined.

I knew this intellectually, but I still clung to some rigid beliefs about my faith, about needing to be right, to be on the safe side, to be approved of by the "white" side of mother church. It became increasingly clear to me that I had to seek beyond the confines of my cloister of notions about who God was. Without a doubt my dream was calling me to release a certain black-and-white mentality about my faith. It was time for me to begin to see God in more beggars, more mosques, in the faces of those who didn't think like me, in the people who didn't like me. It was time to seek him/her in the recesses of my own weaknesses and incompletions, to trust that life itself was an ongoing celebration of the mass. It was time to trust that risking to live my life fully did not mean I would be abandoned, no longer part of the "holy" side of the church. Other parts of this dream experience were not so clear and remain unfinished; yet I trust that as I sit with and ponder them in the dark spaces of the morning, that they will eventually reveal their meaning.

LEARN THIS SONG THE GRANDMOTHER SINGS

When I go back to the Klamath in the fall, I don't know what I'll find. In the spaces of my absence there are bound to have been changes in the road, in the path down to the water, and along the banks of the river itself. I don't expect anything will be exactly the same. The river has taught me that. But year after year, no matter what has happened in the seasons when I have been away, there is still a sameness to the land; a familiarity to the sound of the water tumbling over the rocks, an ancient feel on the trails under my feet. Under the broad expanse of sky above the river I can close my eyes once more and feel the hot sun on my face; I can feel its light penetrate my mind and still the busy nature of my thoughts. I can wonder if I'll see the old black bear again, foraging through the wild grapes that line the banks along the water's edge.

On some days, when the fishing is slow again or when my mind wanders inside, I will build another altar out of stones where I can release the mistakes and failures from the past year. And when I can let go of my regrets, I will sanctify the paradox of my human nature once more. On its smooth stone surfaces I will heap up small treasures from the river's edge; gifts of nature that remind me to celebrate what I have learned and been given in the journey.

In this place the Old Ones will be close to me in every offering of nature. Whether I sleep or dream, I will expect to hear their voices scolding me and praying for me at the same time; reminding me that this road by the river is a holy walk that can only be birthed little by little. That I must walk it with pride and humility, with passion and detachment; that I must share it with beggars and lovers, with heroes and adversaries, with the people I love and the ones who have not loved me enough. In the road their footprints will recall to me that along the journey I must remember to embrace both the abyss and the garment of brightness.

> Learn this song the Grandmother sings
> Pray all your paths are meeting
> Follow this way the Grandfather walks
> Pray all your roads are merging
> Walk this path that speaks of life
> Along its trails see beauty
> Open to the Ancient Hands
> That formed you long ago
> Hear now their holy laughter
> And drink the sky in peace

HO MITAKUYE OYAS' IN

Notes

INTRODUCTION: AS LONG AS THE RIVER SHALL RUN

Epigraph: A tribal song, as quoted in *Walk Quietly the Beautiful Trail* (Kansas City, MO: Hallmark, 1973), 9.

1. THE ROAD BY THE RIVER

Epigraph: Native American prayer, author unknown.

3. THE DEEPER WATERS OF THE SELF: A WAKENING CONSCIOUSNESS

1. Robert Johnson, *Inner Work* (San Francisco: Harper & Row, 1986), 8.
2. Aminah Raheem, *Soul Return, A Guide to Transpersonal Integration* (Aptos, Cal.: Stomel), 21.
3. James M. Robinson, *Nag Hammadi Library* (New York: Harper & Row, 1978), 234.
4. Eknath Easwaran, *Gandhi, the Man* (Petaluma, Cal.: Nilgiri Press, 1975), 60.
5. J. C. Cooper, *An Illustrated Encyclopedia of Symbols* (London: Thames and Hudson, 1978), 98.

4. ROUTES TO THE INNER WOMAN

1. Laurens Van der Post, *The Heart of the Hunter* (New York: William Morrow and Company, 1961), 148.

5. IMAGES OF THE MOTHER

1. Meinrad Craighead, *The Mother's Songs, Images of God the Mother* (New York: Paulist Press, 1986), 11.
2. Nancy Friday, *My Mother, My Self* (New York: Dell, 1977), 75.
3. Francis Wickes, *The Inner World of Childhood* (Englewood Cliffs, New Jersey: Prentice Hall), 1976.

6. FATHERS AS HEROES AND ADVERSARIES

1. Elyse Walkerman, *Father Loss* (Garden City, N.Y: Doubleday, 1984), 56.
2. Linda Leonard, *The Wounded Woman* (Boulder, Col.: Shambhala, 1983).

7. THE WOMAN BEYOND THE MASK

1. Esther Harding, *Women's Mysteries* (New York: Harper & Row, 1971), 75.
2. Penelope Washburn, *Becoming a Woman* (New York: Harper & Row, 1977), 7.
3. Madonna Kolbenschlag, *Kiss Sleeping Beauty Goodbye* (New York: Bantam Books, 1979), 10.
4. *Ibid.*
5. Robert Johnson, *He* (New York: Harper & Row, 1974), 23–24.
6. Jane Sochen, *Herstory* (New York: Alfred, 1974), 367.
7. *Ibid.*
8. Marion Woodman, *Addiction to Perfection* (Toronto: Inner City Books, 1982), 16.

8. AWAKENING RELATIONSHIPS

1. Kabir, *The Kabir Book,* translated by Robert Bly. (Boston: Beacon Press, 1977), 41.
2. Irene de Castillejo, *Knowing Woman* (New York: Harper Colophon Books, 1973), 56.
3. Esther Harding, *Women's Mysteries* (New York: Harper & Row, 1971), 118.
4. *Ibid.,* 36.
5. Joseph C. Pearce, *The Magical Child Matures* (New York: E. P. Dutton, 1985), 37.
6. Jean Bolen, *Goddesses in Every Woman* (San Francisco: Harper & Row, 1984), 148.
7. Arnold Mindell, *Working with the Dream Body* (Boston: Henley, 1985).
8. Kabir, *The Kabir Book,* 35.
9. de Castillejo, *Knowing Woman,* 56.
10. *Ibid.,* 57.
11. Esther Harding, *The Way of All Women* (New York: Harper Colophon Books, 1970), 300.

9. SOUL MAKING

1. Kabir, *The Kabir Book,* translated by Robert Bly (Boston: Beacon Press, 1977), 44.
2. Eknath Easwaran, *Gandhi, the Man* (Petaluma, Cal.: Nilgiri Press, 1978), 115.
3. Thomas Merton, *The Wisdom of the Desert* (New York: A New Directions Book, 1960), 72.
4. Tertullian, quoted in Madonna Kolbenschlag, *Kiss Sleeping Beauty Goodbye* (New York: Bantam Books, 1979), 170.
5. Merlin Stone, *When God Was a Woman* (New York: Harvest/HBJ, 1976), 226.
6. Kolbenschlag, *Sleeping Beauty,* 170.
7. *Ibid.*
8. Helen Luke, *Woman, Earth and Spirit, the Feminine in Symbol and Myth* (New York: Crossroads, 1981), 48.

10. MAY ALL YOUR ROADS MEET

1. Meister Eckhart, *Meditations with Meister Eckhart,* translated by Matthew Fox (Santa Fe: Bear and Company, 1983), 70.
2. Elie Wiesel, *Somewhere a Master* (New York: Summit Books, 1981), 110.
3. *Ibid.,* 98.
4. *Ibid.,* 99.